Media Law in Bosnia & Herzegovina

Media Law in Bosnia & Herzegovina

Tarik Jusić

Sanela Hodžić

This book was originally published as a monograph in the International Encyclopaedia of Laws/Media Law.

Founding Editor: Roger Blanpain
General Editor: Frank Hendrickx
Volume Editors: Peggy Valcke & Eva Lievens

Wolters Kluwer

Published by:
Kluwer Law International B.V.
PO Box 316
2400 AH Alphen aan den Rijn
The Netherlands
E-mail: international-sales@wolterskluwer.com
Website: lrus.wolterskluwer.com

Sold and distributed by:
Wolters Kluwer Legal & Regulatory U.S.
7201 McKinney Circle
Frederick, MD 21704
United States of America
E-mail: customer.service@wolterskluwer.com

DISCLAIMER: The material in this volume is in the nature of general comment only. It is not offered as advice on any particular matter and should not be taken as such. The editor and the contributing authors expressly disclaim all liability to any person with regard to anything done or omitted to be done, and with respect to the consequences of anything done or omitted to be done wholly or partly in reliance upon the whole or any part of the contents of this volume. No reader should act or refrain from acting on the basis of any matter contained in this volume without first obtaining professional advice regarding the particular facts and circumstances at issue. Any and all opinions expressed herein are those of the particular author and are not necessarily those of the editor or publisher of this volume.

ISBN 978-94-035-3854-9

e-Book: ISBN 978-94-035-3855-6
web-PDF: ISBN 978-94-035-3860-0

The Authors

Tarik Jusić, PhD, Lecturer and the guarantor of the study programme, School of Communication and Media, University of New York in Prague, Czech Republic. Tarik holds a PhD from the Institute for Media and Communication Studies, University of Vienna, Austria; an MA in Political Science and an MBA, both from Central European University, Budapest, Hungary; and a BA in Journalism from the Faculty of Political Science, University of Sarajevo. Tarik has previously worked as Managing Director at Analitika – Center for Social Research, an independent think-tank, Sarajevo, Bosnia and Herzegovina (2010-2020); Program Director at the Mediacentar Sarajevo (2002-2011); and Assistant Professor at the Department of Political Science and International Relations, Sarajevo School of Science and Technology (2009-2013). He regularly publishes on media policy issues in Bosnia and Herzegovina and the region of Southeast Europe.

Sanela Hodžić, MA, Independent researcher, previously Lead Researcher at the Mediacentar Sarajevo. Sanela holds a MA in Gender studies from the Center for Interdisciplinary Postgraduate Studies, University of Sarajevo, and a BA in Psychology from the Faculty of Philosophy, University of Sarajevo. She is studying media reforms in BiH and Southeast Europe for over a decade, authoring publications for Mediacentar Sarajevo, European Journalism Network, International Research and Exchange Board and other publishers.

The Authors

Table of Contents

List of Abbreviations

ADSL	Asymmetric Digital Subscriber Line
AGCOM	Autorità per le Garanzie nelle Comunicazioni / Authority for Communications Guarantees
BHRadio 1	Radio of Bosnia and Herzegovina (part of the Public Service Broadcasting of Bosnia and Herzegovina)
BHRT	Bosnia and Herzegovina Radio and Television/Public Service Broadcasting of Bosnia and Herzegovina
BHT	Television of Bosnia and Herzegovina (part of the Public Service Broadcasting of Bosnia and Herzegovina)
BiH	Bosnia and Herzegovina
CAVRMS	Code on Audiovisual and Radio Media Services
CCI	Centres of Civic Initiatives
CENELEC	European Committee for Electrotechnical Standardization
CRA	Communications Regulatory Agency
DPA	Dayton Peace Agreement
DTH	Direct-to-Home Satellite Signal
DTT	Digital Terrestrial Television
ECHR	European Convention on Human Rights
ETSI	The European Telecommunications Standards Institute
EU	European Union
EUMAP	European Union Monitoring and Advocacy Programme
FBiH	Federation of Bosnia and Herzegovina
FOIA	Freedom of Access to Information Act
FTV	Television of Federation of BiH (part of the Public Service Broadcasting of Federation of Bosnia and Herzegovina – RTVFBiH)
GSM	Global System for Mobile Communications
HR	High Representative
HT Mostar	Croatian Telecommunications Mostar *(Hrvatske telekomunikacije Mostar)*

List of Abbreviations

IMC	Independent Media Commission
IPTV	Internet Protocol Television
IREX	International Research and Exchanges Board
ISDN	Integrated Services Digital Network
ITU	International Telecommunications Union
MEC	Media Experts Commission
MW	Medium Wave
NATO	The North Atlantic Treaty Organization
OBN	Open Broadcast Network
OHR	Office of High Representative
OSCE	Organization for Security and Cooperation in Europe
PIC	Peace Implementation Council
PSB	Public Service Broadcasting
Radio FBiH	Radio of Federation of Bosnia and Herzegovina
RF	Radio Frequency
RS	Republika Srpska
RTRS	Radio and Television of Republika Srpska
RTVFBiH	Radio and Television of Federation of Bosnia and Herzegovina / Public Service Broadcasting of Federation of Bosnia and Herzegovina
SAA	Stabilization and Association Agreement
SAI	Supreme Audit Institution
SFOR	Stabilization Force
SMS	Short Message Service
UDHR	Universal Declaration of Human Rights
UN	United Nations

General Introduction

§1. General Background of the Country

I. Political and Legal System of the Country

A. Introduction

1. An independent Bosnian state first emerged in the 1180s.[1] The medieval state of Bosnia developed and territorially expanded between 1180 and 1391.[2] In 1377, Bosnia became 'the Kingdom of Serbian Lands, Bosnia, Coastal Lands and Western Parts'.[3] Conquered in 1463 by the Ottoman forces, Bosnia remained under Ottoman rule until 1878, when it was occupied by Austria-Hungary. With the dissolution of the Austro-Hungarian Empire at the end of World War I, in 1918, Bosnia and Herzegovina (BiH) became an integral part of the new Yugoslav state – the Kingdom of Serbs, Croats and Slovenes. At the end of World War II, it was one of the six republics of the Federal People's Republic of Yugoslavia (as of 1963 the Socialist Federal Republic of Yugoslavia).[4]

2. Democratic reforms began taking place in 1990, when BiH adopted amendments to its constitution, introducing a market economy, a multi-party political system, and a plural democracy. Subsequently, the first free parliamentary elections were held on 18 November 1990. On 20 December 1991, the BiH Government adopted the Decision on statehood, i.e., independence of BiH, and the Assembly of BiH called for a referendum to determine the status of the country.[5] The referendum was held on 29 February and 1 March 1992 and confirmed the country as a sovereign and independent state 'of equal citizens and nations of Muslims, Serbs,

1. Noel Malcolm, *Bosnia: A Short History* 11 (Macmillan London Limited 1994).
2. *Ibid.*, 13.
3. Srđan Dizdarević et al., *Democracy Assessment in Bosnia and Herzegovina* 21 (Open Society Fund Bosnia and Herzegovina 2006).
4. *Ibid.*, 21–22.
5. *Ibid.*, 22.

Croats and others who live in it'.[6] Nevertheless, the referendum was largely boycotted by the Serb population, which wanted the country to remain a part of Yugoslavia.[7] By that time Yugoslavia had already lost three of its republics – Slovenia, Croatia and Macedonia – with only Serbia, Montenegro and BiH remaining a part of it.

3. International recognition of BiH took place on 6 April 1992 at the meeting of the Committee of Ministers of the European Community in Brussels. The country formally ceased to be a part of the Socialist Federal Republic of Yugoslavia.[8]

4. By the time of the recognition of its independence, the country had already collapsed into a full-fledged war that lasted from early 1992 until late 1995. The war resulted in an estimated 104,732[9] dead and 17,000 missing, while some 1.2 million persons fled the country, and more than a million were internally displaced.[10] BiH government authorities have estimated the overall war damages to be between USD 50 and USD 70 billion; estimates for the destruction of productive capacity are ranging between USD 15 and USD 20 billion.[11]

5. The 1995 Dayton Peace Agreement (DPA),[12] mediated by the international community, was reached among representatives of parties to the 1992–1995 war in BiH, including Croatia and the Federal Republic of Yugoslavia (consisting of Serbia and Montenegro), and was signed on 14 December 1995.[13]

6. The DPA established BiH as a democratic state consisting of two entities, the Republika Srpska (RS) with majority Serb population, and the Federation of Bosnia and Herzegovina (FBiH) with majority Bosniak and Croat population.[14] The agreement recognized the need of bringing 'an end to the tragic conflict in the region' and expressed a desire 'to promote an enduring peace and stability'.[15] The agreement's Annex 4 is the Constitution of BiH.

7. The DPA also established the Office of the High Representative (OHR) and charged it with, *inter alia*, monitoring, facilitating and coordinating activities on the

6. Malcolm, *Bosnia: A Short History*, 231.
7. *Ibid.*, 230–231.
8. Dizdarević et al., *Democracy Assessment*, 22; Malcolm, *Bosnia: A Short History*, 234.
9. Taylor B. Seybolt, Jay D. Aronson and Baruch Fischhoff. Counting Civilian Casualties: An Introduction to Recording and Estimating Nonmilitary Deaths in Conflict (New York: Oxford University Press 2013), 4.
10. *Ibid: 21–22.*
11. World Bank, *Bosnia and Herzegovina: From Recovery to Sustainable Growth* 3 (World Bank 1997).
12. The Dayton Peace Agreement is called that way since the negotiations which resulted in the agreement were held in a US military base at Dayton, Ohio, USA. The official title for the DPA is the General Framework Agreement for Peace in Bosnia and Herzegovina (hereinafter 'The General Framework Agreement').
13. Dizdarević et al., *Democracy Assessment*, 22–23.
14. *The General Framework Agreement*, Annex 4, Art. I.3, http://www.ohr.int/dayton-peace-agreement/, accessed 12 Sep. 2020. http://www.ohr.int/dpa/default.asp?content_id=380, accessed 5 Nov. 2012.
15. *Ibid.*, Introduction; Annex 4, Art. I.3.

implementation of the peace agreement's civilian aspects.[16] The High Representative (HR) was given the final authority to interpret the agreement on the civilian implementation of the settlement.[17]

8. The HR is nominated by the Steering Board of the Peace Implementation Council (PIC),[18] and endorsed by the United Nations (UN) Security Council.[19] At the PIC conference in Bonn, Germany, in December 1997, the mandate of the HR was strengthened as it was requested by the PIC to remove public officials who obstruct the legal commitments of the DPA from office, as well as impose laws in case BiH legislatures do not.[20] While OHR was at the time strongly involved in the political life of BiH, for over a decade, it has been favouring engagement and responsibilities of local officials and institutions rather than using its own decision-making powers.[21]

9. The first post-war general elections were held in 1996, and the first municipal elections were held in 1997. Early elections for the RS National Assembly were also held in 1997.[22]

10. As a potential candidate country for the accession of the European Union (EU), BiH signed the Stabilization and Association Agreement (SAA) in 2008. However, the later progress has been slow, with SAA not entering fully into force before 2015. The country submitted the EU membership application in 2016, and in May 2019, the European Commission issued the Opinion on the membership application identifying fourteen priorities (in the areas of democracy, rule of law, fundamental rights and public administration) for the country to fulfil in order to be recommended for opening EU accession negotiations.[23]

---

16. *Ibid.*, Annex 10, Art. I.2; II.1.
17. *Ibid.*, Annex 10, Art. V (available at http://www.ohr.int/dpa/default.asp?content_id=366, accessed 5 Nov. 2012).
18. The PIC was established as a result of a Peace Implementation Conference held in London on 8–9 December 1995, for the purpose of mobilizing international support for the Dayton Peace Agreement. The PIC comprises fifty-five countries and international agencies that give support to the peace process in different ways, such as financially, or by providing troops or directly running country operations; a fluctuating number of observers are also involved. See: Office High Rep., *The Peace Implementation Council and its Steering Board*, http://www.ohr.int/international-community-in-bih/peace-implementation-council/, accessed 12 Sep. 2020. http://www.ohr.int/ohr-info/gen-info/#6, accessed 5 Nov. 2012.
19. Office High Rep., *General Information*, http://www.ohr.int/about-ohr/general-information/, accessed 12 Sep. 2020. http://www.ohr.int/ohr-info/gen-info/#1, accessed 5 Nov. 2012.
20. Office High Rep., *The Mandate of the OHR*, http://www.ohr.int/about-ohr/mandate/, accessed 12 Sep. 2020. http://www.ohr.int/ohr-info/gen-info/default.asp?content_id=38612, accessed 5 Nov. 2012.
21. More on OHR involvement of OHR in legislative production in BiH in Merima Tanović. Constitutional Questions about Sovereignty in Context of the Legislative Process in Bosnia and Herzegovina, Pregled - Journal for Social Issues, 2016, Issue 1. 213-221.
22. Dizdarević et al., *Democracy Assessment*, 24.
23. European Commission, https://ec.europa.eu/commission/presscorner/detail/en/COUNTRY_19_2778, accessed 12 Sep. 2020.

B. *State Structure*

11. BiH remains a heavily divided and administratively complex country. The DPA introduced territorial divisions and power-sharing arrangements to end the conflict and keep the country together.

12. The country includes many layers of government, each with its own political structures and administration. State-level institutions are weak in terms of competencies, while the two entities (FBiH and RS), however, carry a high degree of autonomy and have strong competencies.[24] FBiH comprises ten Swiss-style cantons. Moreover, there are 143 local self-government units in the country, 80 in FBiH and 63 in the RS. A separate Brčko District, independent of the two entities' territories, was established by an HR decision in 2000[25] and is a local self-government unit under the sovereignty of the state.[26]

1. State-Level Institutions

13. At the state level, the legislative branch comprises the Parliamentary Assembly, which has two chambers: The House of Representatives and the House of Peoples. The House of Peoples is made up of fifteen delegates, two-thirds from FBiH (five Croats and five Bosniaks) and one-third from the RS (five Serbs), selected by legislatures of the entity level of government.[27] The House of Representatives (forty-two members) is made up of two-thirds elected from the territory of FBiH and one-third from the territory of RS, in line with the election law.[28] Legislation at the state level requires both chambers' approval,[29] but the majority that decides also needs to include at least one-third of the votes of delegates or members from each entity's territory.[30] A majority of delegates of one of the three ethnic groups in the House of Peoples may declare a proposed decision of the Parliamentary Assembly as destructive of their vital interest, where the decision may pass in case the majority of all three ethnic groups' approval in the House of Peoples.[31] In case, such matters are not resolved in the House of Peoples through further procedures indicated in the Constitution, they can be referred to the Constitutional Court of BiH (*Ustavni sud Bosne i Hercegovine*) for a review of procedural regularity.[32]

24. Competences of the different levels of government will be elaborated on later in the monograph.
25. Office High Rep., *Decision on the establishment of the Brčko District of BiH* (Office High Rep. 2000), http://www.ohr.int/decisions/statemattersdec/default.asp?content_id=359 http://www.ohr.int/decision-on-the-establishment-of-the-brcko-district-of-bih/, accessed 12 Sep. 2020 and 5 Nov. 2012.
26. Official Gazette of BiH, 25/09; for an English translation of the Amendment, see Office High Rep., *Amendment I to the Constitution of Bosnia and Herzegovina* (Office High Rep. 2009), http://www.ohr.int/ohr-dept/legal/laws-of-bih/pdf/001%20-%20Constitutions/BH/BH%20Amendment%20I%20to%20BH%20Constitution%2025-09.pdf, accessed 12 Sep. 2020 and 5 Nov. 2012.
27. *The General Framework Agreement*, Annex 4, Art. IV.1.
28. *Ibid.*, Annex 4, Art. IV.2.
29. *Ibid.*, Annex 4, Art. IV.3.c.
30. *Ibid.*, Annex 4, Art. IV.3.d.
31. *Ibid.*, Annex 4, Art. IV.3.e.
32. *Ibid.*, Annex 4, Art. IV.3.f.

14. A three-member rotating Presidency and the Council of Ministers of BiH represent the executive. The Presidency consists of a Bosniak and a Croat each directly elected from the FBiH territory, and a Serb directly elected from the RS territory.[33] The Presidency is to adopt decisions by consensus; they may be adopted by two members if consensus is not reached, but a dissenting member may declare the decision as destructive of a vital interest of the entity from which they were elected. Such a declaration is then referred to the respective entity legislative body where the respective ethnic group can confirm the declaration and render the challenged decision ineffective.[34]

15. The Presidency's responsibilities are listed in Article V.3 of the Constitution and will be elaborated on later. However, it is important to note that the Presidency nominates the Chair of the Council of Ministers, subject to further approval by the House of Representatives. The Chair nominates state-level ministers and deputy ministers, also subject to the approval of the House of Representatives.[35] The Council of Ministers, responsible for carrying out the policies and decisions at the state level in line with state-level responsibilities listed in the Constitution,[36] reports to the Parliamentary Assembly.[37]

16. The Constitutional Court of BiH has nine members.[38] Its main jurisdiction is to uphold the BiH Constitution,[39] and in that regard, it has exclusive jurisdiction to decide on any dispute that arises between the entities, between BiH and the entities, or between BiH institutions, including deciding on whether a provision of an entity's constitution or law is consistent with the BiH Constitution.[40] Moreover, it has jurisdiction over issues under the Constitution arising out of a judgment of all other courts in the country. It also has jurisdiction over issues referred by any court in the country on whether a law, on whose validity that court's decision may depend, is compatible with the Constitution, the European Convention for Human Rights and

---

33. *Ibid.*, Annex 4, Art. V. Nevertheless, the judgment of the European Court of Human Rights in the case of *Dervo Sejdić and Jakob Finci v. Bosnia and Herzegovina* (Applications No. 27996/06 and 34836/06 of 22 Dec. 2009) established that there is systemic constitutional discrimination of all persons not belonging to the three constituent peoples – Bosniaks, Croats or Serbs – on account of their inability to stand as candidates for position in the Presidency of BiH and the House of Peoples of the BiH Parliamentary Assembly. See more: Edin Hodžić & Nenad Stojanović, *New/Old Constitutional Engineering? Challenges and Implications of the European Court of Human Rights Decision in the Case of Sejdić and Finci v. BiH* (Analitika – Center for Social Research 2011) (available at http://analitika.ba/sites/default/files/publikacije/NEW%20OLD%20CONSTITUTIONAL%20 ENGINEERING%20-%2007062011%20za%20web_0.pdf, accessed 12 Sep. 2020). http://analitika.ba/en/publications/%E2%80%9Cnewold-constitutional-engineering%E2%80%9D, accessed 12 Nov. 2012).
34. *Ibid.*, Annex 4, Art. V. 2.c. and 2.d.
35. *Ibid.*, Annex 4, Art. V.4.
36. *Ibid.*, Annex 4, Art. III.1, 4 and 5.
37. *Ibid.*, Annex 4, Art. V, 4.a.
38. Four are selected by the FBiH House of Representatives, two by the RS Assembly, and three by the President of the European Court of Human Rights (ECHR) upon consultation with the BiH Presidency. See *The General Framework Agreement*, Annex 4, Art. VI.1.a.
39. *The General Framework Agreement,* Annex 4, Art. VI. 3.
40. *Ibid.*, Annex 4, Art. VI. 3.a.; 3.a.2.

Fundamental Freedoms (with protocols) or laws of BiH. The constitutional court also decides on issues referred by any court concerning the existence of or scope of a general rule of public international law that is pertinent to that court's decision.[41] The Court's decisions are final and binding,[42] but the authorities on different levels frequently fail to implement some of them, with relative impunity.[43]

17. A decision by the HR established the Court of BiH (*Sud Bosne i Hercegovine*) on 9 May 2002 and the Office of the BiH Prosecutor (*Tužilaštvo Bosne i* Hercegovine) on 7 May 2002.[44]

2. The FBiH Institutions

18. The FBiH[45] has a complex administrative structure.[46] At the entity level of the government, it consists of a Parliament, consisting of the House of Representatives and the House of Peoples.[47] The delegates of the House of Representatives are directly elected,[48] while the delegates of the House of Peoples are delegated by cantonal assemblies from the ranks of their own MPs, in proportion to the national structure of the population in that canton.[49] Parliamentary decisions need the approval of both chambers.[50] There is a parliamentary procedure for the protection

41. *Ibid.*, Annex 4, Art. VI. 3.b and 3.c.
42. *Ibid.*, Annex 4, Art. VI. 4.
43. Balkan Investigative Reporting Network (BIRN), Duga historija ignorisanja presuda ustavnog suda BiH 2020 [Long history of ignoring the rulings of Constitution court of BiH] https://detektor.ba/2020/02/19/duga-historija-ignorisanja-presuda-ustavnog-suda-bih/, accessed 12 Sep. 2020.
44. Dizdarević et al., *Democracy Assessment*, 24.
45. For the Constitution of FBiH and amendments, *see* Official Gazette of the Federation of BiH, 1/94, 13/97, 13/97, 16/02, 22/02, 52/02, 18/03, 63/03, 9/04, 20/04, 33/04, 71/05, 72/05 and 88/08. A consolidated, unofficial version of the Constitution in local language is referred to here, including all amendments to date: Constitutional Court of FBiH, Constitution of FBiH: Unofficial Consolidated Text (*Ustav Federacije BiH: Neslužbeni prečišćeni tekst*) (available at http://www.ustavnisudfbih.ba/bs/dokumenti/ustav_precisceni_tekst.pdf, accessed 12 Sep. 2020 and 5 Nov. 2012; for an English translation of the Constitution and amendments, see Office High Rep. (n.d.). Constitutions (available at http://www.ohr.int/laws-of-bih/constitutions-2/, accessed 12 Sep. 2020). http://www.ohr.int/ohr-dept/legal/laws-of-bih/constitutions.asp, accessed 5 Nov. 2012).
46. According to Newbury and Behr, FBiH 'seeks to organize the very mixed Bosniak and Croat population under a single federated structure. Respect for local conditions, which, in this instance, are mostly ethnic, has therefore necessitated a highly decentralized organization'. According to the authors, both in terminology used and constitutional organization, it is obvious this constituent entity of the de facto federal state of BiH has the character of a federation, so that federalism can be found at two levels, making it a 'fairly unique solution in the world'. Source: Christopher Newbury & Karsten Behr, *Local and Regional Democracy in Bosnia and Herzegovina, The Congress of Local and Regional Authorities, The Voice of Cities and Regions* para. 19 (Council of Europe 2006) (available at https://wcd.coe.int/ViewDoc.jsp?id=1052891&Site=COE, accessed 12 Sep. 2020 and 5 Nov. 2012).
47. *Constitution of FBiH: Unofficial Consolidated Text*, IV.A.a.
48. *Ibid.*, IV. A.1. Art. 3(1).
49. *Ibid.*, IV. A.2. Art. 8(1).
50. *Ibid.*, IV. A.4. Art. 17 (Except for rulebooks and decisions chambers independently adopt).

of vital interests of the three dominant ethnic groups.[51] *Inter alia*, the FBiH Parliament is responsible for electing an FBiH President and two vice-presidents,[52] approving the Government[53] and enacting laws exercising responsibilities allocated to the FBiH Government.[54]

19. The entity's executive is represented by the President (with two vice-presidents of different constituent peoples)[55] and the Government.[56] The President and vice-presidents can be nominated by respective clubs of the three ethnic groups in the House of Peoples and are elected by both chambers of parliament.[57] The Government, led by a Prime Minister, is nominated by the President and approved by the House of Representatives.[58]

20. The judiciary at the FBiH level consists of a Constitutional Court of FBiH (*Ustavni sud Federacije Bosne i Hercegovine*) and a Supreme Court of FBiH (*Vrhovni sud Federacije Bosne i Hercegovine*).[59] The Constitutional Court of FBiH is, *inter alia*, responsible for resolving disputes between the different levels of government or institutions in FBiH, determining whether laws adopted by legislatures at different levels of government in the FBiH or regulation adopted or enacted by different bodies at different levels of government in the FBiH are in accordance with the Constitution.[60] The Constitutional Court of FBiH gives protection with respect to the right to local self-government, decides on constitutional matters referred to it by other courts in the FBiH, etc. Decisions are final and binding.[61] The Supreme Court is the highest Court of Appeals in FBiH with original jurisdiction as provided by FBiH legislation. Its judgments are also final and binding.[62]

21. The Constitution of FBiH entails provision regarding the distribution of key functions in the executive, legislature and the judiciary among the constituent peoples and representatives of 'others'.[63]

---

51. *Ibid.*, IV. A.6.
52. *Ibid.*, IV. A.7. Art. 20(1) a).
53. *Ibid.*, IV. A.7. Art. (1) c).
54. *Ibid.*, IV. A.7. Art. (1) d).
55. The preamble to the Constitution of BiH states that the sources of the Constitution are: Bosniaks, Croats, and Serbs, as constituent peoples (along with Others), and citizens of Bosnia and Herzegovina. According to the International Crisis Group (ICG) Report: 'to be a "constituent people" (*narod*) amounts essentially to being a "statecreating" people and to not being a national minority (*narodnost*, literally "nationality"), regardless of whether the people in question is a numerical minority in the polity'. Source: ICG – International Crisis Group, *Implementing Equality: The 'Constituent Peoples' Decision in Bosnia & Herzegovina* (International Crisis Group, Sarajevo/Brussels, ICG Balkans Report N° 128, 16 Apr. 2002), https://d2071andvip0wj.cloudfront.net/128-implementing-equality-the-constituent-peoples-decision-in-bosnia-herzegovina.pdf, accessed 28 Nov. 2020.
56. *Constitution of FBiH: Unofficial Consolidated Text*, IV. B.1. Art. 1.
57. *Ibid.*, IV. B.1. Art. 2(1) and (2).
58. *Ibid.*, IV. B.2. Arts 4(1) and 5(1).
59. For more on general provisions regarding the FBiH judiciary, *see* Constitutional of FBiH IV. C.
60. *Constitution of FBiH: Unofficial Consolidated Text*, IV.C 3. Art. 10(1)–(5).
61. *Ibid.*, IV.C.3. Art. 12.
62. *Ibid.*, IV.C.3. Arts 14 and 16.
63. *Ibid.*, IV.D Art. 1.

22. As mentioned above, the FBiH consists of ten federal units, the cantons.[64] Cantons have their own constitutions, which have to be in accordance with the FBiH Constitution.[65]

23. Each of the ten cantons has a legislature, an assembly made up of directly elected members, in charge of enacting cantonal legislation.[66] Mechanisms for the protection of vital national interest also exist in the cantonal legislature.[67] The executive of the canton is the government, led by a prime minister and approved by the assembly. the cantonal government is responsible for enacting and executing cantonal policies and legislation, implementing cantonal and FBiH courts' decisions and responsibilities assigned to the canton by the FBiH government, cantonal police oversight, etc.[68] Courts exist at the cantonal (and municipal) level as well.[69]

24. Municipalities in FBiH have their representative body, the municipal council, and a directly elected mayor as their executive body.[70]

3. The Republika Srpska Institutions

25. The Parliament of RS[71] consists of the National Assembly, which is made up of directly elected deputies, and the Council of Peoples[72] whose members are elected by the relevant caucuses in the National Assembly. Procedures for the Council with respect to the matters of vital interests of constituent peoples as its exclusive competence are elaborated in the Constitution of RS.[73]

26. In addition to the President (and two vice-presidents, from different constituent peoples each), the executive is made up of the Government. The President proposes the candidate for the president of the government, elected by the National Assembly to whom it is responsible.[74]

64. *Ibid.*, I, Art. 2.
65. *Ibid.*, V.1., Art. 4.
66. *Ibid.*, V.2. Arts 5 and 6.
67. *Ibid.*, V.2. Art. 7a and 7b.
68. *Ibid.*, V.3., Arts 8, 8a, 9.
69. *Ibid.*, V.4.
70. *Ibid.*, VI, Arts 1–7.
71. For the RS Constitution and its amendments, *see*: Official Gazette of RS 3/92, 6/92, 8/92, 15/92, 19/92, 28/94, 8/96, 13/96, 15/96, 16/96, 21/96, 21/02, 30/02, 31/02, 69/02, 31/03, 98/03, 115/05, 117/05 and 48/11 Here, the reference is to a consolidated English translation: National Council of RS (nd), *Constitution of Republika Srpska*, https://www.narodnaskupstinars.net/sites/default/files/upload/dokumenti/ustav/eng/USTAV-RS_English.pdf, accessed 12 Sep. 2020 http://www.vijecenarodars.net/materijali/constitution.pdf, accessed 5 Nov. 2012.
72. *Constitution of RS*, V, Art. 69. It should be noted that Thea status of the RS Council of Peoples is however an advisory body rather than a proper legislative chamber in RS is debatable and indeed subject to considerable constitutional debate within Bosnia and Herzegovina.
73. *Ibid.*, V. 1, Arts 70 and 71.
74. *Ibid.*, V. 2, Art. 80; V.3. Art. 94. Art. 92 contains provisions with respect to the ethnic makeup of the government.

27. Judicial powers are vested to the courts in the RS. Constitutionality and legality are to be provided by the Constitutional Court of RS (*Ustavni sud Republike Srpske*).[75] It decides on the conformity of laws, regulations and general acts with the constitution; the conformity of regulations and general legal acts with the law; conflicts of jurisdiction among the legislative, executive and judicial branches; conflicts of jurisdiction among levels of government in the RS, etc. Its decisions are binding and enforceable.[76] As the FBiH, the RS has a Supreme Court of RS (*Vrhovni sud Republike Srpske*) as its highest court.[77]

28. There are constitutional provisions for the distribution of key functions of different branches of government between constituent peoples and others.[78]

29. In addition to the entity level, there is a municipal level of government in the RS: similarly to the FBiH, it contains a municipal assembly and a directly elected mayor as the head of the executive.[79]

4. Brčko District Institutions

30. The status of the Brčko District that is established as a self-governing unit under the jurisdiction of the state of BiH provides for a legislative body – the District Assembly – and the executive which is represented by the mayor. Brčko has its own courts: a basic court and a Court of Appeal.[80]

C. Division of Competences between Different Levels of Government

31. As previously explained, the DPA has granted a broad set of powers to the OHR, especially considering its mandate to impose laws and intervene in any sphere of the country's political or economic life – including media – in order to ensure the implementation of the peace agreement.

32. The powers of the state of BiH are limited. In line with the Constitution of BiH, institutions of BiH are responsible for the following matters: foreign policy; foreign trade policy; customs policy; monetary policy; finances of institutions and international obligation of BiH; immigration, refugee and asylum policy and regulation; international and inter-entity Criminal Code enforcement, which includes

75. *Ibid.*, V, Art. 69.
76. *Ibid.*, VIII, Art. 115; Art. 119.
77. *Ibid.*, VIII, Art. 123.
78. *Ibid.*, V, Art. 69.
79. *Ibid.*, VI, Art. 102.
80. For more, *see: Statute of the Brčko District of BiH: consolidated text* (*Statut Brčko Distrikta BiH: precisceni tekst,* District Assembly of Brčko 2010), https://skupstinabd.ba/images/dokumenti/ba/statut-brcko-distrikta.pdf, accessed 12 Sep. 2020. http://www.skupstinabd.ba/statut/h/Statut%20Brcko%20distrikta%20BiH%20-%20precisceni%20tekst%202-10%20H.pdf, accessed 5 Nov. 2012.

relations with Interpol; establishment and operation of common and international communications facilities; inter-entity transportation regulation; and air traffic control.[81]

33. The two entities – FBiH and RS – have the right to establish special parallel relationships with neighbouring states in line with BiH sovereignty and territorial integrity. They are to provide all necessary assistance to the BiH government to honour international obligations of BiH, provide a safe and secure environment for all persons in their respective jurisdictions through the maintenance of civilian law enforcement agencies operating in line with international standards, entering into agreements with states and international organizations with the consent of the BiH Parliamentary Assembly.[82] According to the Constitution of BiH, all governmental functions and powers not expressly assigned to the institutions of BiH are to be entity functions and powers.[83] Additional responsibilities may be conferred to the state if entities agree, for which additional institutions can be established at the state level.[84]

34. There are some differences with respect to competencies between the RS[85] and FBiH,[86] given that FBiH is divided into cantons. According to the FBiH Constitution, cantons are to have all responsibility not expressly granted to the FBiH government.[87]

---

81. *The General Framework Agreement*, Annex 4, Art. 3.1.
82. *Ibid.*, Annex 4, Art. 3.2.
83. *Ibid.*, Annex 4, Art. 3.3.
84. *Ibid.*, Annex 4, Art. 3.5.
85. According to the amended RS Constitution, Art. 68, the RS is to regulate and ensure integrity, constitutional order and territorial unity of the RS; security; measures in its jurisdiction to be implemented in a state of war or emergency declared by BiH or RS institutions; constitutionality and legality; exercise and protection of human rights and freedoms; ownership and obligation relations, protection of all forms of ownership, legal status of enterprises and other organizations, their associations and chambers, economic relations with countries which have not been transferred to the BiH institutions market relations and planning; banking and tax system; objectives and directions for economic, scientific, technological, demographic and social development, agricultural development, development of rural and urban areas, policies and measures for development planning, and commodity reserves, legality of handling property and resources owned by legal entities and legality of collecting statistical and other data of general interest; organization, powers and functions of state authority bodies; public services system; labour relations, safety in the workplace, employment, social security and other forms of social care, health care, war veteran and disability benefits, child and youth welfare, education, culture and preservation of cultural heritage, physical education and sports; environmental protection; the public information system; international relations, other than those at BiH level; financing for the exercise of rights and duties; other relations of interest to the RS, in line with the Constitution. Ch. V, Art. 68.
86. According to Ch. III, Art. 1, the following are the exclusive responsibility of FBiH; FBiH citizenship, determining economic policies, including planning and reconstructions, and policies of land use at the federal level, adopting regulation on finance and finance institutions of the Federation and the Federation's fiscal policy; combating terrorism, inter-cantonal crime, illegal drug trafficking and organized crime; issuing of electronic frequencies for radio, TV and other purposes, in line with the BiH Constitution; determining energy policy (including distribution between cantons) and ensuring and maintaining the necessary infrastructure, financing the work of federal institutions and bodies. According to Ch. III, Art. 2, Federal and cantonal authorities are jointly responsible for guaranteeing

D. *Overview of the Bosnia-Herzegovina Constitutional Situation in the Context of Media, Communication, Broadcasting and Telecommunications Regulation & Policy*

35. Complex political context, administrative structure, and a slow post-war recovery have decisively shaped the communication, broadcasting and telecommunications regulation and policy in BiH. There are fourteen Constitutions that need to be considered in that respect: Constitution of BiH, Constitution of RS, Statute of Brčko District, and the Constitution of FBiH with the Constitutions of its ten cantons. Additionally, a crucial factor in the shaping of media and communication policy in BiH is the OHR whose powers have been enshrined in the DPA and extended by subsequent decisions of the PIC.

1. Constitution of BiH

36. The Constitution of BiH[88] stipulates that the establishment and operation of common and international communications facilities is the responsibility of the Institutions of BiH.[89] All governmental functions and powers not expressly assigned in the Constitution to the institutions of BiH shall be those of the Entities.[90]

37. Furthermore, the Constitution of BiH stipulates that:

> Bosnia and Herzegovina shall assume responsibility for such other matters as are agreed by the Entities; are provided for in Annexes 5 through 8 to the General Framework Agreement; or are necessary to preserve the sovereignty, territorial integrity, political independence, and international personality of Bosnia and Herzegovina, in accordance with the division of responsibilities

---

and implementing human rights; health; environmental protection policies; policies concerning communication and transportation infrastructure; social policy; implementation of laws and regulations on BiH citizenship and travel documents for the FBiH territory; residence and movement of foreigners; tourism, and the use of natural resources. According to Ch. III, Art. 3, these responsibilities can be met together or separately, but in continuous agreement. See, Constitutional Court of FBiH.

87. Constitutional Court of FBiH (nd). III, Art. 4. According to this article, they are especially responsible for: establishing and oversight of police forces; setting education policies, including provision of education; setting and implementing of cultural policies, setting housing policy; setting policy on the regulation and provision of public services; adopting regulations on the use of local land, including zoning; adopting regulations on improvement of local business and charitable activities; adopting regulations on local energy production facilities and ensuring their availability; setting policy with respect to the provision of radio and television, including adopting regulation on the provision of their work and establishment; implementation of social welfare policy and establishment of social welfare services; creation and implementation of cantonal tourism policy, development of tourism resources; financing activities of cantonal authority or its agencies through taxation, borrowing or other means.

88. *The General Framework Agreement*, Annex IV, Art. III (Responsibilities of and Relations between the Institutions of Bosnia and Herzegovina and the Entities).

89. *Ibid.*, Art. III.1.h.

90. *Ibid.*, Art. III.3.a.

between the institutions of Bosnia and Herzegovina. Additional institutions may be established as necessary to carry out such responsibilities.[91]

2. Constitutions of Federation BiH and Its Cantons

38. The Constitution of FBiH stipulates that the Federation shall have exclusive responsibility for allocating electronic frequencies for radio, TV and other purposes, pursuant to the BiH Constitution.[92] Furthermore, according to Article 2(a), both the FBiH Government and the cantons are to have responsibilities for the infrastructure for communications and transport, in line with the Constitution of BiH. These responsibilities may be exercised jointly or separately, or by the cantons as coordinated by the FBiH Government.[93] Article 4 of the Constitution of FBiH stipulates that the cantons shall have all responsibility not expressly granted to the FBiH Government. They shall have, in particular, responsibility for making policy concerning radio and television facilities, including decisions concerning regulation and provision thereof.

39. The Cantonal Constitutions in an almost identical way, and in accordance with the Constitution of FBiH, stipulate that the cantons shall have all responsibility not exclusively granted to the FBiH Government. This entails the development of broadcasting policy, including the adoption of legislation regarding the functioning of radio and TV broadcasters. Additionally, cantons and FBiH are jointly responsible for communications infrastructure.[94]

40. Consequently, there is no law regulating media and information at the level of FBiH. Instead, six out of ten cantons have introduced the Laws on Public Information or Laws on the Media, depending on the canton.[95] These laws are in many aspects similar and attempt to define the totality of information and media space, covering both print and broadcast media, albeit to a different level of detail. All of these laws guarantee freedom of expression and freedom of access to information.[96] Nevertheless, in practice, these cantonal laws are rather redundant since there are

91. *Ibid.*, Art. III.5.a (Additional Responsibilities).
92. Constitution of FBiH, sec. III (Division of Responsibilities between the Federation Government and the Cantons), Art. 1(a).
93. *Ibid.*, Art. 3.
94. For example: Constitution of Hercegovina Neretva Canton, Art. 16; Constitution of Tuzla-Podrinje Canton, Art. 12; Constitution of Sarajevo Canton, Art. 13.
95. Two cantons – Hercegovačko-neretvanski Canton and Srednjoebosanski Canton – have never adopted such laws while the Canton of Sarajevo abolished its law in 2009 (Official Gazette of Canton Sarajevo 15/09). Mirjana Nadaždin-Defterdarević, *Normativni okvir prava na informisanje u Bosni i Hercegovini, in Medijsko pravo u Bosni i Hercegovini* 99–100 (Mehmed Halilović & Amer Džihana eds, Internews 2012).
96. Nadaždin-Defterdarević, Normativni okvir prava na informisanje u Bosni i Hercegovini, 99.

laws on entity and state levels that sufficiently regulate the area of media and communications.[97] However, some cantons recently considered amending the existing information/media laws.[98]

3. Constitution of Republika Srpska

41. According to Article 3 of the Constitution of RS, 'all State functions and powers shall belong to the Republic, with exception of those which were by the Constitution of Bosnia and Herzegovina explicitly transferred to its institutions'. Article 68(14) stipulates that the RS shall regulate and ensure public information systems.

42. In Republika Srpska, the area of public information is regulated by the Law on Public Information.[99] The Law on Public Information stipulates the freedom of expression and prohibits censorship, and regulates the establishment and registration of the media. It further regulates the limitation to exercise the right to information in specific cases, such as incitement to hatred, endangering the freedoms and rights of others, etc. Nevertheless, the Law does not contain provisions on the protection of journalists and on access to information.[100]

4. Brčko District

43. The Statute of the Brčko District contains no provisions specifically related to communication and media. It is only Article 8 (Exercise of Public Authority in the District) that stipulates that the competencies of the public authorities in the District also include public services and infrastructure, but it does not provide any precise references to media and communication.

5. International Community and OHR

44. There are two important provisions in the DPA that are relevant for the media, and that have been the basis for the subsequent intervention of the HR when it comes to the introduction of media and communication policies in the country.

97. *See* sec, *Confusing Legal Parallelism*, para. 50, *infra*.
98. For instance, Una-Sana Canton, *see* the programme of Cantonal Assembly for 2019, at: http://vladausk.ba/v4/files/media/pdf/5ca2f5e5a88241.63905002_Program_rada_%20Skupstine_2019.pdf, accessed 20 Sep. 2020.
99. The Law on Public Information of RS (*Zakon o javnom informisanju Republike Srpske*, Official Gazette of RS 10/97).
100. Nadaždin-Defterdarević, *Normativni okvir prava na informisanje u Bosni i Hercegovini*, 98–99.

First, signatories of the agreement are to prevent any incitement to ethnic or religious intolerance in the media.[101] Second, the signatories are to secure conditions for fair and free elections, politically neutral surroundings, freedom of expression and freedom of the press.[102]

45. Nevertheless, the political gridlock in the years following the war blocked the decision-making processes and peace implementation efforts. This has made the involvement by the OHR and other international actors rather necessary in order to ensure peace and democratization. The OHR used its power – given to it at the Bonn[103] and Sintra conferences[104] of PIC in 1997 – extensively: for example, the HR established the state-level Court of BiH and the Office of the BiH Prosecutor in 2002,[105] amended Constitutions of FBiH and RS, removed elected politicians, etc.[106]

46. The run up to the first post-war election in late 1996 demonstrated that the mainstream media in BiH are under strong political influence and lack basic standards of professionalism. Such a situation radically reduced the chances for free and fair elections by preventing opposition parties from accessing mainstream media. Moreover, some media outlets continued inciting ethnic hatred and acted as a propaganda tool for discrediting international peace implementation organizations and political opponents.[107]

---

101. *The General Framework Agreement*, Annex 7, Art. 1.3.b.
102. *Ibid.*, Annex 3, Art. 1.1.
103. Following the continuous obstruction of the implementation of the DPA by local political elites, the mandate of HR was strengthened at the PIC conference in December 1997 in Bonn, Germany, having been given the powers to remove from office public officials who obstruct the DPA, as well as to impose laws in cases when BiH legislatures fail to do so and as the HR sees fit.
104. At a ministerial meeting of the PIC Steering Board in Sintra, Portugal, in May 1997, the HR was given the right to take off the air any media network or programme whose output is in persistent and blatant contravention to the DPA. The main reason behind the Sintra Declaration was the destructive behaviour of RS state broadcasters Serb Radio and Television (later renamed to RTRS: Radio-Televislon of Republika Srpska) which attempted to discredit Stabilization Force (SFOR) and North Atlantic Treaty Organization (NATO) peacekeeping troops whom it compared to Nazi occupation forces from World War II, incited ethnic hatred, and generally undermined the Dayton Peace Agreement. As a consequence, on 1 October 1997, the HR requested SFOR troops to take control of crucial Serb Radio and Television transmitters, thus using military force to start the restructuring of the broadcaster. For details, *see*: Mark Thompson & Dan De Luce, *Escalating to Success? The Media Intervention in Bosnia and Herzegovina, in Forging Peace: Intervention, Human Rights and the Management of Media Space* 208–212 (Monroe E. Price & Mark Thompson eds, Edinburgh U. Press 2002).
105. Dizdarević et al., 2006: 24.
106. All OHR decisions are available at http://www.ohr.int/decisions-of-the-high-representative/, accessed 12 Sep. 2020. http://www.ohr.int/decisions/archive.asp, accessed 13 Feb. 2012.
107. Media Experts Commission, *Završni izvještaj: Mediji u izborima* (*Media Experts Commission*, OSCE Mission in Bosnia and Herzegovina, 1998); Kemal Kurspahić, *Zločin u 19:30 – Balkanski mediji u ratu i miru* (Mediacentar Sarajevo and South East Europe Media Organization SEEMO, 2003); Thompson & De Luce, *Escalating to Success?*

47. In such a negative context, the international community was forced to introduce the same basic regulatory principles for the media. The Organization for Security and Cooperation in Europe (OSCE), which was mandated to organize elections, established the Media Experts Commission (MEC) in 1996 that was tasked to enforce the compliance of the media with electoral rules and regulations issued by the Provisional Electoral Commission.[108] The mandate of the MEC expired after the 1998 October elections.[109]

48. In June 1998, the OHR established the Independent Media Commission (IMC)). The IMC was tasked to manage the frequency spectrum, issue broadcasting licenses, draft and enforce codes of conduct for broadcasters and deal with complaints.[110] In 2001, the OHR merged the IMC and the Telecommunications Regulatory Agency into the Communications Regulatory Agency (CRA). This converged regulatory body was put in charge of both broadcasting and telecommunications.[111] In October 2002, the HR imposed the Communications Law of BiH,[112] providing the legal basis for the existence of the CRA.

49. Other important developments in the media sector have taken place thanks to the efforts and intervention of OHR, help from various donors and development agencies, and continuous pressures from important international actors, such as the European Commission and the USA. Hence, the Press Code for the print media was adopted, and the Press Council established. The laws decriminalizing libel and defamation were introduced at state and entity levels. Additionally, a Freedom of Access to Information Act (FOIA) at state and entity[113] levels were introduced, while the transformation of the formerly state-owned broadcasters into the Public Service Broadcasting System (PSB) of BiH has been started.[114]

108. Media Experts Commission, *Završni izvještaj: Mediji u izborima*, 10.
109. *Ibid.*, 19.
110. Hans Bredow Institute for Media Research, Interdisciplinary Centre for Law & ICT (ICRI), Katholieke Universiteit Leuven, Center for Media and Communication Studies (CMCS), Central European University, Cullen International, Perspective Associates (eds.), *INDIREG – Indicators for Independence and Efficient Functioning of Audiovisual Media Services Regulatory Bodies for the Purpose of Enforcing the Rules in the AVMS Directive* 92 (Study conducted on behalf of the European Commission, 2011).
111. Hans Bredow Institute for Media Research et al., *INDIREG*, 176; Thompson & De Luce, *Escalating to Success?*
112. Communications Law of BiH (*Zakon o komunikacijama*, Official Gazette of BiH 31/03; with amendments in Official Gazette of BiH 75/06, 32/10. 98/12).
113. *See* sec. 1. Public Documents, ch. 5. Access to Public Information, *infra.*
114. Especially important was the *Decisions of the High Representative on Restructuring of the Public Broadcasting System in BiH and on Freedom of Information and on Abolishment of Criminal Sanctions for Insult and Defamation* (30 Jul. 1999), which created the basis for the subsequent legislative reforms pertaining to the media and communications in BiH, http://www.ohr.int/decisions-on-the-restructuring-of-the-public-broadcasting-system-in-bih-and-on-freedom-of-information-and-decriminalisation-of-libel-and-defamation/, accessed 13 Sep. 2020. http://www.ohr.int/decisions/mediadec/default.asp?content_id=98, accessed 11 Nov. 2012.

6. Inconsistent Practice and Legislative Stagnation

50. The set of laws introduced by OHR provides a basis for media regulation, anchored to international standards. Nevertheless, a confusing legal parallelism is created by the media laws or public information laws on the level of cantons and the RS that cover some of the same issues,[115] which remain in force despite numerous shortcomings.[116] Moreover, while the legislative and institutional framework introduced by the international community is commendable, its effects have been limited due to inconsistent implementation, political interference, the lack of capacities of the judiciary and the media regulator. Misuse of defamation laws as instruments of pressure on the media,[117] as well as weak FOIA implementation mechanisms,[118] are only some of the examples of uncertainty and inconsistency when it comes to implementation of legal framework. In addition, important professional self-regulatory standards have been introduced as a result of international media assistance efforts, but many media outlets fail to comply with ethical codes of conduct due to particular financial or political interests.[119] Since 2005, the OHR has stopped actively engaging in media regulation, leaving it to the local authorities to deal with media policy issues. However, local actors have failed to adequately address some of the main underregulated areas of the media market, such as media ownership, financial transparency, and government funding.[120]

II. Geography and Population

51. BiH has a population of 3.53 million[121] and is located in the so-called Western Balkan region, surrounded by Croatia, Serbia and Montenegro – all of which gained their independence after the dissolution of the Socialist Federal Republic of

115. Nadaždin-Defterdarević, Normativni okvir prava na informisanje u Bosni i Hercegovini, 99–105. As a positive example, the Assembly of the Sarajevo Canton terminated the validity of the Law on the Media of Sarajevo Canton in 2009, deeming the cantonal law superfluous at the background of the regulatory framework set up at state and entity level. Official Gazette of Sarajevo Canton 15/09.
116. For instance, the Law on Information of RS has been criticized for being outdated, not having changed in twenty years. More in T.Č. RS treba novi zakon o medijima: "RTRS je probio dno, ali Google pamti" (Buka magazine 2018; at https://www.6yka.com/novosti/rs-treba-novi-zakon-o-medijima-rtrs-je-probio-dno-ali-google-pamti, accessed 13 Sep. 2020).
117. Defamation laws have been exploited by not only politicians but also media and related actors through civil lawsuits and high damage payments demands, which in some cases endanger sustainability of media outlets. *Ibid.*, 162.
118. For instance, the representatives of Center for Investigative Journalism have reported that the procedures of pursuing the information after a public body denied access can last for years and be costly for a media outlet. Source: Sanela Hodžić and Anida Sokol. Media Sustainability Index Bosnia and Herzegovina. IREX, 2018. p. 4.
119. Sanela Hodžić and Anida Sokol. MSI IREX Bosnia and Herzegovina, 2019. p. 4.
120. *See*, for instance, Sanela Hodžić, *Bosnia and Herzegovina*, in Petković (ed.) 2014, 122–123.
121. Census data for 2013 at http://www.statistika.ba/, accessed 13 Sep. 2020. Agency for Statistics of Bosnia & Herzegovina, *Bosna i Hercegovina u brojkama* (Agency for Statistics of Bosnia and Herzegovina, 2011), 5, http://www.bhas.ba/tematskibilteni/BIH_brojke_ 11_bh.pdf, accessed 5 Nov. 2012.

Yugoslavia during the 1990s. The population of the country consists of three dominant ethnic groups – referred to in the BiH Constitution as constituent peoples, Bosniaks (Muslims), Serbs (Orthodox) and Croats (Roman Catholic), and several other minority groups, referred to as 'others'. Bosniaks make up 50.11% of the population, Serbs 30.78% and Croats 15.43%.[122] The country covers an area of 51,209 km^2,[123] with the largest city being the capital of Sarajevo, located in FBiH, and the second-largest city Banja Luka, located in the RS.

III. Social and Cultural Values

52. BiH does not have a unified socio-economic space or cultural identity. Social and cultural values correspond to strong ethnonational, religious, and territorial cleavages. There are three official languages (Bosnian, Serbian and Croatian) and two official alphabets (Latin and Cyrillic) in use. Two major ethnic groups have strong ties with neighbouring countries: Serbs with Serbia and Croats with Croatia. Hence, the country has three parallel socio-cultural spaces, each corresponding with the territory dominated by one of the three major ethnic groups: Bosniaks, Serbs and Croats.

§2. The Media Landscape

I. Overview of Media Markets and Main Actors

A. *Introduction*

53. The media landscape of BiH closely mirrors ethnic and political cleavages in the country. There are several parallel media systems that coexist and closely mirror ethnic territorial divisions: The media in RS primarily cater to the interests of the Serb population in that entity; media in the Bosniak-dominated areas such as Sarajevo, Tuzla, Zenica, and Bihać are primarily directed towards the Bosniak population, while media from Croat-dominated parts cater to interests of the Croat population. In addition, there is a strong political bias with the majority of media reporting favourably about a ruling political party within its ethnonational group.[124] There is also a PSB of BiH, consisting of three broadcasters: state-wide Radio and Television of BiH (BHRT); Radio and Television of FBiH (RTVFBiH); and Radio and Television of RS (RTRS). A number of state-wide commercial TV networks and a state-wide Public Service Broadcasting TV channel are targeting the broader

---

122. UNDP Human Development Report 2005, referred to in: Transparency International, *National Integrity System Study – Bosnia and Herzegovina 2007* 17 (Transparency International 2006). *Ibid.*
123. Agency for Statistics of Bosnia and Herzegovina, *Bosna i Hercegovina u brojevimakama*, 2020, 5.
124. *See* Hodžić & Sokol MSI IREX 2019, 8. GfK BiH, *Broadcasting media in Bosnia and Herzegovina* (GfK BiH, Press Release 16 Feb. 2006) http://www.gfk.ba/imperia/md/content/gfkbh/pr_eng/gfk_pr_02-2006_-_tv_and_radio.pdf, accessed 20 Aug. 2012.

population of the country. There is also a strong influence of media systems from neighbouring countries, Serbia and Croatia, and the growing presence of regional and global media groups.

B. TV Broadcasting

54. Estimates on media funding show a sharp decline in advertising revenues in the past decade due to the global economic crisis and advertisers moving away from local media and more towards regional and global media and non-journalistic communication platforms. From the estimated EUR 41 million in 2008, the overall TV advertising revenues dropped to an estimated EUR 20 million by 2017.[125] Majority of these revenues are collected by the bigger televisions with the national coverage, while a large number of smaller TV outlets compete for a minuscule portion of the advertising pie. The public service broadcasters are in addition funded through RTV subscription fees, but the authorities fail to assure an efficient collection, and some political officials advocate against paying the fee, arguing, most notably, that the existing PSB does not represent the interests of Croats in BiH.[126] Public bodies and institutions also allocate considerable funds to media outlets. This is how public service broadcaster RTRS received around EUR 150,000 from the Secretariat General of the Government of Republika Srpska in 2019, under procedures that the audit office deemed as flawed.[127] The data from 2012 show that around 70% of overall broadcasting revenues and 35.4% of broadcasting advertising revenues alone belong to the three public service broadcasters, which makes for harsh competition between a high number of media for the remaining revenues.[128]

1. PSB

55. PSB system in BiH consists of three TV broadcasters: BHT1 (Television of BiH), which is a part of the Radio-Television of BiH (BHRT), at the state level; FTV (Federal TV), which is a part of Radio-Television of Federation of BiH (RTVFBiH) at the level of Federation BiH entity; and Television of Republika Srpska, which is a part of the Radio-Television of Republika Srpska (RTRS), at the

125. Barbara Krajnc & Selma Kadić Maglajlić. Regulacija tržišta oglašavanja [Regulation of Advertising Market]. Mediacentar Sarajevo 2018, 23.
126. In September 2020, the Parliamentary Commission for Traffic and Communications adopted a conclusion that the Council of Ministers BiH should propose a new Law on public RTV system, regulating the collection and distribution of RTV fees between the three public service broadcasters.
127. The Supreme Office for the Republic of Srpska Public Sector Auditing, Izvještaj o provedenoj fin ansijskoj reviziji Konsolidovanog godišnjeg finansijskog izvještaja za korisnike budžeta Republike Srpske za period 01.01-31.12.2019. godine, [Report on financial audit … of Republika Srpska] 2020. http://www.gsr-rs.org/static/uploads/report_attachments/2020/08/31/RI001-20_Lat.pdf, accessed 13 Sep. 2020.
128. Communs. Regulatory Agency, Analiza tržišta emitovanja u BiH [Analysis of Broadcasting Sector in BiH] (Sarajevo: Communications Regulatory Agency of Bosnia and Herzegovina, 2013, https://rak.ba/bs-Latn-BA/brdcst-market-analysis, accessed 14 Sep. 2020).

level of Republika Srpska entity. Additionally, there are eighteen public TV stations[129] (twelve broadcasted terrestrially and six through other communication networks) at the local and regional levels.[130]

2. Private

56. At the end of 2019, there are 26 private terrestrial televisions and 55 televisions in other communication networks at local, regional, entity and state levels.[131] The overall daily reach of TV outlets in BiH in 2018 amounted to 1.9 million individuals, with the highest reach acquired by the three PSBs and four private media with national coverage (Pink BH, OBN, BN, Hayat).[132] The data from 2008 suggest that almost two-thirds of TV broadcasters were covering small areas of less than 500,000 inhabitants.[133]

C. Radio

57. The radio market in BiH is rather small, and in 2017, it was assessed at EUR 2.5 million in advertising revenues.[134] Similarly like in the TV sector, only a few radio stations acquire most of the market revenues. The data from 2006 showed that

129. In the Article 28 of the CRA Rule 77/2015 on Provision of Audiovisual Media Services and Article 27 of Rule 76/2015 on Radio Media Services, 'the public radio/public television is defined as an entity to which at least one of the following is applicable: a) It was established by the state of Bosnia and Herzegovina, the entities, District Brčko, cantons, cities and/or municipalities (political and territorial community); b) It was established by administrative organizations or other administrative bodies of the political and territorial community stemming from indent a) of the item herewith or by institutions with public authorities of the political and territorial community stemming from indent a) of the item herewith; c) It was established on the public-private partnership model and it is in the ownership or it is being financed by more than 51% by legal entities stemming from indent a) and/or b) of the item herewith'. According to the Art. 2 (Definitions) of the CRA's Rule 57/2011 on Public Radio and Television Broadcasters: 'Public radio and television broadcaster means any licensee for radio or television broadcasting for which at least one of the following is applicable: (1) It was established by the state of Bosnia and Herzegovina, the entities, District Brčko, cantons, cities and/or municipalities (political and territorial community); (2) It was established by administrative organizations or other administrative bodies of the political and territorial community stemming from indent 1) of the item herewith or by institutions with public authorities of the political and territorial community stemming from indent 1) of the item herewith; (3) It was established on the public-private partnership model and it is in the ownership or it is being financed by more than 51% by legal entities stemming from indent 1) and/or 2) of the item herewith.'
130. Commun. Regulatory Agency, Annual Report of the Communications Regulatory Agency for the year 2019, 13 (Commun. Regulatory Agency BiH 2020, https://docs.rak.ba//documents/d0e3f02b-c260-42e2-953f-e55919d33762.pdf, accessed 11 Nov. 2020).
131. *Ibid.*
132. Data of agency IPSOS, gathered within the TACSO 3 project funded by the European Union for the needs of the study Sustainability of Professional Journalism in the Media Business Environment of the Western Balkans; unpublished data, on file with the authors.
133. Auth. Commun. Guarantees & Commun. Regulatory Agency, Overview of the Communications Sector, 2008, 110–111.
134. Krajnc & Kadić-Maglajlić, *Regulacija tržišta oglašavanja*, 23.

around 60% of revenues are distributed among more than 130 stations, while ten leading stations share the remaining 40%, and none of the stations makes more than 15% of the total market revenues.[135]

1. Public Radio Broadcasting

58. As a part of the state-wide Public Service Broadcasting System, public radio broadcasting consists of three channels: state-level Radio of Bosnia and Herzegovina (BHRadio 1) (part of Public Broadcasting Service of BiH – BHRT), Radio FBiH (part of RTVFBiH), and Radio Republika Srpska (part of RTRS). Additionally, there are sixty-four public[136] radio stations founded and predominantly financed by the cantonal, city and municipal governments across the country which also have the status of public broadcasters. These public radio stations are of local or regional character, are subject to regulatory provisions that pertain to the public broadcasters but are not a formal part of the state-wide Public Service Broadcasting System, and instead operate as separate legal entities.[137]

2. Private Radio Broadcasting

59. There are seventy-seven private radio stations, two medium wave (MW) private radio licences, one licence for broadcasting in other-than-terrestrial networks and three non-profit radio stations in BiH[138]

D. Print Media

60. According to the BiH Press Council, there are eight daily newspapers published in BiH,[139] all privately owned, and dozens of different magazines.[140] Since the print media market is underdeveloped and in decline, no reliable data on circulation are available as publishers consider such information confidential. Data of

135. *Ibid.*
136. *See* Article 27 of Rule 76/2015 on radio media services. According to the Art. 2 (Definitions) of Rule 57/2011 on Public Radio and Television Broadcasters: 'Public radio and television broadcaster means any licensee for radio or television broadcasting for which at least one of the following is applicable: (1) It was established by the state of Bosnia and Herzegovina, the entities, District Brčko, cantons, cities and/or municipalities (political and territorial community); (2) It was established by administrative organizations or other administrative bodies of the political and territorial community stemming from indent 1) of the item herewith or by institutions with public authorities of the political and territorial community stemming from indent 1) of the item herewith; (3) It was established on the public-private partnership model and it is in the ownership or it is being financed by more than 51% by legal entities stemming from indent 1) and/or 2) of the item herewith.'
137. Commun. Regulatory Agency, Annual Report for 2019, 13.
138. *Ibid.*
139. BH Press Council, *Daily Newspapers in BiH*, http://vzs.ba/index.php?option=com_content&view=article&id=200:dnevne-novine-u-bih&catid=5:tampani-mediji-u-bih&Itemid=8, accessed 13 Sep. 2020 and 20 Aug. 2012.

Agency IPSOS for 2018 show that there is around 0.44 million average issue readership (AIR) in the daily media market and that Dnevni Avaz has the highest readership, followed by EuroBlic, Oslobođenje, Glas Srpske and Nezavisne Novine.[141]

II. Infrastructure

A. *Cable Penetration*

61. As of 31 December 2019, there are 35 distributors of radio and television programmes, of which, 28 distribute via cable (via cable network and via satellite -DTH) and 7 via Internet Protocol Television (via IPTV network and via satellite -DTH). The total number of subscribers is 832,903.[142]

62. Most of the holders of licences for audiovisual services distribution operate within a smaller geographical area. In 2017, CRA identified 'obstacles to the development of effective competition' in the market.[143] Mainly, there is a growing concern about the increasingly strong position of United Group in programme distribution (primarily through Telemach BiH), content production (including through Nova, N1 televisions, Sport Klub), and advertising (mainly through CAS media agency) in BiH and the wider region.[144] Such vast cross-ownership may enable practices that can put the competitors in a disadvantageous position.

63. Three decisions of the Competition Council of BiH[145] indicate that United Group has been misusing its dominant position by applying different conditions in the distribution of its sports channels. These issues arise particularly in relation to premium sports content, which brings high advertising revenues to broadcasters. While the United Group claimed it was pressured to lower the prices and that the case against them was ungrounded, the association of cable operators and distributors in BiH, ACOP claims that the problematic practices continued.[146]

---

140. There are around 180 periodicals, but only a minority are journalistic in nature. List available at BH Press Council, *Print Media in BiH*, https://www.vzs.ba/index.php/vijece-za-stampu/printani-mediji-u-bihhttp://vzs.ba/index.php?option=com_content&view=category&id=5&Itemid=8, accessed 20 Aug. 2021.
141. IPSOS agency, Regional media market Bosnia and Herzegovina, on file with the authors.
142. Commun. Regulatory Agency, Annual Report for 2019, 14.
143. Commun. Regulatory Agency, Annual Report for 2017, https://docs.rak.ba//documents/2933bd93-d5f6-4b8a-83b2-8604f5bebc0a.pdf, 31, accessed 14 Sep. 2020.
144. *See* Hodžić and Sokol, MSI IREX report 2019, 13.
145. Competition Council of BiH, decision at: http://bihkonk.gov.ba/datoteka/Rjesenje-BH-Telecom-d.-d.-20122017-bos.pdf. also see press release, at:http://bihkonk.gov.ba/saopcenje-za-medije-sa-116-sjednice-konkurencijskog-vije-ca-bosne-i-hercegovine.html, accessed 14 Sep. 2020.
146. Kapital.ba, AKOP pozvao državne institucije da spriječe medijski monopol Telemacha [ACOP called the state institutions to prevent the media monopole by Telemach] https://www.capital.ba/akop-bih-pozvao-drzavne-instituci-je-da-sprijece-medijski-monopol-telemacha/, accessed 14 Sep. 2020.

64. Cable distributors and broadcasters sign contracts so that the cable operators acquire the right to transmit specific TV channels.[147] There is also an obligation to submit signed individual agreements on the basis of the Collective Agreement on cable retransmission of audiovisual copyrighted works in BiH for the period 2016–2018 signed between the Association of Cable Operators (AKOP) and Association of the Film Industry (UFI).[148] In 2019, the CRA required the distributors to submit the information and proof of resolved copyrights and issued measures against those that failed to do so.[149]

65. The value of the market of distribution of audiovisual and radio media services has been stable over the previous years. The main source of revenues is the user subscriptions to cable/IPTV distribution services. The overall revenues on the telecommunication market in 2018 amounted to EUR 650 million, out of which a majority comes from telephone services while 11.09% is acquired from cable TV services.[150]

B. Mobile Market

66. There are three licensed operators for the provision of mobile telephony services Global System for Mobile Communications (GSM)/Universal Mobile Telecommunications System (UMTS): *BH Telecom* Sarajevo, *Telekomunikacije Srpske* Banja Luka, and *Hrvatske Telekomunikacije Mostar* (*HT Mostar*). Several more operators emerged in the past year, but their overall share in the telecommunication market amounted to only 0.1% at the end of 2019.[151] The number of subscribers for mobile services totalled 3.76 million by the end of 2019, with a slight increase as compared to 2018.[152] At the end of 2019, the level of penetration of mobile telephony amounts to 106.35%. Commercial provision of 4th generation mobile services in Bosnia and Herzegovina began on 9 May 2019.[153]

67. There is a strong resistance to the privatization of state-owned telecom operators. Hence, two operators are still majority-owned by the state: FBiH still owns 90% of *BH Telecom*, despite the indicators of a sharp decline of its revenues and repeated calls by civil society for changes in investments, business operations,

147. Auth. Commun. guarantees & Commun. Regulatory Agency, Overview of the Communications Sector 147. *Ibid.*, 150.
148. 'Official Gazette of BiH', No: 4/19.
149. Commun. Regulatory Agency, Annual Report for 2019, 16–17.
150. *See* Commun. Regulatory Agency, Report on telecommunication market in 2018, 2, https://docs.rak.ba/documents/21b80755-fe0f-45ec-bf22-76ad0f5b5327.pdf, accessed 24 Oct. 2020.
151. Commun. Regulatory Agency, Kvartalni uporedni podaci tržišta elektronskih komunikacija [Quartal comparative data on electronic communication market] 2019. https://docs.rak.ba//documents/58784e9e-57f9-42d9-9227-e1188dabe273.pdf, accessed 15 Sep. 2020.
152. Commun. Regulatory Agency, Annual report for 2019, 23.
153. *Ibid.*, 21.

management, and ownership.[154] FBiH also owns 50.1% of HT Mostar, while other owners include T-Hrvatski telekom, Zagreb and Hrvatska pošta d.d., Zagreb.[155] *Telekom Srpske* has undergone the privatization process in 2002, and 65% of the stake was sold to *Telekom Serbia*[156](which is 58.11% owned by the Republic of Serbia[157]).

68. All the services in the market of electronic communication in BiH were formally liberalized by 2006,[158] but the European Commission notes that there is still a lack of legislation enabling liberalization of the telecommunication and electronic media sector.[159] At the end of 2019, there were 12 providers of fixed public telephone services, but a major market power in the services market of fixed telephony belongs mainly to three large telecom operators (mentioned above).[160]

C. Internet Services

69. At the end of 2019, there were overall sixty-five Internet service providers in BiH.[161] Internet penetration has been growing over the years and from 55% in 2015 reached 94.32% in 2019. The estimated total number of internet users in December 2019 amounted to 3.33 million.[162]

70. There were overall 746.271 internet subscribers as of 31 December 2019, of which, 745.887 (99.95%) had broadband access. The number of broadband subscribers in 2019 amounted to 21.12% of the overall population. In the structure of broadband connections, ADSL access led with 55.49% of the total number of broadband connections and continued to increase (2.25% increase compared to 2018).

---

154. Centre for Policy and Governance. Perspektive razvoja BH Telekoma [Perspective of development of BH Telekom], CPU 2017. http://www.cpu.org.ba/media/31663/Perspektive-razvoja-BH-Telecoma.pdf, accessed 15 Sep. 2020.
155. HT Eronet corporate website: https://www.hteronet.ba/upoznajte-nas/o-nama-s143, and Inforadar, Za i protiv privatizacije BH Telekoma [For and against privatization of BH Telekom]https://inforadar.ba/za-i-protiv-privatizacije-bh-telecoma-kako-ce-zavrsiti-stranacka-zlatna-koka-ciji-se-profit-godinama-topi/, accessed 15 Sep. 2020.
156. M:tel annual report for 2017, 14 https://docs.google.com/document/d/1VPpocfhyEWs7gi72oG6xJ7ETYloPbNiG/edit#, accessed 15 Sep. 2020.
157. Telekom Serbia corporate website, https://mts.rs/O-Telekomu/Investitori-i-akcionari?tab=315/577, accessed 15 Sep. 2020.
158. Decision on the Adoption of Politics of Sector of Electronic Communication of B&H for the period 2017–2021, section 2.1. http://www.sluzbenilist.ba/page/akt/WBr1TX3CmYY=, accessed 15 Sep. 2020.
159. European Commission, Analytical report from 2019, 107, https://ec.europa.eu/neighbourhood-enlargement/sites/near/files/20190529-bosnia-and-herzegovina-analytical-report.pdf, accessed 16 Oct. 2020.
160. Commun. Regulatory Agency, *Annual report for 2019*, 17–18.
161. Commun. Regulatory Agency, *Annual report for 2019*, 25.
162. *Ibid.*, 26.

There was also an increase in Fixed Wireless Access (amounting to 60,936 subscribers in 2019) while cable Internet access (with 239,551 subscribers in 2019) decreased compared to 2018.[163]

III. Technological and Economic Developments on the Media Markets

A. *Digital Television*

71. The switchover from analogue to digital terrestrial TV signal should have been completed by June 2015, as envisaged by the Geneva 2006 (GE-06) Agreement. The agreement has the status of a binding international treaty. It establishes frequency plans for analogue and digital environments in Europe, Africa and parts of Asia.[164] The Digital Terrestrial Television (DTT) Forum was created in 2006, tasked to draft the *Strategy on the digital switchover* and to guide the introduction of DTT in the country. Although the Strategy was formally adopted in 2009 by the Council of Ministers of BiH, during the next two years not much has been put into practice. It is only when the Expert Commission of the DTT Forum was established in September 2011 that the process of developing an Action Plan for the switchover actually started. The Action Plan was then adopted by the Council of Ministers in 2014.[165] Further delays, of both procedural and political nature, followed and even five years after the deadline passed, the switchover is yet to be realized. Some steps forward were made by setting up the Multiplex A and B (MUX A and B) and by performing a test digital broadcasting in 2006. However, the issue of managing the infrastructure and technical resources of multiplexes remains unsolved. The public service broadcasting system (with its three TV and radio broadcasters) is in charge of MUX A and B, but fragmented as it is, it never formed a joint body that would coordinate the use of MUX A and B. A step towards the transition from analogue to digital terrestrial for private TV stations was made when the licence for operating the Multiplex C (MUX C) was granted to a private company Multiplex Service BHJ, in October 2019.[166] A public call for broadcasters to apply for entering Multiplex C was published in February 2020. However, some critics point to overpricing of the distribution services that might jeopardize the sustainability of broadcasters. Additional criticism concerns delays and shortcomings in the introduction of the MUX C infrastructure.[167] Hence, it remains to be seen how and with what dynamics the switchover is going to unfold.

163. *Ibid.*, 26–29.
164. *See* http://www.digitag.org/DTTResources/IBC06/Digital_future.pdf, accessed 5 May 2011. https://www.itu.int/en/ITU-R/terrestrial/broadcast/plans/Documents/GE06-End%20of%20transition%20period_information%20document-Final.pdf, accessed 19 Sep. 2020.
165. Commun. Regulatory Agency, Bosnia and Herzegovina Media Landscape, presentation for the 49th EPRA meeting, at: https://cdn.epra.org/attachments/files/3548/original/Media_landscape_BiH.pdf, accessed 19 Sep. 2020.
166. Commun. Regulatory Agency, *Annual report for 2019*, 16.
167. *See*, for instance, articles at Zenica.info: https://zenicainfo.ba/2020/03/13/lokalni-medijski-servisi-na-udaru-pojedinima-prijeti-gasenje/ and Nezavisne novine: https://www.nezavisne.com/novosti/drustvo/Multiplex-Service-BH-za-100-dana-nije-izradio-mrezu-i-poceo-emitovanje/587979, accessed 19 Sep. 2020).

B. Convergence of Media Products

72. All major classic media – dailies, weeklies, radio, and TV stations – have websites. Nevertheless, only a handful have made serious progress in introducing truly converged newsrooms. In most cases, websites are used primarily to re-publish, in identical or reduced format, what is already being published in print or broadcast formats. Important exceptions are web operations of major regional television programmes such as N1 and Al Jazeera Balkans; a daily newspaper, Dnevni avaz; Radio Sarajevo; and to some extent, the web portal, Federalna.ba, run by RTVFBiH public service broadcaster. There is also a joint desk that integrates the daily Oslobođenje, the redaction of informative programmes of television O kanal (O Channel), and its related websites and magazines. The most visited is the web portal of Dnevni Avaz, followed by the news web portal www.klix.ba which hosts a large community around its blogging and forum services.[168] There is also a growing number of web-only media, such as Žurnal (www.zurnal.info) and Buka (http://www.6yka.com/). There are also thirty-five licences issued by the CRA for TV broadcasting over other electronic communication networks.[169]

§3. Sources of Media Law

Constitution

Constitution of Bosnia and Herzegovina, General Framework Agreement for Peace in Bosnia and Herzegovina (Dayton Peace Agreement), Annex 4; Amendment I (Official Gazette of BiH 25/09)

Constitution of FBiH (*Ustav Federacije Bosne i Hercegovine*, Official Gazette of FBiH 1/94, 3/97, 16/02, 22/02, 52/02, 60/02, 18/03, 63/03, 9/04, 20/04, 33/04, 71/05, 72/05, 88/08)

Constitution of RS (*Ustav Republike Srpske*, Official Gazette of RS 21/92, 28/94, 8/96,13/96, 15/96, 16/96, 21/96, 21/02, 30/02, 31/02, 69/02, 31/03, 98/03, 115/05, 117/05, 48/11)

Statute of Brcko District (*Statut Brčko Distrikta Bosne i Hercegovine*, Official Gazette of Brčko District 3/07, 17/08, 39/09)

General Laws on Communications

Communications Law of BiH (*Zakon o komunikacijama BiH*, Official Gazette of BiH 31/03, 75/06, 32/10, 98/12)

Defamation Law of Brčko District (*Zakon o zaštiti od klevete Brčko Distrikta BiH,* Official Gazette of Brčko District 14/03)

Defamation Law FBiH (*Zakon o zaštiti od klevete FBiH*, Official Gazette FBiH No. 19/03, 73/05)

Defamation Law RS (*Zakon o zaštiti od klevete RS*, Official Gazette RS No. 37/01).

168. Alexa.com, http://www.alexa.com/topsites/countries/BA, accessed 19 Sep. 2020 and 20 Aug. 2012.
169. *Commun. Regulatory Agency Register of License Users*, https://www.rak.ba/bs-Latn-BA/brdcst-license-holdershttp://www.rak.ba/bih/index.php?uid=1273787112, accessed 19 Sep. 2020 and 20 Aug. 2012.

FOIA BiH /Freedom of Access to Information Act BiH (*Zakon o slobodi pristupa informacijama u BiH*, Official Gazette of BiH 28/00, 45/06, 102/09, 62/11, 100/13)
FOIA FBiH / Freedom of Access to Information Act FBiH (*Zakon o slobodi pristupa informacijama u Federaciji Bosne i Hercegovine*, Official Gazette of FBiH 32/01, 48/11)
FOIA RS/ Freedom of Access to Information Act RS (*Zakon o slobodi pristupa informacijama u Republici Srpskoj*, Official Gazette of RS 20/01)
The Law on Public Information of RS (*Zakon o javnom informisanju Republike Srpske*, Official Gazette of RS 10/97)

Public Radio and Television

Law on the Radio-Television of Federation of BiH (*Zakon o Javnom servisu radio-televizije Federacije Bosne i Hercegovine*, Official Gazette of FBiH 48/08)
Law on the Radio-Television of Republika Srpska (*Zakon o Radio-Televiziji Republike Srpske*, Official Gazette of RS 49/06, 73/08, 42/10, 89/13, 44/16)
The Law on the Public Service Broadcasting System in BiH (*Zakon o javnom radio-televizijskom sistemu BiH*, Official Gazette of BiH 78/05, 35/09, 32/10. 51/15, 25/16)
Law on the Public Service Broadcasting of BiH (*Zakon o Javnom radio-televizijskom servisu Bosne i Hercegovine*, Official Gazette of BiH 92/05, 32/10)

Other Laws

Election Law of BiH, (*Izborni zakon BiH,* Official Gazette of BiH 23/01, 7/02, 9/02, 20/02, 25/02, 4/04, 20/04, 25/05, 52/05, 65/05, 77/05, 11/06, 24/06, 32/07, 33/08, 37/08, 32/10, 18/13, 7/14, 31/16)
Competition Act BiH (*Zakon o konkurenciji BiH*, Official Gazette of BiH 48/05, 76/07, 80/09).
Law on the Protection of Secret Data of BiH (*Zakon o zaštiti tajnih podataka BiH*, Official Gazette of BiH 54/05, 12/09).
Law on the Protection of Personal Data of BiH (*Zakon o zaštiti ličnih podataka BiH*, Official Gazette of BiH 49/06, 76/11, 89/11).
Law on Public Order and Peace of RS (Zakon o javnom redu i miru RS, Official Gazette of RS 11/15)

Rules and Codes of the Communications Regulatory Agency (CRA)

(CRA rules available at URL: https://rak.ba/bs-Latn-BA/brdcst-regulations)

Rule 90/2018 on Provision of Electronic Communications Network Management Services in Digital Terrestrial Broadcasting (Pravilo 90/90/2018 o pružanju usluga upravljanja elektronskim komunikacijskim mrežama u digitalnoj zemaljskoj radiodifuziji)
Rule 89/2018 on license fees of the Communications Regulatory Agency (Pravilo 89/2018 o naknadama za dozvole Regulatorne agencije za komunikacije)
Rule 79/2016 on Licenses for the Distribution of Audiovisual Media Services and Radio Media Services (Pravilo 79/2016 o dozvolama za distribuciju audiovizuelnih medijskih usluga i medijskih usluga radija)

Rule 77/2015 on the Provision of Audiovisual Media Services (Pravilo 77/2015 o pružanju audiovizuelnih medijskih usluga)

Rule 76/2015 on the Provision of Radio Media Services (Pravilo 76/2015 o pružanju medijskih usluga radija)

Rule 71/2013 on the Registry of Communications Regulatory Agency Licence Holders (*Pravilo 71/2013 o Registru korisnika dozvola Regulatorne agencije za komunikacije*)

Code on Audiovisual Media Services and Radio Media Services, CAVRMS, (*Kodeks o audiovizuelnim medijskim uslugama i medijskim uslugama radija*) (Official Gazette of BiH 3/16)

Code on Commercial Communications (*Kodeks o komercijalnim komunikacijama*) (Official Gazette of BiH 3/16)

Rule 12/2001 on Technical Requirements for Radio and Telecommunications Equipment in Public Telecommunications Networks (*Pravilo 12/2001 o tehničkim zahtjevima za radio i telekomunikacijsku opremu u javnim telekomunikacijskim mrežama,* URL: https://rak.ba/hr/articles/53.) Rule 35/2008 on Unbundled Access to the Local Loop (*Pravilo 35/2008 o pristupu izdvojenoj lokalnoj petlji*, Official Gazette of BiH 54/08) Rule 51/2010 on Interconnection (*Pravilo 51/2010 o interkonekciji*, Official Gazette of BiH 109/10)Rule 54/2011 on Electronic Communications Market Analysis (*Pravilo 54/2011 o analizi tržišta elektronskih komunikacija*, https://www.rak.ba/bs-Latn-BA/articles/59) *Other Rules and Codes*

Central Election Commission of BiH: The Rulebook on the Media Representation of Political Subjects during the Electoral Campaign (*Pravilnik o medijskom predstavljanju političkih subjekata u periodu od dana raspisivanja izbora do dana održavanja izbora,* Official Gazette of BiH 29/18)

Court of BiH: Rules on Freedom of Access to Information controlled by the Court and on the Cooperation of the Court with Community (*Pravilnik o ostvarivanju pristupa informacijama pod kontrolom suda i saradnji suda sa zajednicom*, Court of BiH, March 20, 2012)

Press Council BiH: The Press and Online Media Code (*Kodeks za štampu i online medije,* URL: http://english.vzs.ba/index.php?option=com_content&view=article&id=218&Itemid=9&lang=en)

Decisions by the Office of the High Representative

(OHR decisions available at the URL: http://www.ohr.int/decisions/archive.asp)

Decision on Amending the Structure of Expenditure of the Communications Regulatory Agency for 2002, 2 December 2002

Decision Regulating various matters of a transitional nature arising out of previous Decisions of the High Representative as aforesaid and Enacting the Law on Communications of Bosnia and Herzegovina, 21 October 2002

Decision imposing the Law on the Basis of the Public Broadcasting System and Public Broadcasting Service of Bosnia and Herzegovina, 23 May 2002

Decision imposing the Law on Radio-Television of Republika Srpska, 23 May 2002 and 31 August 1999

Decision imposing the Law on Radio-Television of the Federation BiH, 23 May 2002
Decision on the liquidation procedure to be applied in the winding-up of the Public Enterprise Radio-Television of Bosnia and Herzegovina, 23 May 2002
Decision combining the competencies of the Independent Media Commission and the Telecommunications Regulatory Commission (establishing the Communications Regulatory Agency), 2 March 2001, *Official Gazette BiH* No. 8/01; *Official Gazette FBiH* No. 11/01 and *Official Gazette RS* No. 12/01
Decision appointing new members to the Council of the Communications Regulatory Agency (CRA), 29 November 2001
Second Decision on restructuring of the Public Broadcasting System in BiH, 23 October 2000
Decision on the appointment of the Board of Governors of Radio-Television of the RS, 27 July 2000
Decision on changes and amendments of the Law on RTRS, 1 September 1999
Decision amending the decision on Public Radio-Television of BiH, 16 March 2000
Decision on the implementation of the Law on Radio-Television of the Federation, 6 December 1999
Decisions on restructuring of the Public Broadcasting System in BiH and on freedom of information and on abolishment of criminal sanctions for insult and defamation, 30 July 1999
Decision imposing the Law on Telecommunications in BiH, 11 September 1998, *Official Gazette BiH* No. 10/99
Decision on establishing the Independent Media Commission, 11 June 1998

Part I. Freedom of Speech

§1. Constitutional Framework

73. Constitutional and legal framework relevant for the freedom of speech in BiH consists of a complex set of legal documents, institutions and practices. The country has fourteen constitutions: Constitution of BiH at the state level; Constitution of FBiH entity; Constitution of RS entity; Statute of the Brčko District; and Constitutions of each of the ten cantons within the FBiH entity. Consequently, numerous laws and regulations at these various administrative levels are relevant for the exercise and the protection of the freedom of speech.

74. Freedom of speech and the freedom of the media are guaranteed by the Constitutions of BiH,[170] FBiH,[171] RS,[172] and the Statute of the Brčko District.[173] BiH is a member of the Council of Europe and has thus accepted international legal standards established by the European Court of Human Rights and numerous recommendations and declarations of the Council of Europe.[174]

75. In article 2, section 3, Enumeration of Rights, the Constitution of BiH specifies that 'all persons within the territory of BiH shall enjoy human rights and fundamental freedoms' including Freedom of Expression. The BiH Constitution guarantees full enjoyment of human rights, including non-discrimination on the basis of political opinion.[175] Furthermore, the European Convention on Human Rights (ECHR) is a part of the Constitution of BiH[176] which states that 'the rights

170. Constitution of BiH (*Ustav Bosne i Hercegovine*) http: http://ccbh.ba/osnovni-akti/ustav/?title=preambula //www.ohr.int/dpa/default.asp?content_ id=379, accessed 20 Sep. 2020 and 14 Jul. 2012.
171. Constitution of FBiH (Ustav Federacije Bosne i Hercegovine, Official Gazette of FBiH 1/94), http://www.ohr.int/laws-of-bih/constitutions-2/ http://skupstinabd.ba/ustavi/f/ustav_federacije_bosne_i_hercegovine.pdf, accessed 20 Sep. 2020 and 14 Jul. 2012.
172. Constitution of RS (Ustav Republike Srpske, Official Gazette of RS 28/94), http://www.ohr.int/laws-of-bih/constitutions-2/ http://www. ustavnisud.org/upload/4_8_2009_48_ustav_srpski.pdf, accessed 20 Sep. 2020 and 14 Jul. 2012.
173. Article 13, Fundamental Rights and Obligations, Statute of Brčko District (*Statut Brčko Distrikta Bosne i Hercegovine*, Brčko District Official Gazette 17/08, 39/09), http://www.ohr.int/laws-of-bih/constitutions-2/ http://www.ohr.int/ohr-offices/brcko/arbitration/default.asp?content_id=43564, accessed 20 Sep. 2020 and 20 Aug. 2012.
174. Mehmed Halilović & Mirjana Nadaždin-Defterdarević, *Ustavno i zakonsko jamstvo slobode izražavanja*, in *Medijsko pravo u Bosni i Hercegovini* 35 (Mehmed Halilović & Amer Džihana eds, Internews, 2012).
175. Constitution of BiH, Art. 2, para. 43.
176. *Ibid.*, sec. 2. International Standards.

and freedoms set forth in the European Convention for the Protection of Human Rights and Fundamental Freedoms and its Protocols shall apply directly in Bosnia and Herzegovina. These shall have priority over all other laws'.[177]

76. The Constitution of FBiH in its Article 2 states that 'the Federation will ensure the application of the highest level of internationally recognized rights and freedoms provided in the documents listed in the Annex to the Constitution'. In particular: (1) All persons within the territory of the Federation shall enjoy the rights: (a) To fundamental freedoms: free speech and press; freedom of thought, conscience, and belief; freedom of religion, including private and public worship; freedom of assembly; freedom of association, including to form and belong to and labour unions and the freedom not to associate; and freedom to work; (b) To political rights: to participate in public affairs; to have equal access to public service; to vote and stand for election. Furthermore, the Constitution of FBiH[178] lists a total of twenty-one international conventions and declarations, including the 1948 Universal Declaration of Human Rights (UDHR), 1950 European Convention for the Protection of Human Rights and Fundamental Freedoms, and the 1966 International Covenant on Civil and Political Rights.

77. The Constitution of RS in Article 25 states that 'freedom of thought and orientation, conscience and conviction, as well as of public expression of opinion shall be guaranteed'. Additionally, Article 26 stipulates that: 'freedom of press and other media of communication shall be guaranteed. Free establishment of newspaper and publishing houses, publishing of newspapers and public information by other media in accordance with law shall be guaranteed. Censorship of press and other public information media shall be forbidden. Public information media shall be obliged to inform the public on time, truthfully and impartially. The right to correction of incorrect information shall be guaranteed to anyone whose right or legally determined interest has been violated, as well as the right to a compensation for damage arising therefrom'.

78. Furthermore, Article 32 defines that:

---

177. Article 10 (Freedom of expression) of the European Convention for the Protection of Human Rights and Fundamental Freedoms states that 'Everyone has the right to freedom of expression. This right shall include freedom to hold opinions and to receive and impart information and ideas without interference by public authority and regardless of frontiers. This article shall not prevent States from requiring the licensing of broadcasting, television or cinema enterprises. (…) The exercise of these freedoms, since it carries with it duties and responsibilities, may be subject to such formalities, conditions, restrictions or penalties as are prescribed by-law and are necessary in a democratic society, in the interests of national security, territorial integrity or public safety, for the prevention of disorder or crime, for the protection of health or morals, for the protection of the reputation or rights of others, for preventing the disclosure of information received in confidence, or for maintaining the authority and impartiality of the judiciary.'

178. Annex to the Constitution of FBiH, Instruments for the Protection of Human Rights with the Legal Status of Constitutional Provisions (*Instrumenti za zaštitu ljudskih prava koji imaju pravnu snagu ustavnih odredaba*), http://predstavnickidom-pfbih.gov.ba/bs/page.php?id=103, accessed 16 Oct. 2020.

citizens shall have the right to publicly express their opinion on the work of State agencies and other bodies, to submit petitions, complaints and proposals to them and to receive answers thereto. No one may be held responsible or suffer other adverse consequences because of the public expression of his opinion on the work of State agencies or his statements publicly presented in a complaint, petition and proposal, unless thus committing a criminal offence.

79. Although the RS Constitution is more detailed than the Constitutions of BiH and FBiH, it does not contain any references to specific international conventions, resolutions, and declarations. Article 5 stipulates that the constitutional arrangement shall guarantee and protect human freedoms and rights in accordance with international standards.[179]

80. Statute of the Brčko District in Article 13 (Fundamental Rights and Obligations), stipulates that:

(1) Everyone is entitled to the enjoyment of all rights and freedoms guaranteed under the Constitution and laws of Bosnia and Herzegovina, this Statute and the laws of the District, without discrimination of any kind, including discrimination on the basis of gender, race, sexual orientation, colour, language, religion, national or social origin, political or other opinion, membership of a national minority, property, birth or other status. (…) (4) All persons shall be entitled within the territory of the District to all the rights and freedoms accorded to them by the European Convention on Human Rights and Fundamental Freedoms. Within the District, those rights and freedoms shall prevail over all conflicting laws. All institutions of the District shall observe those rights and freedoms. The District Courts shall enforce those rights and freedoms in accordance with procedures provided for in District legislation. When entertaining cases in which allegations of violation of those rights and freedoms are at issue, the District courts shall take account of the case law of the European Court of Human Rights.

81. Constitutions of the ten cantons in FBiH in principle refer to the provisions of the Constitution of BiH and the Constitution of FBiH in respect to the protection of human rights, including the freedom of speech. According to their constitutions, under no circumstances can the Assembly of the canton or any other public institution reduce the human rights and freedoms guaranteed by the Constitution of BiH and the Constitution of FBiH.

82. Freedom of speech and of the media is also guaranteed by the Communications Law of BiH which stipulates that the regulatory principles of broadcasting shall include 'The protection of freedom of expression and diversity of opinion

179. Also see: Halilović and Nadaždin-Defterdarević, *Ustavno i zakonsko jamstvo slobode izražavanja*, 35.

while respecting generally accepted standards of decency, non-discrimination, fairness, accuracy, and impartiality.'[180] Additionally, relevant Codes and Rules of the CRA[181] that apply to the broadcasting media outlets provide guarantees for freedom of expression and freedom from interference with their editorial policy and work, in accordance with Article 19 of the UDHR. These freedoms are also guaranteed by the Laws on Protection from Defamation,[182] as well as by the Law on Public Information in RS, and the laws on media and public information in six out of ten cantons in Federation BiH[183] in which such laws exist. The state-level and the entity-level freedom of information acts, as well as the cantonal laws on information/media, guarantee the right to access information of public interest held by public bodies.

§2. Scope

83. Freedom of expression is guaranteed by the Constitutions of BiH, FBiH and RS,[184] Article 10 (Freedom of expression) of the European Convention for the Protection of Human Rights and Fundamental Freedoms, which is the part of the Constitution of BiH. Since the wording of the Constitution of BiH and FBiH is technologically neutral, and wording of the Constitution of RS explicitly encompasses different media platforms, it can be understood that the freedom of expression applies to all types of media – press, radio, televisions, movies and the Internet. Such a position is also reflected in the regulatory and self-regulatory arrangements, with the CRA having the authority over the broadcasting media sector, and the Press Council of BiH defining itself as the self–regulatory body for print and online media.[185]

§3. No A Priori Censorship

84. According to the provisions of the Constitution of RS, Article 26, the censorship of the press and other public information media is forbidden. Constitutions of BiH and FBiH do not entail explicit prohibition of censorship, but since an integral part of both of these Constitutions is the European Convention for the Protection of Human Rights and Fundamental Freedoms,[186] which clearly state that the

180. Communications Law of BiH, Art. 4.
181. See Part III. Regulation of Audiovisual Media, *infra.*
182. *See* sec. 2. Defamation and Libel, ch. 3. Journalists' Liability, *infra.*
183. Halilović & Nadaždin-Defterdarević, *Ustavno i zakonsko jamstvo slobode izražavanja*, 37.
184. Constitution of RS, Art. 26.
185. *See* BH Press Council website: http://vzs.ba, accessed 20 Sep. 2020 and 5 Nov. 2012.
186. European Convention for the Protection of Human Rights and Fundamental Freedoms as amended by Protocols No. 11 and 14 and supplemented by with Protocols Nos 1, 4, 6, 7, 12,13 and 164, https://www.echr.coe.int/Documents/Convention_Eng.pdf, accessed 20 Sep. 2020, http://ustavnareforma.ba//files/docs/en.CONVENTIONFORTHEPROTECTIONOFHUMANRIGHTSANDFUNDAMENTALFREEDOMS.pdf, accessed 5 Nov. 2012.

freedom of expression will be exercised without interference by public authority;[187] one can understand that both constitutions prohibit censorship.

85. Also, the Defamation Law FBiH, Article 10, stipulates that:

> 2. A court order prohibiting or limiting the making or dissemination of an expression of false fact is not allowed prior to the publication of that expression. 3. Preliminary court orders to prohibit disseminating or further disseminating of an expression of false fact may only be issued where publication has already occurred and the allegedly injured person can make probable with virtual certainty that the expression caused harm to his or her reputation and that the allegedly injured person will suffer irreparable harm as a result of further dissemination of the expression. Permanent court orders to prohibit the dissemination or further dissemination of an expression of false fact may only be applied to the specific expression found to be defamatory and to the specific person found to be responsible for the making or dissemination of the expression.[188]

86. Almost identical provision is contained in Article 11(2) and (3) of the Defamation Law RS[189] as well.

§4. SPECTRUM OF A POSTERIORI RESTRICTIVE MEASURES

87. The Constitutions of BiH, FBiH and RS, and the Statute of Brčko District do not prevent the imposition of a posteriori restrictions on the freedom of expression. As a result, there are broad restrictive measures aimed at protecting a wide range of public interests and individual rights, including:

– Protection of court proceedings (e.g., The Criminal Code of BiH,[190] Article 237).

187. *Ibid.*, Art. 10 (Freedom of expression).
188. Article 10, Defamation Law FBiH (*Zakon o zaštiti od klevete FBiH*, Official Gazette FBiH No. 19/03).
189. Defamation Law RS (*Zakon o zaštiti od klevete RS*, Official Gazette RS No. 28/94).
190. Criminal Code of BiH (*Krivični zakon BiH*, Official Gazette of BiH 3/03; 32/03; 37/03; 54/04; 61/04; 30/05; 53/06; 55/06; 32/07; 8/10; 47/14; 22/15; 40/15; 35/18).

- Protection of honour, reputation and rights of others (e.g., Defamation Law FBiH, Article 10; Criminal Procedure Code BiH, Article 437;[191] Law on Obligations[192]).
- Protection against hate speech (e.g., Article 4, CAVRMS – Code on Audiovisual and Radio Media Services).[193]
- Protection of privacy (e.g., CAVRMS, Article 17).
- Protection of minors (e.g., CAVRMS, Articles 18 to 25).
- Protection of public health (e.g., Code of Commercial Communications).[194]
- Protection of consumers (e.g., Code of Commercial Communications).
- Protection of commercial interests (e.g., FOIAs).[195]

§5. Prior Authorization for Publishing

88. There are no major legal obstacles for publishing, but the Law on Public Information of RS[196] contains the provision of obligatory registration of the media within the registry of publishers at the responsible state institution prior to the start of publishing activities.[197] Some cantonal laws on information/media require media only to register in the local court registry,[198] as any other type of business is obligated to do.

89. Web and print publishing is not subject to prior authorization or any similar duty or requirement. In other words, publishing on the Internet is free. In accord with international standards, providers of audiovisual media services, such as broadcasters and content distributors are required to obtain the licence from the CRA.[199]

---

191. Article 437 (Compensation of Damages Inflicted by Media) stipulates that 'If a case involving unjust conviction or groundless apprehension of a person was covered by media, inflicting damage upon the reputation of that person, the Court shall, at the person's request, publish in newspapers or other media a statement on its decision confirming that the previous conviction was unjust or that the apprehension was groundless', Criminal Procedure Code BiH (*Zakon o krivičnom postupku*, Official Gazette of BiH, 3/03, 32/03, 36/03, 26/04, 63/04, 13/05, 48/05, 46/06, 76/06, 29/07, 32/07, 53/07, 76/07, 15/08, 58/08, 12/09, 16/09, 93/09, 72/13, 65/18).
192. Law on Obligations FBiH (*Zakon o obligacionim odnosima*, Official Gazette of SFRJ 29/78; 39/85; and 57/89; Official Gazette of the Republic of BiH 2/92; 13/93; 13/94; 29/03; 42/11) and the Law on Obligations RS (*Zakon o obligacionim odnosima*, Official Gazette of RS 17/93; 3/96; 37/01; 39/03; 74/04).
193. CAVRMS/Code on Audiovisual and Radio Media Services (Commun. Regulatory Agency 2015 2011).
194. Code on Commercial Communications (Commun. Regulatory Agency 20151)
195. *See* sec. 1. Public Documents, ch. 5. Access to Public Information, *infra*.
196. Law on Public Information of RS, Art. 10.
197. Nadaždin-Defterdarević, *Normativni okvir prava na informisanje u Bosni i Hercegovini*, 104.
198. *See* Law on Public Information of Tuzla Canton (Zakon o javnom informisanju, Official Gazette of Tuzla Canton 15/00).
199. *See* Part III. Regulation of Audiovisual Media, *infra*.

Part II. Regulation of Print Media

Chapter 1. The Journalists' Profession

§1. Notion

90. There is no clearly established notion of a journalist in relevant legislation. There are no legal or other obstacles for the journalistic profession in BiH, and journalists are not required to obtain a license. Hence, journalism is an open profession that can be practised disregarding the educational profile of a journalist. The Constitution of BiH and all other relevant laws protect the right of journalists and the media to practice their profession freely.

91. From Articles 9 and 10 (Protection of Confidential Sources) of the Defamation Laws in FBiH and in RS respectively, a notion of journalist could be extracted to mean any natural person 'regularly or professionally engaged in the journalistic activity of seeking, receiving or imparting information to the public'.

§2. Subsidies to the Press

92. There are no systematic policies for the provision of subsidies and financial support to the press in BiH. Nevertheless, press and electronic media often receive support from the budget of governments at various levels, from local to entity government. Especially prominent is the role of local and cantonal governments that often subsidize media that operate in a specific municipality or canton under their jurisdiction. This type of support is provided through ad hoc commercial contracts, donations and grants, for example, for coverage of municipal government activities, cultural events, or for the production of specific types of content that is relevant for a particular local community. Estimates range between EUR 15 million and over EUR 50 million of annual government funding for media in BiH,[200] but the majority is allocated to two public news agencies (funded predominantly by entity governments) and local public broadcasters (funded mainly through municipal, city and

200. Some data and estimates available in Sanela Hodžić & Anida Sokol. Transparent and legitimate media financing from public budgets. Mediacentar Sarajevo 2018, 9, https://www.media.ba/sites/default/files/transparent_and_legitimate_media_financing_from_public_budgets_-_guidelines_for_public_bodies_of_bih_-_eng.pdf, accessed 20 Nov. 2020.

cantonal budgets). Print media do not enjoy state subsidies in the form of reduced value-added tax, nor are there other government policies aimed at advancing their sustainability.

93. Important sources of revenues for media, including the print sector, are grants given by international donors for various media democratization projects, often providing funding for media content (i.e., such as investigative journalism, reporting on corruption, coverage of EU integration process, etc.), or for core operations and enabling environment. The financial support from international donors to media sector in BiH has decreased over the past decades, but in recent years some media, including the print ones, have been receiving valuable donor support.

Chapter 2. Journalists' Rights

§1. Role of Journalists as Watchdogs of Society

94. Declaration on freedom of political debate in the media of the Council of Europe[201] strongly emphasizes the importance of the public being informed about matters of public concern in democratic societies. The media is seen as having a central role in that process, by collecting and disseminating such information to the public. Hence, the Declaration stipulates that:

> the state, the government or any other institution of the executive, legislative or judicial branch may be subject to criticism in the media. Because of their dominant position, these institutions as such should not be protected by Criminal Code against defamatory or insulting statements.[202]

95. Furthermore, Articles III and IV state that 'Political figures and public officials must accept that they will be subject to public scrutiny and criticism, particularly through the media, over the way in which they have carried out or carry out their functions' and should not 'enjoy greater protection of their reputation and other rights than other individuals'.[203]

96. Also, the practice of the European Court of Human Rights emphasizes the importance of critical reporting of the media about political institutions, politicians and public officials. ECHR has taken a principal stand that the criticism of public officials should not be restricted as it contributes to the democratic process and since the public officials have voluntarily chosen positions exposed to public and media scrutiny.[204]

97. In principle, in BiH, the particular responsibility of the press as a watchdog of society that acts in the public interest has so far been confirmed by the case law in respect to the Defamation Laws at BiH, RS and FBiH level, where judicial practice has established the standard of issuing minimal penalties to media and journalists.[205]

---

201. Council of Europe – Committee of Ministers, *Declaration on freedom of political debate in the media* (adopted by the Committee of Ministers on 12 Feb. 2004 at the 872nd meeting of the Ministers' Deputies), https://wcd.coe.int/ViewDoc.jsp?id=118995&Lang=en, accessed 21 Sep. 2020 and 3 Jul. 2012.
202. *Ibid.*, Art. II.
203. *Ibid.*, Art. VI.
204. Mladen Srdić, *Izražavanje o pitanjima od javnog interesa*, in *Medijsko pravo u Bosni i Hercegovini* 79 (Mehmed Halilović & Amer Džihana eds, Internews, 2012).
205. Mehmed Halilović, *Primjena novog zakona o zaštiti od klevete u BiH: novinari nisu previše profitirali* (Mediacentar Online 2005), http://www.media.ba/bs/etikaregulativa-novinarstvo-etika/primjena-novog-zakona-o-zastiti-od-klevete-u-bih-novinari-nisu, accessed 22 Sep. 2020.

98. Furthermore, according to the Defamation Laws,[206] in the cases of expression of untruthful or incorrect information about issues of public interest, politicians, public officials or candidates for public functions, the author is responsible only if he/she knew that the expression was untruthful or incorrect or the defamatory expression was a result of negligence. This is a milder form of liability in comparison to defamation in relation to private persons in which case it is only relevant that the harm occurred, no matter if the author of such expression knew about the untruthfulness of the expression.[207] Hence, such provisions of Defamation Laws allow for the media to avoid being sanctioned for defamation if they have acted in good faith, and have undertaken all reasonable measures to avoid publishing non-factual information about issues of public interest, or about public figures and public officials.

99. The courts in BiH have mostly reinforced such interpretation of the Defamation Law, and have upheld the importance of the watchdog role of the media. According to Čolaković and Bubalo, for example, the County Court in Banjaluka reversed the ruling of the basic court on libel stating that the plaintiff, at that time the president of municipal assembly and member of a political party, was as such '(…) herself showing a readiness that her actions, both in private and public life, be exposed to more intense critique than persons who are not public figures' (ruling of the District Court in Banja Luka 011 0Gž 08 001293 from 21. 7. 2008, upheld by the Constitutional Court BiH in the case AP 2806/08 from 20. 4. 2011. godine). Similarly, the Basic Court of Bihać in the ruling No. 17 0P 011380 05 P from 16. 1. 2012 concluded there was no liability for defamation, primarily on the rationale that persons who are public figures must tolerate negative opinions.[208] On the same grounds, the Basic Court of Banja Luka (*Osnovni sud Banja Luka*) in the case P-2033/01, ruled in January 2004 in favour of a daily paper which reported critically on a public official in the Government of RS. Referring to Article 10 of the European Convention for the Protection of Human Rights and Fundamental Freedoms, the Court ruled that the imposition of penalty on the media outlet and its journalists could have a chilling effect on journalists who might refrain from public discussions on the issues important for the community and thus limit the access of the public to relevant information. [209] In a ruling in the case AP 2501/15, the Constitutional Court of BiH overturned the previous ruling of District and Municipal court in Banja Luka, concluding that the Municipal court failed to consider all the circumstances of the case, such as the public interest of publishing information about the 'irregularities in the operations of the legal person that the plaintiff supervised (… .) as the president of Governing Board, against which a criminal proceeding was initiated … '. The ruling confirmed that the Municipal court diverged from

206. The Defamation Law FBiH, Art. 6; the Defamation Law RS, Art. 5.
207. Srdić, 'Izražavanje o pitanjima od javnog interesa', 83.
208. Maja Čolaković & Lana Bubalo. Građanskopravna odgovornost za klevetu u sudskoj praksi Bosne i Hercegovine [Civil Law Liability for Defamation in the Court Practice of BiH], 2018, 13. https://www.researchgate.net/publication/327824313_Gradanskopravna_odgovornost_za_klevetu_u_sudskoj_praksi_Bosne_i_HercegovineCivil_Liability_for_Defamation_in_Jurispridence_of_Bosnia_and_Herzegovina, accessed 25 Nov. 2020.
209. *Srdić* 'Izražavanje o pitanjima od javnog interesa', 84.

the practice of ECHR, basing its decision on the judgement that the defendant did not prove the truthfulness of its reporting.[210] The decision of the Constitutional Court thus reinforced the protection of freedom of expression and reiterated the responsibility of the court to consider all the circumstances of the case.

100. In a ruling P-19/04 of the Cantonal Court of Sarajevo (*Kantonalni sud u Sarajevu*), it was concluded that even a president of the sub-municipal self-governance unit of 'local community' or 'ward' (*mjesna zajednica*) is a public official and has to tolerate greater scope of criticism than a private person.[211]

101. Moreover, the role of journalists as watchdogs of society is firmly inscribed in the Press and Online Media Code of the BiH Press Council. According to the General Provisions of the Code:

> 'It is the duty of journalists and publishers to respect the needs of citizens for useful, timely and relevant information and to defend the principles of freedom of information and the right of fair comment and critical journalism. (…) Journalists shall protect the rights of the individual, while at the same time upholding the right to information in the public interest.'

102. Article 1 (The Public Interests) of the Press and Online Media Code stipulates that the:

> The public interest … is … the procedure and/or information which has the intention of helping the public create personal opinions and decisions about issues and events, including the efforts to detect criminal and/or civil offenses, and to prevent the public from being misled by certain statements or actions of individuals or organizations.

§2. Journalists' Independence

I. Print Media

103. Editorial policy and content of written press in BiH are not subject to any form of regulation. Print media rely on self-regulatory mechanisms and ethical codes of conduct, institutionalized through the Press Council and the Press and Online Media Code – a key self-regulatory instrument.[212]

210. Official Gazette of BiH 90/17.
211. *Srdić* 'Izražavanje o pitanjima od javnog interesa', 84–85.
212. *See*, ch. 6, Press Council, Part II, Regulation of Print Media, *infra*.

II. Audiovisual Media

104. Pursuant to Article 4 of the Communications Law BiH, principles of regulation of the RTV sector are: protection of freedom of expression and thought, development of a professional and sustainable commercial and public RTV sector, and freedom of radio and television from political control and manipulation.[213]

105. As for electronic media and in compliance with the practice of western democracies, regulation rests with the CRA.[214]

§3. Protection of Journalistic Sources

106. The right of journalists, editors, and any other natural persons involved in regular journalistic activity to protect their sources is embedded in Article 9 of the Defamation Law of FBiH the Defamation Law of Brčko District and Article 10 of the Defamation Law RS. Article 10 of the Defamation Law of Brčko District reads as follows:[215]

1. A journalist, and any other natural person regularly or professionally engaged in the journalistic activity of seeking, receiving or imparting information to the public, who has obtained information from a confidential source has the right not to disclose the identity of that source. This right includes the right not to disclose any document or fact which may reveal the identity of the source, particularly any oral, written, audio, visual or electronic material. Under no circumstances shall the right not to disclose the identity of a confidential source be limited in proceedings under this Law.
2. The right not to disclose the identity of a confidential source is extended to any other natural person involved in proceedings under this Law who, as a result of his or her professional relationship with a journalist or other person referred to in paragraph 1 of this Article, acquires knowledge of the identity of a confidential source of information.

The equivalent stipulations in laws on the level of RS and FBiH are almost identical.

107. One can conclude that the right to the protection of sources is applicable to a much broader range of actors who are 'regularly or professionally engaged in the journalistic activity of seeking, receiving or imparting information to the public', and essentially applies not only to journalists and editors but also to bloggers and to

213. For more details, please *see*, Part III. Regulation of Audiovisual Media, *infra*.
214. For more details, please *see*: Part V. Supervision: Media Regulator, *infra*.
215. Defamation Law of Brčko District (*Zakon o zaštiti od klevete*), Official Gazette of Brčko District 14/03), https://skupstinabd.ba/ba/zakon.html?lang=ba&id=/Zakon%20o%20zas--titi%20od%20klevete, accessed 20 Aug. 2012.

any other natural person who, as a result of professional relationship with a journalist, knows the identity of a confidential source of information.

108. Additionally, Article 13, Confidentiality of Sources, of the Press and Online Media Code, says that:

> whenever possible, journalists should rely on open, identified sources of information. These are to be preferred to anonymous sources, whose honesty and accuracy cannot be gauged by the public. Journalists and their publications, however, have an obligation to protect the identity of those who provide information in confidence, whether or not they explicitly request confidentiality.

109. Hence, the BiH laws referred to here go even beyond the ECHR and the case law of the European Court of Human Rights. Thanks to such a precise definition, there have mostly been no problems in the application of these legal provisions in the practice. However, a case from December 2014, pointed to an important collision between the good norms and the actions of governmental bodies. Namely, the police of Republika Srpska raided the offices of popular news website Klix, in search of the recordings featuring then the Prime Minister of Republika Srpska, revealing how the ruling coalition bought-of the MPs in the National Assembly of Republika Srpska in order to form a parliamentary majority. Klix published this recording in November 2014, without revealing the source. While the legal basis of the raid was the suspected wiretapping, seizing of the equipment and materials of Klix clearly jeopardized the right to protection of journalistic sources. Another worrying development dates to the beginning of 2015 when the Law on Public Order and Peace of Republika Srpska was adopted, introducing a category of "insult" and "affront", not defined precisely enough to limit arbitrary implementation that can restrict freedom of speech.[216] The Law also envisages punishment for endangering peace and order on the internet, which raised concerns on possible chilling effects on public discussion. While in some cases these but also other legal norms on public order might have been misused for limiting the freedom of expression,[217] the draft amendments of the Law on Public Order and Peace in Republika Srpska from 2019 brought additional distress. The drafted amendments opened a possibility to forbid any recordings (video, audio, photo) of officials, which would impede or prevent the officials from performing their duty. Some representatives of civil society believed that in the background of the citizens' protests 'Justice for David', [218] these amendments were designed with the intention to prevent citizens from recording police brutality and to limit the critique of the government during the protests. In

---

216. Nihada Jele, Zaštita novinarskih izvora u BiH [Protection of Journalist Sources in BiH], bulletin of the association BH novinari, E-novinar, No. 43. 2016, 2.

217. On a case of a fine against a journalist for a negative comment about a politician in Tuzla Canton, *see*: https://www.media.ba/bs/vijesti-i-dogadaji-vijesti/ostre-osude-za-novcano-kaznjavanje-vahidi na-durica, and on a police requests for initiation of civil procedure for violation of Law on Public Order and Peace in Republika Srpska, on: https://www.slobodnaevropa.org/a/29669323.html.

218. These protests were organized around a murder of David Dragičević in Banja Luka, from March 2018, primarily due to a conviction that the murder has been covered up and that high-ranking officials have been implicated; the protests involve a strong critique of the RS government.

addition, the fact that it was not clearly defined what constitutes such 'impediment' of the work of officials incited fears of future misuse. After a strong critique by the civil society and international community, the amendments were retracted. In the background of the COVID-19 pandemic, the intensified monitoring of online spaces by the police forces in Federation of BiH, and a legislative decree in Brčko District and Republika Srpska adopted in March 2020 that forbids spreading of panic and disorder[219] brought additional concerns as the lack of transparency and precision in terms of definition and/or modalities of enforcement enabled arbitrary interpretations and actions that can limit media freedoms.[220] The decision in Republika was however retracted, faced with a resistance of civil society and the international community. On the other hand, journalists are sometimes also using the right to protect their sources as an excuse for liability for defamation, claiming that the defamatory information was obtained from a confidential source and that they have not been able to verify its factuality.[221]

110. Moreover, the cantonal laws on public information stipulate the right of journalists to protect their sources, and in some of the cantons, such a right is extended to editors, publishers, book authors and authors of published items who are not journalists. Journalists are obliged to reveal their sources only upon the court order.[222]

219. *See* Mehmed Halilović & Amer Džihana, Ograničavanje prava na slobodu izražavanja u BiH u toku trajanja panemdije (Sarajevo: BH novinari, 2020) https://bhnovinari.ba/wp-content/uploads/2020/06/Ograni%C4%8Davanje-prava-na-slobodu-izra%C5%BEavanja-BOS.docx, accessed 26 Nov. 2020.
220. In one case for instance a medical doctor was fined for criticising the state of health sector, an a blogger was penalized for criticising the response of Republika Srpska to the pandemic. *Ibid.*, 5--6.
221. Mladen Srdić, *Osnovni standardi postupanja Evropskog suda*, in *Medijsko pravo u Bosni i Hercegovini* 59 (Mehmed Halilović & Amer Džihana eds, Internews, 2012).
222. Nadaždin-Defterdarević, *Normativni okvir prava na informisanje u Bosni i Hercegovini*, 102.

Chapter 3. Journalists' Liability

§1. LIABILITY

111. According to the Defamation Law FBiH, Article 6:

> 1. Any person who causes harm to the reputation of a natural or legal person by making or disseminating an expression of false fact identifying that legal or natural person to a third person is liable for defamation. 2. For defamation made through media outlets the following are jointly responsible: author, editor, or publisher of the expression or someone who otherwise exercised control over its contents.

112. Similarly, the Defamation Law RS, in its Article 5 (Liability for Defamation) is basically identical to the law in FBiH, except that it even more precisely stipulates that liability for defamation can be attributed to any work-capable person who causes harm to a private or legal person.

113. Both laws stipulate that defamation exists in the case of dissemination of harmful expression, including the re-publishing of expression that was already published elsewhere. This was confirmed by the decision GŽ-20/05 of the Supreme Court of FBiH (*Vrhovni sud FBiH*) which ruled that the fact that if other media had previously published specific harmful expressions, it does not excuse from liability the media outlet that later re-published such expressions.[223]

114. Nevertheless, this does not mean that any dissemination and re-publishing of untruthful expression will automatically be sanctioned – the courts will carefully consider each case in order to establish if there is evidence of defamation. The ruling will largely depend on the way harmful statements have been re-published, whether the conduct of journalists was responsible and careful, and whether both sides have been offered the chance to comment and negate the defamatory statement prior to its re-publishing and dissemination.[224]

115. Hence, the basic criteria for the establishment of liability are work capability; non-factual information; existence of harm or damage; availability of harmful information to third persons; and the existence of intention or negligence.[225]

> The problems can occur in respect to establishing who is the author in the case when a specific expression is re-published or re-transmitted in the media. The decision 71-0-P-033381-09-Gž from November 2009 at the District Court Banja Luka (*Okružni sud u Banja Luci*) demonstrates well how courts can have

223. Mladen Srdić, *Kleveta u sudskoj praksi*, in *Medijsko pravo u Bosni i Hercegovini* 157 (Mehmed Halilović & Amer Džihana eds, Internews, 2012).
224. *Ibid.*, 156.
225. *Ibid.*, 152.

the problem in defining the term 'author' and establishing the liability for defamatory expression that was transmitted through the media. Namely, the Court ruled in the second instance that the person who wrote and send letters that contained defamatory statements, and that have been published in print media, cannot be considered the liable author, since her letters have been published in print media, and she is neither author nor editor nor publisher in that print media outlet.[226] Similarly, the Supreme Court of FBiH (*Vrhovni sud FBiH*) in the decision GŽ-155/05 from December 2005 ruled that the person who gave defamatory statements in an interview cannot be held accountable for defamation in accordance with the Defamation Law FBiH since that person is not an author of the text that was published in the media.[227] At the same time, several cases at the level of Cantonal Courts and even at the Supreme Court of FBiH (GŽ-132/04) have demonstrated that the persons who gave interviews and statements to the media can be held accountable for their expressions published in the media.[228] According to Srdić, such court rulings are the result of inadequate interpretation of the Defamation Laws in RS and in FBiH[229] and of the imprecise wording of the laws.[230]

116. The Defamation Law FBiH (Article 7) and the Defamation Law RS (Article 6) also set out the exemptions from liability. Accordingly, there shall be no liability for defamation where: the expression was an expression of opinion rather than of facts; the expression is substantially true while being false only in insignificant segments; the person who allegedly caused the harm was under a statutory obligation to make or disseminate the expression, or was required in the course of legislative, judicial or administrative proceedings to make or disseminate the expression.

117. Also, there shall be no liability for defamation when the making or dissemination of the expression was reasonable. The criteria for determining reasonableness are:

> the manner, form and time of the making or dissemination of the expression; the nature and degree of harm caused; good faith and adherence to generally accepted professional standards by the person who allegedly caused the harm; consent by the allegedly injured person; the likelihood that the harm would have occurred had the expression not been made or disseminated; whether the expression constitutes a fair and accurate report of the expressions of others; and whether the expression concerns a matter of the allegedly injured person's private life, or involves a matter of political or public concern.[231]

226. *Ibid.*, 152.
227. *Ibid.*, 154–155.
228. *Ibid.*, 154.
229. *Ibid.*, 151–152.
230. *Ibid.*, 155.
231. Defamation Law FBiH, Art. 7(2); Defamation Law RS, Art. 6(c).

118. According to the Criminal Code of BiH,[232] Criminal Code of FBiH,[233] Criminal Code of RS,[234] and Criminal Code of Brčko District,[235] any person that illegally obtains information classified as a secret is liable for a criminal act and can be prosecuted. This inevitably includes both journalists and their sources of information.[236] Possible sanctions are up to ten years in prison depending on the status of the offender and the contextual conditions. Furthermore, Law on the Protection of Secret Data[237] stipulates that any citizen of BiH who obtains secret information in a lawful way also has an obligation to protect that information. According to Sali-Terzić,[238] the problem is that these definitions are too broad and that the laws apply to any classified information disregarding the type of information and the level of its secrecy. Unlike the RS Criminal Code, laws of other administrative units contain a provision that excludes the existence of criminal act in the cases when someone publishes secret information with content contradictory to the constitutional order, in an attempt to inform the public about the violation of the constitution, and when such publishing will not have negative consequences for the administrative unit (BiH; FBiH and Brčko District).[239]

§2. Defamation and Libel

119. Up until 1999, Libel and Defamation were considered criminal offences in BiH. As a consequence, in the years after the 1992–1995 war, there have been dozens of criminal proceedings against journalists and editors in the country.[240] Hence, the OHR brought a decision that eliminated the criminal offence status of libel and defamation.[241] The Decision involved an order that both entities in BiH should adopt necessary laws that will establish, in the course of civil proceedings, legal remedies for defamation and libel in accordance with the ECHR. Accordingly, the working groups consisting of local and international experts prepared the draft of

---

232. Article 164, Criminal Code of BiH (Krivični zakon BiH, Official Gazette of FBiH 3/03; 32/03, 54/04; 61/04; 30/05; 53/06; 55/06; 8/10; 47/14; 22/15; 40/15; 35/18).
233. Article 158, Criminal Code of FBiH (*Krivični zakon FBiH*, Official Gazette of FBiH 36/03; 37/03; 21/04; 69/04; 18/05; 42/10; 42/11; 59/14; 76/14; 46/16; 75/17).
234. Article 292, Criminal Code of RS (*Krivični zakonik RS*, Official Gazette of RS 64/17; 104/18).
235. Article 156, Criminal Code of Brčko District (*Krivični zakon Brčko Distrikta*, Official Gazette of Brčko District33/13; 47/14;26/16; 13/17; 50/18).
236. Sevima Sali–Terzić, 'Odavanje tajne u krivičnim zakonima u BiH', in *Medijsko pravo u Bosni i Hercegovini* 228–229 (Mehmed Halilović & Amer Džihana eds, Internews, 2012).
237. Article 11, Law on the Protection of Secret Data BiH *(Zakon o zaštiti tajnih podataka BiH*, Official Gazette of BiH 54/05; 12/09).
238. Sali-Terzić, *Odavanje tajne u krivičnim zakonima u BiH*, 228–231.
239. *Ibid.*, 231.
240. Mehmed Halilović & Mladen Srdić, 'Zakoni o zaštiti od klevete', in *Medijsko pravo u Bosni i Hercegovini* 124 (Mehmed Halilović & Amer Džihana eds, Internews, 2012).
241. OHR, Decision on Restructuring of the System of Public Broadcasting in BiH and on Freedom of Information and Elimination of Criminal Prosecution for Defamation (*Odluka o restruktuiranju Sistema javnog emitiranja u Bosni i Hercegovini i o slobodi informisanja i ukidanja krivičnih kazni za uvredu i klevetu)*, http://www.ohr.int/decisions-on-the-restructuring-of-the-public-broadcasting-system-in-bih-and-on-freedom-of-information-and-decriminalisation-of-libel-and-defamation/, accessed 22 Sep. 2020.

the law which was then submitted to the parliaments of FBiH and RS by OHR and the Mission of OSCE to BiH. The law was promptly adopted by the Assembly of RS, while the FBiH Parliament failed to do so which forced the OHR to enforce the adoption of the law in 2002 by a decree.[242]

120. Today, the Defamation Law is in force in FBiH,[243] RS,[244] and Brčko District,[245] in almost identical form. The Law decriminalizes defamation, placing it into civil law, jurisprudence and civil procedure. According to Halilović and Srdić,[246] the practice and the standards of the European Court of Human Rights have had a decisive influence over the content of defamation laws in BiH.

121. Hence, the three defamation laws in BiH provide for the protection of public debate on important public matters; support the watchdog function of the media; protect the freedom of expression;[247] require public figures, politicians and public institutions to demonstrate a larger degree of tolerance to public scrutiny; and make important distinctions between facts that can be proven, and opinion whose truthfulness cannot be proven.[248] The law encourages freedom of expression and of the press, including expression which may offend, shock or upset,[249] but it also requires that the press and journalists act in a responsible and professional manner. Journalists are held accountable for defamation if they deliberately or as a consequence of recklessness, publish untrue information. Furthermore, the laws eliminate the protection of national symbols and of state officials; guarantee the protection of

242. OHR, Decision Enacting the Law on the Protection against Defamation in Federation of BiH (*Odluka kojom se proglašava Zakon o zaštiti od klevete Federacije Bosne i Hercegovine*), http://www.ohr.int/decision-enacting-the-law-on-protection-against-defamation-of-the-federation-of-bosnia-and-herzegovina/, accessed 22 Sep. 2020; also see: Halilović & Srdić, *Zakoni o zaštiti od klevete*, 124.
243. Defamation Law FBiH, Official Gazette of FBiH 19/03; 73/05.
244. Defamation Law RS, Official Gazette of RS 37/01.
245. Defamation Law of Brčko District, Official Gazette of Brčko District 14/03.
246. Halilović and Srdić, *Zakoni o zaštiti od klevete*, 129–130.
247. For example, according to Art. 7 (Standard of Proof) of the Defamation Law RS, 'The necessity of any interference with the right to freedom of expression, through the finding of liability and the awarding of compensation under this Act, must be convincingly established in accordance with Article 10(2) of the European Convention on Human Rights and Fundamental Freedoms and the court practices of the European Court on Human Rights.'
248. For example, Constitutional Court of BiH decision AP 787/04 (20 Dec. 2005) firmly distinguished between facts and opinion and ruled that there was no defamatory statements in the particular article since the authors only expressed their opinion rather than untruthful facts and information that could be proven as such. Source http://sup.ustavnisud.ba/public/down/Blt-2005-II-dio.pdf, p. 755, accessed 26 Sep. 2020; Similarly, the distinction between opinion and facts as a basis for determining the presence of defamation has been upheld by the decision GŽ-125/05 (29 Sep. 2005) of the Supreme Court of FBiH; See: Srdić, *Kleveta u sudskoj praksi*, 140–141.
249. According to Srdić, a good example from the court practice is the Cantonal Court of Sarajevo decision P-75/03 (12 Nov. 2004) which rejected the defamation claims even though the expression contained the elements of exaggeration, since it did not contain factual information but authors opinions, and it had elements of metaphor as well. The Court ruled that the Defamation Law FBiH in the Art. 2(b) protects the freedom of expression and that also applies to expression which might offend, shock or upset; *see*: Srdić, *Kleveta u sudskoj praksi*, 138–139.

sources; establish a balance between freedom of expression and protection of dignity and honour; encourage the resolution of disputes through mediation; and in the case of FBiH Defamation Law, Article 14 classifies the court proceedings on defamation as urgent.

122. Importantly, the Laws encourage the plaintiff to first approach the media outlet for redress, and only to seek protection through courts if the media response to the complaint was unsatisfactory or when the damages caused are such that they cannot be remedied other than through courts. Additionally, public authorities – the government, the assembly, courts, public enterprises and institutions – cannot act as plaintiffs. Only members of government, public officials, judges, etc., may be plaintiffs but as private individuals.

123. According to the laws, for defamation to exist, all of the following five criteria have to be met: publishing of untruthful information; identification of the plaintiff;[250] harm caused to a private or legal person; distribution of information to third person; and intent or a certain degree of negligence.[251]

124. Journalists and the media can defend themselves even if they publish untruthful and defamatory information when the expression was reasonable:

> depending on the degree of harm caused; good faith; adherence to generally-accepted professional standards; whether the expression constitutes a fair and accurate report of the expressions of others; and whether the expression concerns a matter of the allegedly injured person's private life, or involves a matter of political or public concern.[252]

125. Hence, the courts in BiH regularly consult the Press and Online Media Code and the relevant codes of the CRA to assess the good faith and the level of professional conduct of journalists' actions when making decisions in such cases.[253]

126. The Defamation Laws in FBiH, RS and Brčko District cover only the offence of defamation, defined as the expression of untruthful or non-factual information, and do not recognize the insulting expression, understood as discrediting of the third person by the way of expressing derogatory opinion and statements.

---

250. An expression must refer to clearly identified person in order to be classified as defamation (Art. 4, Defamation Law RS; Art. 5, Defamation Law FBiH). Nevertheless, in practice, the issue of identification can pose problems. For example, the Cantonal Court of Sarajevo in the decision P-117/03 (17 Aug. 2004) that was in the second instance upheld by the decision GŽ-130/04 of the Supreme Court of FBiH, ruled that in the particular case, where a name of a person was linked to the war-crimes in a particular municipality in BiH, this was not enough to identify the plaintiff as that particular person, since many persons have the identical names and no other characteristics of that person have been mentioned in the concerned press article, such as his occupation, education, his address, etc.; See: Srdić, *Kleveta u sudskoj praksi*, 142.
251. Halilović & Srdić, *Zakoni o zaštiti od klevete*, 132.
252. Defamation Law FBiH, Art. 7(2); Defamation Law RS, Art. 6(c); Also see sec. 1, Liability, *supra*.
253. Halilović & Srdić, 'Zakoni o zaštiti od klevete', 131–132.

Hence, the offence of insulting expression is regulated through the Law on Obligations of FBiH and the Law on Obligations of RS, which do not recognize the difference between defamation and insult, and Article 200 stipulate the compensation for non-material damage in the case of harm to the honour and reputation. In the case when the court determines that there is no defamation the court is not bound by the legal qualification of the prosecutor's request (i.e., defamation), and can, where appropriate, issue a decision on compensation of non-material damage caused by insult, in accordance with the relevant provisions of the Laws on Obligations in FBiH and in RS. This has been confirmed in the decision AP 1064/05 of the Constitutional Court of BiH.[254]

127. After the introduction of the Defamation Laws in BiH, under the civil law jurisprudence, the number of defamation cases in front of the courts rapidly increased, to almost 300 in the first two years – almost three times more than in the previous two years.[255] Nevertheless, the number of cases has been reduced to less than one hundred for the period from early 2010 until mid-2012.[256] A similar trend continued the following years as well, with around a hundred defamation cases per year.[257] In July 2020, there were at least 289 active defamation lawsuits against the media and journalists, and in 2019, there were 21 new defamation lawsuits filed.[258] Initial plaintiffs' claims have been rather ambitious, often requiring compensation between BAM 10,000 and BAM 100,000 and in some cases over half a million of BAM. Nevertheless, the case law established the standard of relatively low financial penalties that ranged between BAM 500 and BAM 2,500 in most cases, and rarely up to BAM 5,000 or BAM 10,000. Furthermore, the fact that the court tax (court proceedings costs) is proportional to the amount requested for compensation had a discouraging effect on the requested amounts.[259]

128. Such a practice of courts is based on the provisions of the defamation laws that stipulate that compensations must be proportional to the inflicted harm to the honour of the plaintiff.[260] Furthermore, the courts must consider all relevant circumstances, such as the actions taken by the authors and publisher of defamatory expression to remedy the damage, for example, through publishing of a correction; the type of the article or a broadcast where the expression was made;[261] and the

254. Srdić, *Kleveta u sudskoj praksi*, 175.
255. Halilović, Mehmed 2004. *Kako se u BiH primjenjuje novi zakon o zaštiti od klevete: novinare tuže političari, ali i – novinari!* (Media Online, 24 August 2004).
256. Halilović and Srdić, *Zakoni o zaštiti od klevete*, 129.
257. Rea Adilagić, Indikatori nivoa medijskih sloboda i sigurnosti novinara [Indicators on the level of media freedom and journalists' safety], BH journalists association, 2018, 8.
258. According to the registry of the association BH novinari, https://bhnovinari.ba/bs/2020/07/09/blizu-300-aktivnih-tuzbi-za-klevetu-protiv-novinara-u-bih-u-posljednjih-pet-godina/, accessed 26 Sep. 2020, there is no central registry of defamation cases in judiciary and the cases against journalist and media in a large number of court registries are not differentiated from the cases against other actors.
259. Halilović and Srdić, *Zakoni o zaštiti od klevete*, 128.
260. For example, Art. 10, The Defamation Law FBiH.
261. Depending on the type of the article or broadcast where the expression was published, different treatment will be given to, for example, an investigative report as opposed to a satirical article. This

eventual negative financial consequences the compensation might have for the publisher.[262] In essence, the case law has established the practice of 'objectification of the amount of financial fines' for the harm caused by defamation – the courts have issued the amounts of financial fines based on their own free assessment in the case when the plaintiff does not submit evidence for the financial implications of the caused harm. In such circumstances, the courts issue fines in accordance with the free assessment of established social norms and standards, while the requested financial compensation by the plaintiff in that respect is not of crucial importance.[263]

129. As Halilović and Srdić[264] emphasize, the implementation of the Law on Defamation in FBiH, RS, and Brčko District, and the decriminalization of libel and defamation, have had a significant positive effect on the advancement of freedom of expression and of the freedom of the media in BiH. First, the court practice has strongly upheld the principles of freedom of expression and has largely adhered to the case law of the European Court of Human Rights. Second, financial fines for non-material harm caused by defamation have been issued in rather limited amounts, thus not having a chilling effect on the freedom of the media. And third, the courts place a strong emphasis on the professional conduct of journalists and the media, referring to the Press and Online Media Code and the Broadcasting Code of Practice in their decisions.[265]

130. Nevertheless, the key problems in the implementation of the laws on defamation are the slowness in resolving defamation cases through civil proceedings; different court practices when it comes to proving the emotional and psychological pain caused by defamation; and literal interpretation of specific legal provisions, especially in respect to deciding about who is the author of expressed information.[266] The court practice concerning the financial compensation in libel cases is mostly judged as adequate, as it is based on consideration of all circumstances (such as publishing retractions, financial gains from publishing defamatory content, evaluating the damage caused by libel, as well as the financial circumstances and impact of the financial compensation on the defendant). [267] Some sources, however, suggest that the court practice is in some respects inconsistent, particularly with regard to compensation for libel[268] and differentiation between facts and opinions,[269] that

has been also acknowledged in the relevant case law: Supreme Court of FBiH, decision no. GŽ-21/05 (12 Apr 2005); Constitutional Court of BiH decision no. AP 1423/05, Official Gazette BiH no. 60/05,. *See*: Srdić, *Kleveta u sudskoj praksi*, 147.

262. Srdić, *Kleveta u sudskoj praksi*, 147.
263. Supreme Court of FBiH, decision GŽ-91/04 (26 October 2004); Constitutional Court of BiH, decision AP 1145/04 (2 Dec. 2005); *Source*: Srdić, *Kleveta u sudskoj praksi*, 148.
264. Mehmed Halilović & Mladen Srdić, *Osnovni zaključci o tretmanu klevete pred bh. sudovima*, in *Medijsko pravo u Bosni i Hercegovini* 177 (Mehmed Halilović & Amer Džihana eds, Internews, 2012).
265. *Ibid.*, 177.
266. *Ibid.*, 177.
267. Čolaković & Bubalo, *Građanskopravna odgovornost za klevetu u sudskoj praksi Bosne i Hercegovine*, 15–16.
268. *Ibid.*, 22.

court rulings were in some cases politically biased,[270] and that the stipulations on the possibility of issuing a court order prohibiting the relevant expression before the court ruling remain contestable.[271] There are also some indicators that the libel court proceedings and compensations have on occasions financially overburdened media and could have discouraged critical reporting. For instance, the compensation costs in the libel cases were one of the reasons why political magazine Slobodna Bosna was so financially weakened that it stopped publishing in print form in 2015.[272]

§3. Privacy

131. Constitution of BiH,[273] Constitution of RS,[274] and the Constitution of FBiH[275] recognize the right to privacy as a basic human right. According to the Constitution of BiH,[276] the definition of the right to privacy from Article 8 of the European Convention of Human Rights is directly applied in BiH and has a priority over domestic legislation.

132. The right to privacy, in its various aspects, is protected through a number of different laws in BiH. For example, the FOIAs at state and entity levels regulate the access to, *inter alia*, personal data of citizens which are in possession of public institutions; the Law on the Protection of Personal Data of BiH[277] stipulates the right to secrecy in respect to the processing of personal information of citizens; the Criminal Codes on all levels involve stipulations against unauthorized use of personal data, and the Communications Law of BiH defines the responsibilities of the CRA in respect to the protection of personal data and privacy. Furthermore, legislation and different rules of courts in BiH provide the principles for the protection of privacy in court proceedings.[278] Furthermore, with respect to the audiovisual media, the right to privacy is enshrined in Article 17 (Protection of Privacy) of the CAVRMS.

133. Additionally, there is a practice of relying on the Defamation Law in attempts to protect privacy, but that is not an appropriate mechanism since violation

269. Anida Sokol, Tužbe za klevetu i dalje opterećuju BH novinarstvo (Mediacentar Sarajevo 2018) https://media.ba/bs/magazin-novinarstvo/tuzbe-za-klevetu-i-dalje-opterecuju-bh-novinarstvo, accessed 21 Sep. 2020.
270. Sanela Hodžić, *Bosnia and Herzegovina*, in *Media Integrity Matters: Reclaiming Public Service Values in Media and Journalism* 121 & 162 (Brankica Petković ed, Ljubljana: Peace Institute, Institute for Contemporary Social and Political Studies, 2014).
271. Sokol, Tužbe za klevetu i dalje opterećuju BH novinarstvo. *Also see* Article 11.3 of the Defamation Law of RS, Article 10.3. of the Defamation Law of FBiH.
272. *Ibid.*
273. Constitution of BiH, Art. 2, sec. 3.
274. Constitution of RS, Art. 13.
275. Constitution of FBiH, Art. 2, sec. g.
276. Constitution of BiH, Art. 2, sec. 2.
277. Law on the Protection of Personal Data of BiH (*Zakon o zaštiti ličnih podataka BiH*, Official Gazette of BiH 49/06, 76/11, 89/11).
278. *See*, Part II. Regulation of Print Media, ch. 5, Access to public information, sec. 2. Court Hearings and Documents, *infra*.

of one's privacy does not necessarily imply the existence of defamation.[279] Hence, the judicial practice demonstrates that the protection of privacy can be granted by referring to the infringement of basic human rights in accordance to the ECHR or by referring to the entities' Laws on Obligations in FBiH and RS, which stipulate that each person has to restrain him/herself from inflicting harm on other persons, including harm to personal and family life.[280] However, the authorities so far failed to adopt the legal framework for protection of personal data in accordance with the norms of the Council of Europe and European Union adopted in 2018, although the Agency for Protection of Private Data prepared the draft law with needed revisions.[281] In addition, the Agency that should monitor protection of private data continuously warns about the lack of capacity to do so and reports on frequent violations of the right to protection of data, including those inflicted by the public bodies.[282] For instance, they warned against some public bodies publishing personal data on persons who do not respect the prohibition measures concerning the COVID-19 pandemic (such as quarantine). While the Agency considers that publishing a minimum of such data can serve public interest, it deems that publishing such information in a generalized and proactive manner is at odds with the relevant laws on protection of personal data and privacy.[283]

134. According to Article 9 of the Press and Online Media Code, the press shall 'avoid interference with anyone's private life, other than cases when such interference is necessary in public interest. Reports involving personal tragedies shall be processed with full consideration, and persons affected by it will be dealt with discretely and compassionately'. Additionally, Article 11 of the Code also establishes standards for the protection of children and minors:

> Journalists shall not interview or photograph children younger than 15 on issues related to the child's family, in the absence of or without the consent of a parent or guardian. Journalists shall not identify children under the age of 18 when they are victims of crimes. Journalists must not, under any circumstances, identify children under the age of 18 who are involved in criminal cases as witnesses, victims or defendants.

---

279. Amer Džihana & Mladen Srdić, *Zaštita privatnosti*, in *Medijsko pravo u Bosni i Hercegovini* 212 (Mehmed Halilović & Amer Džihana eds, Internews, 2012).

280. Džihana & Srdić, *Zaštita privatnosti*, 212–213; *Also see*: Ljiljana Krunić-Zita, *Mediji u BiH i prava djeteta – pravni osnov* (Mediacentar Online, 2008), http://www. https://www.media.ba/bs/etikaregulativa-novinarstvo-pravda-i-sigurnost-etika/mediji-u-bih-i-prava-djeteta-pravni-osnov, accessed 27 Sep. 2020.

281. Agency for Protection of Personal Data, Izvještaj o zaštiti ličnih podataka u BiH za 2019. Godinu [Report on Protection of Personal Data in BiH for 2019] (Agency for Protection of Personal Data, 2020).

282. Dženana Halimović, Privatnost građana krše svi pa i institucije [Privacy of Citizens Violated by Everyone, including Institutions] (Radio Slobodna Evropa, 29. Jan. 2018), https://www.slobodnaevropa.org/a/zastita-licnih-podataka-u-bih/29005003.html, accessed 27 Sep. 2020.

283. *See*, for instance, A.Z. AZLP: Objavljivanje podataka o osobama koje krše mjere zabrane nije u skladu sa zakonom [APPL: Publishing of data on persons who violate prohibition measures are not in accord with the law] (klix.ba, 10 Apr. 2020). https://www.klix.ba/vijesti/bih/azlp-bih-objavljivanje-podataka-o-osobama-koje-krse-mjere-zabrane-nije-u-skladu-sa-zakonom/200410122, accessed 27 Sep. 2020.

135. Twenty complaints filed to the Press Council in 2019 were related to violation of the right to privacy in accordance with Article 9 of the Press and Online Media Code.[284] What Press Council reported sixteen years ago continues to be relevant today:

> Daily newspapers are, in most cases, violating Article 9 of the Code on pages generally titled 'black chronicle' (though not just there), where there are interferences with other persons' lives, even when it is not in the public interest, or there are stories about personal tragedies not made with due consideration, and persons affected by such tragedies are not approached discreetly and compassionately.[285]
>
> The Press Council has previously indicated serious violations of provisions for the protection of minors, stating: 'The most frequent cases of violations of the Code are contained in texts revealing the identity of children victims of crime, as well as the identity of children under the age of 15 involved in offences, or accused of offences, as well as photographs of children (abandoned babies, child beggars), etc.'[286] In 2019 none of the processed cases was concerning the violations of the privacy of children and minors.[287] Some analyses of the media reporting on juvenile crime however point to overly simplified representation of juvenile crime which emphasizes the responsibility of the individuals, portray sensationalized images of social deviants, neglecting the background and social context that contributes to such behaviour.[288]

136. There is still only limited attention dedicated to the protection of privacy in print media in BiH. In the period from 2001 until 2009, out of the total of 229 complaints submitted to the Press Council, only 10 (3%) referred to the violation of the privacy provisions outlined in Article 9 of the Press and Online Media Code. In 2010, there were 16% and in 2011, only 11% of complaints related to the violation of privacy.[289] The number of cases has reduced in recent years. More precisely, there were only eight (i.e., 2.5%) of such complaints in 2018, and 20 (i.e., 3.2%) in 2019, which might indicate some progress in terms of the respect of the right to privacy in print and online media.

---

284. See the list of cases of Press Council for 2019, at: https://www.vzs.ba/images/2019/BHS_2019.pdf, accessed 27 Sep. 2020.
285. Press Council BiH, Report No. 2 on permanent monitoring of print media in BiH April-May 2004 10 (Press Council BiH 2004).
286. *Ibid.*, 12.
287. Press Council, the list of cases for 2019, at: https://www.vzs.ba/images/2019/BHS_2019.pdf, accessed 27 Sep. 2020.
288. Mediacentar Sarajevo, *Analiza praćenja slučajeva maloljetničkog sukobljavanja sa zakonom u štampanim medijima u BiH* (Mediacentar Sarajevo/Save the Children UK, 2005), 36; Ivana Dračo, Mediji i konstrukt maloljetnog "predatora" [Media and the Construct of Minors "Predators"] (Mediacentar Sarajevo 2020) https://www.media.ba/bs/etikaregulativa-novinarstvo-etika/mediji-i-konstrukt-maloljetnog-predatora, accessed 27 Sep. 2020.
289. Džihana & Srdić, *Zaštita privatnosti*, 214; *Also see*, Press Council BiH, *Short Overview of Complaints for Each Year*, http://vzs.ba/index.php?option=com_content&view=category&id=22&Itemid=23, accessed 27 Sep. 2020.

137. When it comes to the case law in the field of privacy protection that involve media outlets, the Constitutional Court of BiH in the decision AP 427/06 dismissed the request for compensation for the slander in the print media. The Court ruled that the published article related to the public function that the appellant has held, and not to the appellant's private life.[290]

290. Džihana & Srdić, *Zaštita privatnosti*, 211.

Chapter 4. Right to Reply

138. The right to reply in relation to print and online media is defined in Article 7 of the Press and Online Media Code of BiH – Opportunity to Reply – which stipulates that: 'A right to reply shall be extended to relevant persons if the editor determines that such a step contributes to accuracy and impartiality. If at all possible, the opportunity for an immediate response shall be made available in the same edition of the publication as the one containing the accusation and/or incorrect information, not exceeding the originally published article in length.' Hence, according to the Code, the conditions to exercise the right to reply are to be determined by the publication concerned, in the cases when fairness and impartiality principles require the reply from the affected party.

139. Nevertheless, Article 8 of both the Defamation Law FBiH and Defamation Law RS, stipulates the obligation to mitigate harm, requiring an allegedly injured person to 'undertake all necessary measures to mitigate any harm caused by the expression of false fact and in particular requesting a correction of that expression from the person who allegedly caused the harm'. Furthermore, Article 10 of the Defamation Law FBiH and Article 11 of the Defamation Law RS stipulate that the court, when 'determining compensation (…) is obliged to have regard for all of the circumstances of the case particularly any measures undertaken by the person who allegedly caused the harm to mitigate the harm, such as: the issuance of a correction and retraction of expression of false fact or issuance of an apology (…)'. Such provisions encourage both sides to act in good faith and seek for reply and correction to be published in order to mitigate harm.

Chapter 5. Access to Public Information

§1. Public Documents

140. Freedom of Access to Information Act in BiH was adopted at the state level in November 2000[291] and was amended several times. The first amendment involved introducing the obligation of state authorities to issue a formal decision (*rješenje*),[292] instead of notification (*dopis*) upon the receipt of requests for access to information,[293] and the second involved introducing the possibility of financial penalty for public institutions and individuals who prevent the access to information.[294] The amendment from 2013 specified the supervision over the implementation of the law, placed under the authority of the Administrative Inspectorate of the Ministry of Justice, which should, upon complaint, decide if a public body violated the law and order it to deliver the requested (and previously denied) information. If the said body fails to do so, the administrative inspector, under the official duty, has to initiate a court proceeding.[295] The Ombudsmen BiH however reports that this complaint mechanism has so far been ineffective and confusing, as well as that the citizens often fail to submit complaints under the stipulated deadline.[296] At the level of FBiH,[297] the FOIA was adopted in February 2002 and in 2011 amended with outlined complaints procedure and the possibility of initiating an administrative dispute.[298] The law at the level of RS[299] was adopted in November 2001 and has not been amended so far. The two entity laws do not envisage that an inspectorate monitors the implementation of FOIA but points to the possibility of addressing the complaints to the Ombudsman.

141. The three FOIAs require public authorities and institutions to grant access to information in their possession. Citizens are granted the right to access the information in the possession of public authorities and institutions to the largest possible extent. That applies to all public authorities, institutions, organizations, companies, schools, state agencies, etc., but is not applicable to the private sector. However,

291. FOIA BiH (*Zakon o slobodi pristupa informacijama u BiH*, Official Gazette of BiH 28/00).
292. Official Gazette of BiH 45/06.
293. Decision (rješenje), unlike the notification (dopis), is an administrative act, and thus in line with the principle of two-instance procedure. The FOIA at the level of RS still envisages response in the form of notification and should be changed in this respect.
294. Official Gazette of BiH 102/09.
295. Article 22b of the FOIA BiH, Official Gazette of BiH 100/13. The third amendments are published in the Official Gazette of BiH 62/11.
296. Ljubinko Mitrović, Jasminka Džumhur & Nives Jukić. Specijalni izvještaj o iskustvima u primjeni zakona o slobodi pristupa informacijama u BiH [The special report on experiences in implementation of the freedom of information acts in BiH], Ombudsman BiH, 2019, 15.
297. FOIA FBiH (*Zakon o slobodi pristupa informacijama u Federaciji Bosne i Hercegovine*, Official Gazette of FBiH 32/01).
298. Amendments to FOIA FBiH, Official Gazette of FBiH 48/11.
299. FOIA RS (*Zakon o slobodi pristupa informacijama u Republici Srpskoj*, Official Gazette of RS 20/01).

public companies are to an extent protected from delivering information that constitutes a business secret.[300] According to the three FOIAs, public authorities and institutions are required to respond to the request within fifteen days.

142. The FOIAs grant access to each person, regardless of their citizenship, nationality, ethnicity or place of residence. Access to information is granted to both, private persons and legal persons, and no special provisions exist in respect to the media and journalists. In other words, the media and journalists enjoy the same rights as any other private or legal person.[301]

143. The FOAIs grant access to a wide variety of public information, such as documents, registers, and other types of information in the possession of public institutions. Furthermore, access is to be granted to all types of information, regardless of its format, date of its creation and its formal classification. This means that even documents that are classified as secret or confidential according to the Law on the protection of secret data[302] can potentially be accessed.

144. Access to information may be limited or denied only in cases where disclosure of such information could reasonably be expected to harm the legitimate aims of the state (e.g., defence interests, public safety, crime prevention, etc.), where such information relates to confidential commercial interests of a third party, or where personal privacy of a third person is related to such information. However, even in such cases, disclosure may be permitted if it is justifiable by a greater public interest.[303] In other words, no information might be automatically excluded from the access. Instead, public authorities and institutions are required to apply the test of public interest before a decision for limiting or prohibiting access to requested information is made.[304] Moreover, it is prohibited to classify the whole categories of information as non-accessible. In 2016, the Ministry of Justice of BiH opened a process of public consultations on a preliminary draft of the new FOIA, by which the test of public interest would have been abolished, and thus the right to free access to data would have been severely limited. The initiative was however abandoned after the civil society and international community expressed strong disagreement.[305]

---

300. Sanela Hodžić & Anida Sokol. Oglašavanje i drugi komercijalni odnosi između javnog sektora i medija [Advertising and other commercial relations between public sector and media] Mediacentar Sarajevo, 2018, 21, https://media.ba/sites/default/files/izvjestaj_o_oglasavanju_mediacentar_sarajevo.pdf, accessed 5 Nov. 2020.
301. Mehmed Halilović, *Zakoni o slobodi pristupa informacijama*, in *Medijsko pravo u Bosni i Hercegovini*, 108 (Mehmed Halilović & Amer Džihana Internews, 2012).
302. Law on the Protection of Secret Data BiH, Art. 19.
303. FOIA BiH, Arts 6, 7, 8 and 9.
304. *Ibid.*, Art. 9.
305. Mitrović et al. *Specijalni izvještaj o iskustvima u primjeni zakona o slobodi pristupa informacijama*, 9.

145. Although Article 25 of the entity FOIAs and Article 26 of the state-level FOIA stipulate that 'legislation passed subsequent to this Law that is not specifically aimed at amending this Law shall in no way restrict the rights and obligations established herein' some of the laws that were passed later, such as the Criminal Procedure Code of FBiH[306] or the Law on the Protection of Secret Information in BiH, have been found to be in breach of the FOIAs.[307]

146. For example, Criminal Codes at all administrative levels and the Law on the Protection of Secret Information define what is to be considered as secret data. Nevertheless, given definitions are too broad, restrictive, and in contradiction with the Johannesburg Principles.[308] More specifically, the laws define the 'secret data' and 'secret' in such a way as to prevent the access to such information in contradiction to the FOIAs. Namely, FOAIs define a narrow scope of exceptions when the access to information can be restricted, and stipulate that even when the information access can be legitimately denied (like in the cases of 'secret' information), even such information can be made available if it is justifiable by public interest. Nevertheless, the Law on the Protection of Secret Data in Article 8 stipulates that all information is to be considered secret if its release might cause damage to the integrity of BiH, especially in the areas of:

- public security;
- defence;
- international relations and interests;
- intelligence and security interests;
- communication and other systems which are of importance for state's interests, judiciary, projects and plans important for defence, intelligence and security activities;
- scientific, research, technological, economic and financial activities of importance for the secure functioning of institutions of BiH, i.e., of its security structures at all levels of government.

147. Such a definition is too broad and can refer to a wide variety of information access to which might be in the public interest. Furthermore, the Law on the Protection of Secret Data does not allow for any exceptions as is stipulated in FOIAs, which means that according to the Law on the Protection of Secret Data the public authorities do not apply the 'public interest test' on the case-by-case basis in respect to the information classified as 'secret'. Sevima Sail Terzić argues that such a broad definition is in contradiction to the FOIAs, and leaves the possibility for the total prohibition of access to a wide range of information of public interest.[309] In

306. Criminal Procedure Codes of FBiH (*Zakon o krivičnom postupku FBiH*, Official Gazette of FBiH 35/03, 78/04, 28/05, 55/06, 27/07, 53/07, 9/09, 12/10, 8/13, 59/14).
307. Halilović, *Zakoni o slobodi pristupa informacijama*, 111; Sevima Sali-Terzić, 'Odavanje tajne u krivičnim zakonima u BiH', 235.
308. The *Johannesburg Principles on National Security, Freedom of Expression and Access To Information* (London: Art. 19, 1996) http://www.article19.org/data/files/pdfs/standards/joburgprinciples.pdf, accessed 27 Sep. 2020.
309. Sali-Terzić, *Odavanje tajne u krivičnim zakonima u BiH*, 233.

the Special report of the institution of Ombudsman BiH from 2019, several problems in the responses of public institutions to the requests for information are identified, including: a) tendency towards protecting private interests of third persons, without conducting the test of public interest for the specific information; b) negligible extent of the use of the possibility to identify and redact personal information, while providing other requested information that are in the public interest; c) questionable capacities of some institutions to implement FOIA and particularly lack of understanding of the principles and procedures of "test of public interest", and d) difficulties in waging between the right to protection of personal data and the right to access to information,[310] etc., which all indicate that more should be done to assure better and more consistent implementation of FOIAs.

148. Furthermore, based only on the Law on the Protection of Secret Data, one might conclude that public authorities do not have any obligation to respond to the requests for access to the classified information.[311] If the public authority would reject the request for access to the classified information, the Law on the Protection of Secret Data does not offer a possibility to challenge the decision through courts. Also, there are no provisions about the eventual review of the status of classified information on a periodic basis, nor are there clear deadlines for the duration of the status of specific classification.[312]

149. Last but not least, the Law on the Protection of Secret Data and the Criminal Codes provides for criminal prosecution of individuals, including journalists, for publishing such classified information. The punishment for revealing such information ranges from six months up to five years in prison at BiH, FBiH and Brčko District level for unauthorized persons. At the RS level, there is no differentiation between unauthorized and authorized persons, and the same punishments apply to both: from one to ten years in prison, or six months to five years in cases where secret data are revealed out of negligence.[313]

150. The Criminal Code at the BiH and FBiH level provides for exemption from prosecution in the case when revealing such information was in the function of uncovering anti-constitutional activities and if it does not have negative consequences for BiH, FBiH or Brčko district.[314] Nevertheless, the RS Law does not have even this narrow exception. Also, the Law on the Protection of Secret Data of BiH in Article 9 stipulates that the information cannot be classified as secret if the intention of such classification is to hide abuse of office, unlawful conduct, or administrative mistake. Nevertheless, none of the laws recognizes the duty of public

310. Mitrović et al, Specijalni izvještaj o iskustvima u primjeni zakona o slobodi pristupa informacijama u BiH, 73-77.
311. Sali-Terzić, *Odavanje tajne u krivičnim zakonima u BiH*, 233.
312. *Ibid.*, 234.
313. Criminal Code of RS, Art. 292.
314. Criminal Code of FBiH, Art. 158(5); Criminal Code of Brčko District, Art. 157(5); Criminal Code of BiH, Art. 164(9).

officials to uncover classified information internally or to the responsible supervisory body, in the cases of unlawful conduct, such as the infringement of human rights, abuse of office, corruption, public health hazard, environmental threats, etc.[315]

151. For instance, public company Elektroprivreda BiH, the branch offices of Tuzla, denied the requested information on contracts on procurement of meat signed with private companies, revoking the protection of commercial interests of third parties, without elaborating them and without considering the public interest. The second-instance administrative organ also failed to conduct the test of public interest and refused access to the requested information. The Ombudsmen BiH, after a received complaint, recommended granting the right to the requested information, in line with the FOIA.[316]

152. It is only the state-level FOIA that has provisions on penalties for responsible institutions and individuals: BAM 500–BAM 7,500 (EUR 250–EUR 3750) for institutions and BAM 100–BAM 2,500 (EUR 50–EUR 1250) for individuals. Other FOIAs refer to the relevant criminal and administrative laws concerning sanctioning non-compliance. The FOIA laws also provide for the possibility of a court appeal. By December 2019, the Center for Investigative Journalism had a dozen court decisions upon an appeal concerning the access to information, ruled in their favour. In one case, after their requests for information on salaries and contributions of the members of the Presidency of BiH from 2017 was denied, and the decision of the Appeal Council of Councils of Ministers also decided to refuse access to the information, the Court BiH ruled that this was a breach of the law as the test of public interest was never conducted. The court also emphasized that the right to protection of personal data cannot be a reason for ad hoc denial of information.[317]

153. All public bodies are required to produce the register of the information in their possession, and to appoint officials in charge for the access to information, and while most of them comply with these provisions, there are a number of institutions that failed to do so by the end of 2019.[318] Furthermore, a number of them failed to deliver information on the officials responsible for managing the requests for information to the Ombudsmen BiH, despite the fact that they are requested by the law to do so.[319]

---

315. Sali-Terzić, *Odavanje tajne u krivičnim zakonima u BiH*, 235.
316. Mitrović et al. Specijalni izvještaj o iskustvima u primjeni zakona o slobodi pristupa informacijama u BiH (Ombudsman BiH, 2019), 17. For other cases see Halilović, *Zakoni o slobodi pristupa informacijama*, 113.
317. See MC Online, CIN dobio desetu presudu protiv institucija, https://www.media.ba/bs/vijesti-i-dogadaji-vijesti/cin-dobio-desetu-presudu-protiv-institucija, 2019, and CIN dobio tužbu protiv Razvojne banke FBiH, 2019, https://www.cin.ba/cin-dobio-tuzbu-protiv-razvojne-banke-fbih/ (both accessed 28 Sep. 2020).
318. At least nineteen public bodies failed to appoint a FOIA officer. Mitrović et al. Specijalni izvještaj o iskustvima u primjeni zakona o slobodi pristupa informacijama u BiH, Ombudsman BiH, 2019, 55-61.
319. *Ibid.*

154. The situation regarding access to information improved significantly over time. For example, within the IREX ProMedia study from 2002, only 27% of public institutions responded to the requests for access to information (nineteen out of sixty institutions).[320] The Transparency International BiH study from 2005 recorded a 59% response rate, while the Mediacentar Sarajevo study from 2006 on the sample of 240 public institutions obtained 68.7% of responses – 58.8% in accordance with the FOIAs and 8.8% contrary to the FOIAs.[321] The study conducted by Jusić in 2010 that tested the compliance of municipal governments in BiH with the FOIAs involved sending 141 requests to all municipal governments, and it resulted in the total of 116 received responses (82%), out of which some 86% within the fifteen days prescribed by the FOIAs.[322] Since the introduction of the FOIAs, the Ombudsman of FBiH received on average 130–160 complaints per year from citizens that have been denied access to information. Around 90% of the complaints were resolved positively. In some cases, access to information was granted. In others, the formal decision by a public authority that denied access was issued, which enabled judicial complaint.[323] In 2015, this institution was closed at the level of the Federation of BiH, but the state-level institution of Ombudsmen oversees the implementation of FOIAs. In 2015, the Ombudsmen of BiH received 223 complaints, and the number increased to 340 in 2018.[324] The case law on FOIA over the previous years is for the most part going in favour of good practices of access to information held by public bodies. However, the appeals are usually finalized years after the initial request for information is filed, and by that time, the requested information becomes much less relevant. There is also a need for improvement of the laws, the capacities and practice of public bodies, as well as the citizens' understanding of the FOIA procedures. Experts for instance recommend amending FOIAs with stipulations on proactive publishing of information, strengthening the institutional framework for supervising the implementation of FOIA, and improving the procedure of accessing information based on request.[325]

§2. Court Hearings and Documents

155. According to the relevant laws of FBiH,[326] RS[327] and the Brčko District,[328] the work of the courts is public if not otherwise stipulated by law. Transparency of

320. Mirna Jusić, *Procjena budžetske transparentnosti u općinama u Bosni i Hercegovini* 38 (Analitika – Centar za društvena istraživanja 2011). https://www.analitika.ba/bs/publikacije/procjena-budzetske-transparentnosti-u-opcinama-u-bosni-i-hercegovini, accessed 28 Sep. 2020.
321. Amer Džihana, *Monitoring demokratskog razvoja u Bosni i Hercegovini: Indeks otvorenosti javnih institucija, organizacija i agencija* 32–33 (Mediacentar Sarajevo 2006); https://www.media.ba/bs/publication/monitoring-demokratskog-razvoja-u-bosni-i-hercegovini-indeks-otvorenosti-javnih, accessed 28 Sep. 2020.
322. Jusić, *Procjena budžetske transparentnosti,* 47.
323. Halilović, *Zakoni o slobodi pristupa informacijama,* 116.
324. Mitrović et al. Specijalni izvještaj o iskustvima u primjeni zakona o slobodi pristupa informacijama u BiH, 14.
325. *Ibid.*, 11.
326. Article 8 (Publicity and Transparency), in the Law on the Courts in FBiH (*Zakon o sudovima u FBiH*, Official Gazette of FBiH 38/05); the Law on Changes and Amendments to the Law on the

the courts is provided by the public debates in the proceedings before courts; by the publishing of the information about the court members; and by providing information to the public during court proceedings, under the conditions stipulated by law. Transparency can also be achieved by publishing court decisions and other information of public interest.

156. The general public has the right to access court documents and registries, in accordance with the law.[329] The Law on Courts in FBiH, Article 58, stipulates that information from the court register is public, and everyone can transcribe them or require the certified notification from the court register, except when otherwise prescribed by the law for specific information from the court register.

157. In the cases of the Constitutional Court of BiH and the Court of BiH, access to court hearings and documents is regulated by the courts' rules and procedures. For example, Article 13 of the Rules of the Constitutional Court of BiH[330] stipulates that the work of the Constitutional Court is public. The public character of the proceedings before the Constitutional Court of BiH is ensured by informing the public about the preparation of the court's sessions and public discussions before the Constitutional Court; providing the information about the status of proceedings; distribution of official press releases to the media; holding press conferences; providing the parties in the proceedings the access to the court documents and to public sessions of the Court, except when the president of the Constitutional Court decides otherwise, in the interest of morale, public order, and national security; publishing court decisions, etc. According to Article 14, except for the public debates, the presence of the members of the public during the sessions of the Constitutional Court is excluded. Finally, Article 15 stipulates that information on court sessions and public hearings of the Constitutional Court is published on the court's website and in the media.

158. Likewise, the Court of BiH provides guidelines for journalists[331] that stipulates that journalists accredited as visitors by the court have free access to the areas for the public in the courtrooms, and to the press centre. Video filming and taking photographs in the courtrooms, except in special cases such as press conferences, must be approved by the information office of the Court of BiH, upon prior approval

---

Courts in FBiH (*Zakon o izmjenama i dopunama Zakona o sudovima u FBiH*, Official Gazette of FBiH 22/06 and 63/10; plus, the corrections in the Official Gazette of FBiH 72/10 and 7/13.

327. Article 9 of the Law on the Courts in RS (*Zakon o sudovima RS*, Official Gazette of RS 37/12); the Law on Changes and Amendments to the Law on the Courts in RS (*Zakona o izmjenama i dopunama Zakona o sudovima RS*, Official Gazette of RS 100/17) and decisions of Constitutional Court 44/14, 44/15, 39/16).

328. Article 9, the Law on the Courts of Brčko District (*Zakon o sudovima Brčko Distrikta BiH*, Official Gazette of Brčko District 18/20);).

329. Article 58, Law on the Courts in FBiH; Article 88, Law on the Courts in RS; Article 66, Law on the Courts of Brčko District.

330. Rules of the Constitutional Court of BiH (*Pravila Ustavnog suda BiH*, Official Gazette of BiH 94/14).

331. Court of BiH http://www.sudbih.gov.ba/?opcija=sadrzaj&kat=7&id=92&jezik=b, accessed 28 Sep. 2020.

by the president of the Court. Video/audio recording and photographing from the courtroom gallery is strictly prohibited, and so is bringing cellular phones to the courtroom gallery. The requests of journalists and media representatives for the issuance of audio-video records will be addressed with special urgency, normally within the same day in which such a request has been filed by the media to the Court whenever possible. No fee will be charged by the Court for making audio-video copies, except the costs of the DVD-R/CD when such is provided by the Court. These aspects of the access of the media and the broader public to the information controlled by the Court of BiH have been regulated in more detail with the Rules on Freedom of Access to Information controlled by the Court and on the Cooperation of the Court with Community.[332]

159. Moreover, Criminal Procedure Codes of BiH,[333] FBiH,[334] and RS,[335] as well as the Civil Procedure Codes of RS[336] and FBiH[337] stipulate that the main trial is open for the general public, but that the general public can be excluded from the hearings at any moment. In the criminal procedure codes, this is specified as follows:

---

332. *Pravilnik o ostvarivanju pristupa informacijama pod kontrolom suda i saradnji suda sa zajednicom*, Court of BiH, adopted 20 Mar. 2012; consolidated text from 2016 is available at: https://www.google.com/url?sa=t&rct=j&q=&esrc=s&source=web&cd=&ved=2ahUKEwjIy9TEzIvsAhXOyIUKHayzDZYQFjAAegQIBBAB&url=http%3A%2F%2Fwww.sudbih.gov.ba%2Ffiles%2Fdocs%2FPIOS%2FSu-197-4%2520Pravilnik%2520o%2520ostvarivanju%2520pristupa%2520informacijama%2520%2520%2520%2520%2520precisceni%2520tekst.pdf&usg=AOvVaw1RiAJ_8Ug_3OpaBEssiKT2, accessed 28 Sep. 2020.
333. Article 234 (General Public), Article 235 (Exclusion of the Public), Article 237 (Decision on the Exclusion of the Public) and Article 365 (Exclusion of the Public) of the Criminal Procedure Code of BiH; the Law on Changes and Amendments to the Criminal Procedure Code of BiH (*Zakon o izmjenama i dopunama Zakona o krivicnom postupku BiH*, Official Gazette of BiH 32/03, 36/03, 26/04, 63/04, 13/05, 48/05, 46/06, 76/06, 29/07, 32/07, 53/07, 76/07, 15/08, 58/08, 12/09, 16/09, 53/09, 93/09, 72/13, 65/18).
334. Article 249 (General Public), Article 250 (Exclusion of the Public) Article 252 (Decision on the Exclusion of the Public) and Article 386 (Exclusion of the Public) of the Criminal Procedure Codes of FBiH; and the Law on Changes and Amendments to the Criminal Procedure Code of FBiH (*Zakon o izmjenama i dopunama Zakona o krivičnom postupku FBiH*, Official Gazette of FBiH 37/03, 56/03, 78/04, 28/05, 55/06, 27/07, 53/07, 9/09,22/09, 12/10 & 8/13).
335. Article 250 (General Public) and Article 251 (Exclusion of the Public), Article 279, 4 (Special Rules on Proves in Cases of Sexual Delicts) Article 300, 4 (Date and Place of Verdict Announcement)of the Criminal Procedure Code of RS (*Zakon o krivičnom postupku RS*, Official Gazette of RS 53/12); and the Law on Changes and Amendments to the Criminal Procedure Code of RS (*Zakon o izmjenama i dopunama Zakona o krivičnom postupku RS*, Official Gazette of RS 91/17, 66/18).
336. Articles 118, 119, 121 and 122 of the Civil Procedure Code of RS (*Zakon o parničnom postupku RS*, Official Gazette of RS 58/03); and the Law on Changes and Amendments to the Civil Procedure Code of RS (Zakona o izmjenama i dopunama Zakona o parničnom postupku RS, Official Gazette of RS 85/03, 74/05, 63/07, 105/08, 49/09, Decision of Constitutional Court BiH 49/09 & 61/13).
337. Articles 118, 119, 121 and 122 of the Civil Procedure Code of FBiH (*Zakon o parničnom postupku FBiH*, Official Gazette of FBiH 53/03); and the Law on Changes and Amendments to the Civil Procedure Code of FBiH (*Zakona o izmjenama i dopunama Zakona o parničnom postupku FBiH*, Official Gazette of FBiH 73/05, 19/06 & 98/15).

> The judge or the Panel of judges may at any time, ex officio or on motion of the parties and the defence attorney, (…) exclude the public for the entire main trial or a part of it if that is in the interest of the national security, or if it is necessary to preserve a national, military, official or important business secret, if it is to protect the public peace and order, to preserve morality in the democratic society, to protect the personal and intimate life of the accused or the injured party or to protect the interest of a minor or a witness.

160. The decision on exclusion of the public must be explained and publicly announced.

161. Finally, in 2006 the Press Council in BiH issued *Recommendations for Court Media Reporters Regarding Reporting on Investigations and Court Processes*,[338] which emphasize that:

> 'the public has a right to obtain fair information on court activities'. It further reads as follows:
> With objective to report more professionally on investigations and court processes, by these recommendations, reporters are reminded to: (1) carefully and sensitively report on investigations and court processes on crime acts, crime prosecutions and court verdicts; (2) professionally, objectively, timely, correctly and impartially report on crime acts and work of courts, respecting ethical standards assigned by the Press Code of BiH, and appreciating rules and legislation of BiH courts, where such procedures are being conducted (…); (6) remember that their reports and published information must neither interfere, nor jeopardize implementation of justice in current processes, nor influence the outcome of court trials and verdict; (7) remember if they have already named the accused/suspect person in their reports, or identified that person in any way so the public might recognize her/him, they are obliged to print information on charge dismiss and/or termination of court trial, if it comes to that; (8) not publish names of sexually abused victims or victims of violence, suicide, or publish materials that might help to identify the victim, unless the victim of violence and/or family of suicide victim allows it, and if disclosure is necessary for the investigation (…); (10) show utmost care and sensitivity when reporting on investigations and crime processes against minors, bearing in mind future of those persons, as well as to show care and sensitivity for minor crime victims (…); and (14) carefully report on 'cases in procedure' thus avoiding to jeopardize procedure in the appeal period.

338. *Recommendations adopted in December 2006, in cooperation with other journalist associations*, https://english.vzs.ba/index.php/guidelines-and-laws/guidelines-and-recommendations/8-recommendations-for-the-media, accessed 29 Sep. 2020.

162. The coverage of the court proceedings of the audiovisual media is additionally regulated in Article 15, The Coverage of Court Proceedings, of the CRA's CAVRMS.[339]

163. The judiciary practice regarding publishing personal information has been inconsistent and in some cases, the public is deprived of the information of public relevance.[340] The documents introduced in 2012: the *Guidelines on anonymization of Court Decisions, Audio/Video Recording of Court Proceedings, and of other Informative Content*[341] and the *Rules on Freedom of Access to Information controlled by the Court and on the Cooperation of the Court with Community,*[342] which regulated in detail the way the Court of BiH enforces the anonymization of private information, incited an outrage within the expert and wider community. The Guidelines and the Rules introduced an extensive range of anonymization measures that protect the private information of accused and prosecuted private and legal persons, information on cities related to the cases, even information on public institutions related to the particular cases, including the cases of war-crimes trials. The changes and amendments to the Law on Courts of Republika Srpska from 2012 (Article 9.3) stipulate as well that the court should 'anonymize personal data' before issuing the judgement and publishing other information of public interest. Many critics find such measures contradictory to the very mission of the court, especially when it comes to communicating the truth about severe war-crimes atrocities.[343] According to Sevima Sali-Terzić:

> … "The Regulation does not annul the public character of the trial and the pronouncement of the judgment. However, it lacks sufficient clarity in order to avoid misinterpretation of the rules on anonymization of audiovisual and other 'informative material' that Court of BiH provides to media and general public in relation to the on-going cases and in order to preserve the right of public to be informed as well as the right of a private person to have his/her personal data protected in an appropriate manner."[344]

339. For details please, *see* Part III: Regulation of Audiovisual Media, ch. 6, Right to Information, sec. 1 Access to Major Events, *infra.*
340. *See* more in Emina Cerimović, Edin Hodžić & Amra Mehmedić. Anonimizacija sudskih i tužilačkih akata u BiH [Anonymization of court and prosecution documents in BiH](Analitika 2014).
341. Guidelines on Anonymization of Court Decisions, Audio/Video Recording of Court Proceedings, and of other Informative Content (*Upute o načinu anonimizacije sudskih odluka, audio/video zapisa ročišta i drugog informativnog sadržaja*, Court of BiH, 21 Mar. 2012), http://sudbih.gov.ba/files/docs/Upute_o_nacinu_anonimizacije_sudskih_odluka,_audio_video_zapisa.pdf, accessed 20 Sep. 2020.
342. Rules on Freedom of Access to Information controlled by the Court and on the Cooperation of the Court with Community (*Pravilnik o ostvarivanju pristupa informacijama pod kontrolom suda i saradnji suda sa zajednicom*, Court of BiH, 20 Mar. 2012.
343. Jusić, Asim, *Pravna analiza: Neizravna cenzura i obesmišljavanje sudskog postupka* (BIRN – Balkan Investigative Reporting Network, 24 May 2012), https://www.justice-report.com/bh/sadr%C5%BEaj-%C4%8Dlanci/pravna-analiza-neizravna-cenzura-i-obesmi%C5%A1ljavanje-sudskog-postupka, accessed 29 Sep. 2020.
344. Sevima Sali-Terzić, *Anonimizacija ili cenzura sudskih odluka? Problemi s Pravilnikom Suda BiH* 15 (Fondacija Centar za javno pravo – CJP 2012).

164. However, in the later changes of the *Rules on Freedom of Access to Information controlled by the Court and on the Cooperation of the Court with Community*, the practice of ad hoc anonymization is abandoned, and publishing of court judgements that are of public relevance (i.e., those pertaining to war-crimes, terrorism, organized crime, corruption, tax evasion and other cases that involve particular public interest) is envisaged. The court can, however, in order to protect personal or intimate life of the accused or the victim, plaintiff or defendant, or to protect the interest of a minor or a witness, decide to exclude personal data from the judgements published on the website of the court. These data can include name, surname, date and birthplace, name and surname of parents, address, e-mail, and URL address (Article 25.6). However, the criteria for establishing public interests (in particular in the wording 'other cases that involve particular public interest') are not specified.[345] Furthermore, the Rules are far from being uniformly implemented, and for instance, the proactive publishing of court decisions is still not a common practice.

345. See Cerimović et al. *Anonimizacija sudskih i tužilačkih akata u BiH.*

Chapter 6. Press Council

165. The Press Council is a self-regulatory body for print and online media established in 2006 by the active associations of journalists in BiH.[346] The Press Council consists of representatives of print media publishers, journalists, and citizens. The Press Council tries to resolve disputes between the public and the press through the right to respond, to provide correction, apology and rebuttal and cannot impose sanctions. The principles upon which the Council makes its decisions are embedded in the Press Code – a key self-regulatory instrument for the journalists in BiH.

166. According to Article 12 of the Statute, the objectives and activities of the Press Council are:

1. improvement and protection of the journalism profession through improvement and protection of ethical standards in print and online media, as well as through strengthening self-regulation in print and online media in Bosnia and Herzegovina;
2. monitoring the implementation of professional standards in newspaper and online coverage in Bosnia and Herzegovina.
3. advocating for media freedom and freedom of information.
4. providing expert assistance and advice to members of the Association [i.e., the Press Council] and the general public
5. organizing seminars, workshops, conferences, debates, in order to improve the work of its members and the general public.
6. starting the initiative towards the relevant authorities to create conditions for undisturbed development of a sustainable self-regulatory body for print and online media in Bosnia and Herzegovina, through legislative and other legal regulations.
7. exchanging experiences and information with similar Associations and other non-government organizations in the country and abroad.
8. publishing books, brochures, bulletins and other publications, as well as launching websites and radio shows in order to achieve the objectives of the Association [i.e., the Press Council].

167. The most important body of the Press Council is the Complaints Commission[347] which acts as an advisory body and is nominated by the Board of Directors of the Press Council. The Complaints Commission consists of nine members: including members of the Press Council, representatives of civil society, and the media and academic community. Article 41 of the Statute stipulates that 'Members of the Complaints Commission cannot be members of the Board of Directors (…)

346. Mandate of the Press Council in BiH (PC BiH) was extended to online media as of January 2011. Mission, vision and values of PC BiH is available at: https://english.vzs.ba/index.php/press-council-in-bih/about-us/mission-vision-values, accessed 29 Sep. 2020.
347. Articles 40 through 44 of the Statute of the Press Council.

politicians, prominent party activists, members of political bodies or activists in electoral headquarters in Bosnia and Herzegovina.'

168. According to Article 42 of the Statute:

> The duties and responsibilities of Complaints Commission are to consider public complaints about the writings of the press and online media in Bosnia and Herzegovina; consider the monitoring results of the press and online media; monitor the implementation and initiate issues of breaches of the Press and Online Media Code of BiH in all newspaper editions and internet portals in Bosnia and Herzegovina; and publicly react to breaches of ethical journalism standards foreseen by the Code. According to Article 43 'The Complaints Commission of the Association can validly reach and adopt decisions upon the presence of the more-than-half majority of its members (…) Adjudications are reached by a more-than-half majority vote of the total number of Commission members.' The Complaints Commission receives hundreds of complaints per year, in 2019 overall 623 complaints, out of which 186 complaints on editorial content and 437 complaints on user generated content.[348]

169. The Press Council and the Press and Online Media Code are a direct result of extensive efforts and financial support provided by numerous international cooperation and development organizations and donors, and the Press Council until today receives important donor support.[349] The Press Council promotes professional ethical standards. The breach of those standards is however relatively common. Many platforms are not members of the Council and do not abide by its ethical standards. Some platforms do not publish information on persons responsible for their content or contact information, thus making it difficult for the Council to even initiate a direct dialogue about compliance with its ethical standards.[350]

348. Data on the website of Press Council BiH, at: https://www.vzs.ba/.
349. Source, List of donors and partners of Press Council BiH at: https://english.vzs.ba/index.php/press-council-in-bih/about-us/531-donors-and-partners, accessed 30 Sep. 2020.
350. *See* more on models of problematic communication practices in BiH in Anida Sokol. Propaganda, Disinformation and Hate Models of Media and Communication in Bosnia and Herzegovina (SEENPM 2020). https://www.media.ba/sites/default/files/rsl_researchtemplate_20-09-16_bih-eng_chapter1.pdf, accessed 29 Sep. 2020.

Part III. Regulation of Audiovisual Media (Broadcasting)

170. The regulatory framework for broadcasting was updated and aligned with the EU acquis communautaire in 2015. At the session of the CRA Council from 17 December 2015 the new rules and regulations were adopted: Rule 77/2015 on Audiovisual media services and Rule 76/2015 on Radio Media Services, the new Code on Audiovisual Media Services and Radio Media Services and the Code on Commercial Communications. In the following years, the regulatory framework was additionally amended, primarily with the new Rule on Licenses for the Distribution of Audiovisual Media Services and Radio Media Services (Rule 79/2016) and the Rule on Provision of Electronic Communication Network Management Services in Digital Terrestrial Broadcasting (Rule 90/2018), adopted in view of the upcoming stages of the process of the switch to the digital broadcasting.

Chapter 1. Public Service Broadcasting

171. According to Article 27 of Rule 76/2015 on the Provision of Radio Media Services and Article 28 of Rule 77/2015 on the Provision of Audiovisual Media Services, public radio and TV stations is each holder of the licence for television/radio broadcasting to which at least one of the following criteria apply: 'a) the founder is the state of Bosnia and Herzegovina, entity, Brčko District of Bosnia and Herzegovina, canton, city and/or municipality (political and territorial community); b) the founder is an administrative organization or other administrative body of a political and territorial community under a point a) of paragraph (1) of this Article, or an institution with public authorities of the political and territorial community under a point a) of paragraph (1) of this Article; c) it has been established under a public-private partnership model, whereby the legal entities under points a) and/or point b) of paragraph (1) of this Article have more than 51% share in the property or financing.'

172. ' As stated earlier, apart from three Public Service Broadcasters with their radio and TV channels, currently there are eighteen TV stations and sixty-one radio stations that fulfil these criteria and are formally considered public service broadcasters.[351] Nevertheless, the following sections within this chapter will primarily focus on the PSB at state and entity levels and will only marginally take into account the cantonal and municipal public broadcasters.

§1. The Concept and Mission of Public Service Broadcasting

I. History and Evolution

173. Former state-controlled broadcasters have undergone a thorough transformation since 1998, pushed by the OHR and the PIC,[352] who called for the creation of a PSB system in BiH that would consist of one state-level broadcaster and two entity-level broadcasters, each with one TV and one radio channel.[353] Consequently, in 1999, the OHR established the state-wide Public Service Broadcasting of BiH and the Public Service Broadcaster for the FBiH entity.[354] Furthermore, the OHR requested the assembly of RS to establish a public broadcaster for that entity as well.[355] Nevertheless, due to the failure of local authorities in BiH to implement

351. *See* Commun. Regulatory Agency registry of licence holders at: https://rak.ba/en/brdcst-license-holders, accessed 30 Jan. 2020; Also see Part I. General Introduction, sec. 2. The Media Landscape, *supra*.
352. *See* Thompson & De Luce, *Escalating to Success?*
353. Tarik Jusić & Amer Džihana, *Bosnia and Herzegovina*, in *Divided they Fall: Public Service Broadcasting in Multiethnic States* 92 (Sandra Bašić-Hrvatin, Mark Thompson & Tarik Jusić eds, Mediacentar Sarajevo 2008).
354. *High Representative Decisions on the restructuring of the Public Broadcasting System in BiH and on freedom of information and decriminalization of libel and defamation* (Office High Rep. 1999).
355. *High Representative Decisions amending the Law on Radio-Television of the RS* (Office High Rep. 1999).

these decisions, the HR issued the *Second Decision on Restructuring the Public Broadcasting System in Bosnia & Herzegovina*.[356] After three more years of delays, and the failure of state and entity authorities to adopt laws necessary for actual implementations of these decisions, the HR in 2002 imposed the *Law on the Basis of the Public Broadcasting System and on Public Service Broadcasting in Bosnia and Herzegovina* (hereafter, PSB Law 2002).[357] Furthermore, HR imposed three more decisions: the *Decision Imposing the Law on Radio-Television of Republika Srpska*;[358] the *Decision Imposing the Law on Radio-Television of the FBiH*;[359] and the *Decision on the Liquidation Procedure to be applied in Winding-up the Public Enterprise Radio and Television of Bosnia and Herzegovina*.[360] In effect, the PSB of Bosnia-Herzegovina was thus officially created, consisting of the following segments:

- Radio and Television of Bosnia and Herzegovina (*BHRT*), the state-level public broadcaster, with one TV channel (*BHT*) and one radio channel (*BH Radio 1*).
- Radio-Television of the Federation of Bosnia & Herzegovina (*RTVFBiH*), consisting of one TV channel (*FTV*) and one radio channel (*Radio FBiH*).
- *RTRS*, consisting of one TV channel and one radio channel.[361]

174. Nevertheless, the legal framework that was put in place was not fully implemented – three public broadcasters failed to create a joint Transmission Corporation that was supposed to manage the transmission network. Additionally, the three public broadcasters also failed to act as partners and members of the same system, and instead continued to behave as competitors.[362] Decreasing ratings, insufficient collection of the monthly licence fee, debts, and overstaffing have further complicated the situation and prevented the development of a functional PSB in

356. *High Representative Second Decision on restructuring the Public Broadcasting System in BiH* (Office High Rep. 2000), http://www.ohr.int/second-decision-on-restructuring-the-public-broadcasting-system-in-bih/, accessed 30 Sep. 2020.
357. High Representative Decision Imposing the Law on the Basis of the Public Broadcasting System and on the Public Broadcasting Service of Bosnia and Herzegovina (Office High Rep. 2002), (available at http://www.ohr.int/decision-imposing-the-law-on-the-basis-of-the-public-broadcasting-system-and-on-the-public-broadcasting-service-of-bosnia-and-herzegovina/?print=pdf, accessed 30 Sep. 2020); Law on the Basis of Public Broadcasting System and Public Broadcasting Service of Bosnia and Herzegovina (Official Gazette of BiH 29/02).
358. High Representative Decision Imposing the Law on Radio-Television of Republika Srpska, http://www.ohr.int/decision-imposing-the-law-on-radio-television-of-republika-srpska/, accessed 30 Sep. 2020; Law on Radio and Television of the Republika Srpska (Official Gazette of RS 22/03).
359. High Representative Decision Imposing the Law on Radio-Television of the Federation of Bosnia and Herzegovina, https://www.google.com/url?sa=t&rct=j&q=&esrc=s&source=web&cd=&cad=rja&uact=8&ved=2ahUKEwjN8NCCq5HsAhVNOhoKHRXNBaUQFjACegQIBBAB&url=http%3A%2F%2Fwww.ohr.int%2F%3Fp%3D66697%26print%3Dpdf&usg=AOvVaw19V9Bhj6bmZthliMtCwUe8, accessed 30 Sep. 2020. Law on Radio and Television of the Federation BiH (Official Gazette of FBiH 40/02).
360. Decision on the Liquidation Procedure to be Applied in Winding-up the Public Enterprise Radio and Television of Bosnia and Herzegovina, http://www.ohr.int/decision-on-the-liquidation-procedure-to-be-applied-in-the-winding-up-of-the-public-enterprise-radio-and-television-of-bosnia-and-herzegovina/, accessed 30 Sep. 2020.
361. PSB Law 2002, Art. 3.
362. See, for example: Jusić & Džihana, *Bosnia and Herzegovina*.

BiH. Consequently, strong pressures by the HR and the EC have resulted in the adoption of two new laws on the state level in 2005: *The Law on the PSB in BiH* (hereinafter 'PSB System Law')[363] and the *Law on the Public Service Broadcasting of BiH* (hereinafter 'BHRT Law').[364] These Laws replaced the state-level PSB Law 2002 that was imposed by HR in 2002.[365]

175. The System Law of 2005 regulates the relationships among the three broadcasters: BHRT, RTRS, and RTVFBiH, and specifies the principles for the creation of the Corporation of the Public RTV Services of BiH (hereafter, the Joint Corporation). The Joint Corporation is supposed to be funded and managed by the three public broadcasters and should be tasked to fulfil numerous important roles, such as transmission network and technical resources management, advertising, etc. The state-level broadcaster BHRT is regulated by the *BHRT Law*.[366] Additionally, the EU required that the laws regulating entity broadcasters *RTVFBIH* (hereinafter 'RTVFBiH Law')[367] and *RTRS* (hereinafter 'RTRS Law')[368] are amended in accordance with this new state-level legislation.

176. In spite of all legislative engineering, the persistent political obstacles prevented the true development of the PSB system in the country. Even in 2020, the Joint Corporation is still non-existent. The modes of collection of RTV fees are inefficient, the formula for the distribution of funds among the three broadcasters is not operational, and there is no true programming cooperation among them.[369]

II. Mission

177. Public broadcasters have specific programme requirements. CRA *Rules 76/2015 (Article 28) and 77/2015 (Article 29)* define programmatic obligations for the local public broadcasters, including for instance 40% of news and other informative and educational content. As for the public service broadcasters (BHRT, RTVFBiH and RTRS), their general programmatic obligations include reserving the majority of their programmes for European content, 40% to domestic programmes of all genres, and at least 10% of programmes (excluding informative programmes,

363. PSB System Law (*Zakon o javnom radio-televizijskom sistemu BiH*, Official Gazette of BiH 78/05, later amendments and changes Official Gazette of BiH 35/09, 32/10. 51/15, 25/16).
364. BHRT Law (*Zakon o Javnom radio-televizijskom servisu Bosne i Hercegovine*, Official Gazette of BiH 92/05, later amendments and changes: 32/10).
365. Jusić & Džihana, *Bosnia and Herzegovina*, 94–95.
366. *Ibid.*, 95–96.
367. RTVFBiH Law/Law on the Radio-Television of Federation of BiH (*Zakon o Javnom servisu radio-televizije Federacije Bosne i Hercegovine*, Official Gazette of FBiH 48/08).
368. RTRS Law/Law on the Radio-Television of Republika Srpska (*Zakon o Radio-Televiziji Republike Srpske*, Official Gazette of RS 49/06, later amendments and changes: 73/08, 42/10, 89/13, 44/16).
369. See, for instance, the Report on Financial Audit of Public Service Broadcaster RTV of Federation BiH for 2018 (Izvještaj o finansijskoj reviziji javnog servisa RTV Federacije BiH) https://parlamentfbih.gov.ba/v2/userfiles/file/Materijali%20u%20proceduri_2019/Izv-fin_revizija_RTV%20FBiH_2018.pdf, accessed 30 Sep. 2020; also see Jusić & Džihana, *Bosnia and Herzegovina*, 96–97.

sports and advertising content) from independent producers or commercial radio-televisions.[370] The Statutes of the public service broadcasters also outline the general principles such as respect for ethical and quality standards, promoting democratic freedoms, social justice, and peace. While these documents mention that the programme of the public service broadcasters must involve news and information, culture, education, entertainment and sport, it is the document System Licence that further specifies their obligations, including at least: a) 40% of weekly broadcasting reserved for domestic programme of all genres excluding sport and news; b) 51% of yearly content for European work, and at least 10% for European work of independent producers (excluding sport, news, games, advertising, teletext and teleshopping); c) broadcasting of informative, culture, educational, fiction and documentary programmes adapted to persons with invalidity and development difficulties, in particular those with hearing and sight impairments; at least one informative programme in primetime per day must be in sign language; d) At least 10% of overall programme accessible to persons with disability or developmental difficulties in the first year of the validity of the licence (starting September 2020), with continuous increase of that percentage and at least 25% of such programme by the end of the validity of the licence (end of April 2025); e) adapting the content and programme policies to the needs of gender equality and equal representation of interests of both sexes in media; and f) at least 1 hour per week intended for members of national minorities, making sure they are equally represented.[371] In addition, each of the three public service TV and radio broadcasters has its own weekly minimum programme quota (more below).

178. The laws on entity public service broadcasters stipulate that an advisory body, Programmatic Council will be established, including representatives of different social groups, such as youth or retired persons. The members of the Council are appointed based on a public call, after which the Supervisory board suggests the members, and the legislative body appoints the members.[372] The Council has an advisory role particularly concerning programmatic politics and plans and appointments of members of the managerial personnel within the broadcaster. RTV FBiH does not provide any information on such a body, the RTRS provides info on its 11 members on its website, while the BHRT also established the Programmatic Council, including nine members, in 2019.[373] Overall, these bodies in practice have a rather marginal role and their members meet only a few times per year.

370. Article 29 of the Law on Public Service of BiH. Similar stipulations are a part of Law on Radio-Television of Republika Srpska (Articles 13– 16) and Law on Radio-television Service of Federation BiH (Articles 13– 41).
371. Dozvola Sistema (System License) from 26 Apr. 2020, Article 6 (Programme quotas), the licence is on file with the authors.
372. Article 50, Law on RTRS; Article 30 of RTV FBiH.
373. Klix.ba, Sanja Vlaisavljević, Ivica Gudelj i Zija Dizdarević među članovma Viijeća (Klix.ba, 2020), https://www.klix.ba/vijesti/bih/sanja-vlaisavljevic-jurica-gudelj-i-zija-dizdarevic-medju-clanovima-vijeca-uo-bhrt-a/190122042, accessed 26 Oct. 2020.

A. BHRT: Radio and Television of BiH

179. According to the BHRT Law which relates to the state-level Radio and Television of BiH, BHRT is required to implement in its activities and staffing structure the constitutional requirements pertaining to the equal status of constitutional peoples and others in BiH. Programmes will be adjusted to the needs of constitutional peoples and citizens of BiH and will be edited and broadcasted equally in three official languages (Bosnian, Croatian and Serbian) and the two alphabets (Latin and Cyrillic).[374] The BHRT is required to provide coverage of the most important cultural, sport, entertainment and other events in BiH and internationally.[375]

180. The Statute of the BHRT stipulates that the broadcaster is responsible to the public of BiH for its activities, and is required to respect and promote public interest while adhering to the highest professional and ethical standards of independent journalism.[376]

181. The BHRT has an obligation to establish cooperation with entity-level public service broadcasters – RTRS and RTVFBiH – in order to ensure the production of programmes of the highest quality for the public in BiH and for BiH citizens who live abroad.[377] Its task is to broadcast truthful and diverse information on political, economic, social, health, cultural, educational, scientific, religious, ecological, and sports and other events.

182. The majority of the BHRT programming, outside of informative programmes, entertainment and advertising, should be of European origin whenever possible.[378] At least 40% of the programmes must be originally produced by the BHRT or by other members of the PSB System of BiH (i.e., RTRS and RTVFBiH) or procured by any of them. At least 50% of those programmes must be audiovisual works of fiction, documentary, animated or entertaining character, the purpose of which is in essence educational. At least 10% of the total programming of the BHRT, except informative and sports programmes and advertising, must be commissioned from domestic independent producers or commercial broadcasters. The System Licence further specifies the programme requirements for BHT1, including at least: 10 hours of informative programmes; 5 hours of children and youth programmes; 3 hours of programmes of educative character (magazines, documentary,

374. Article 8 of the Law; similar are stipulations in the laws on RTRS and RTVFBiH (Article 8 and 38(5) of the Law on RTVFBiH, article 13 (4) and 18 of the Law on RTRS); Additionally, The Statute of BHRT in its Programming Principles (Art. 9) requires BHRT journalists to use Bosnian or Croatian or Serbian language, while programmes should be equally produced in all three official languages and two alphabets. Similar are the Article 13 of the Statute of RTRS and Article 8 of the Statute of RTFBiH. The latter stipulates the use of three languages but only Latin alphabet in television program.
375. BHRT Law, Art. 10.
376. Statute of the BHRT, Art. 3.
377. *Ibid.*, Art. 5. Also Law on Public Broadcasting Service of BiH, Article 29.
378. *Ibid.*, Art. 10.

factual or studio programmes for different age groups); 3 hours of culture and art programme; 3 hours of music and entertainment programmes; and 1 hour of religious programmes (taking into account specificities of constituent people and others in BiH).[379]

B. RTVFBiH: Radio and Television of FBiH

183. The programming principles outlined in the RTVFBiH Law[380] stipulate that the RTVFBiH will provide truthful, comprehensive, impartial, and timely information on political, economic, educational, scientific, religious, cultural, sport and other events in BiH and abroad. The RTVFBiH is required to ensure open and free debate on issues of public interest so that all interests and tastes are taken into consideration, and that pluralism of political, religious and other ideas is respected and encouraged in order to strengthen democracy, mutual understanding and tolerance. The RTVFBiH must nurture and develop all forms of creativity that support the development of culture, art and entertainment, and contribute to the respect and promotion of fundamental human rights and liberties, democratic values and institutions, and promote the culture of public dialogue/deliberation. Additionally, the broadcaster has an obligation to respect privacy, dignity and honour of individuals, and especially of youth and children. Its programmes are to be adjusted to the needs of persons with hearing impairment and other special needs while news must be impartial, independent and factual.

184. Incitement of national, racial or religious hatred and intolerance, anti-Semitism, xenophobia, or discrimination against individuals or groups based on their origin, race, political beliefs, religion, health, gender, sexual orientation and any other characteristics are strictly prohibited in the programmes of the RTVFBiH. Furthermore, it is also prohibited to negate or inappropriately treat the genocide committed in Srebrenica. The RTVFBiH cannot broadcast immoral or pornographic content; instigate violence and criminal behaviour or promote the use of alcohol, drugs, narcotics or tobacco products among youth. It will not broadcast any programmes that can have a negative impact on the physical, psychological or moral development of children and youth in the period when children and youth are likely to be exposed to such programmes. The RTVFBiH will not breach generally accepted cultural standards of decency.[381]

185. Most of the RTVFBiH programmes will be reserved for European production whenever possible, except for the time dedicated to the news, sports events, entertainment, advertising, and teletext and teleshopping services. At least 40% of

379. Dozvola Sistema (System License) from 26 Apr. 2020, Specific Programmatic Conditions for BHT1.
380. RTVFBiH Law, Art. 39.
381. *Ibid.*, Art. 40.

the time will be reserved for domestic programmes, except news and sports programmes. At least 10% of broadcasting time, except informative broadcasts, sports programmes and advertising, must be commissioned from independent producers and/or commercial broadcasters.[382]

186. In its Statute,[383] the RTVFBiH is required to establish cooperation with other public service broadcasters within the PSB System of BiH – BHRT and RTRS – in order to ensure the production of programmes of the highest quality for the public in BiH. RTVFBiH broadcasts truthful and diverse information on political, economic, social, health, cultural, educational, scientific, religious, ecological, sport, and other events.

187. Its programmes are to be prepared in the languages of constituent people of FBiH, with the use of the Latin alphabet in its TV programmes.[384] Certain programmes should be broadcast in the languages of minorities that live in the territory of FBiH.[385] Programme quotas for FTV include at least: 9 hours of informative programmes, 6 hours of children and youth programmes, 3 hours of sports programmes, 2 hours of educative programmes, 1.5 hours of culture and art programmes, the same amount of music and entertainment programmes, and 1 hour of religious programmes.[386]

C. RTRS: Radio and Television of RS

188. The mission of the RTRS is to encourage the democratic process and ensure adequate presence of unbiased news and current issue programmes, informative, cultural, educational, children, sport and entertainment programming so that the programmes of the highest quality are available to the public in RS. Through the broadcasting of diverse and factual information, the RTRS should inform the public about political, economic, social, health, cultural, educational, scientific, religious, ecological, sports, and other events.[387]

189. The programming principles of the RTRS require the broadcaster to have programmes that serve the public interest and to be in accordance with the professional standards and rules and regulations of the CRA. The RTRS is obliged to ensure a diverse and balanced programme in accordance with the ethical and quality standards, respect to human life, dignity and physical integrity of persons, and to promote democratic freedoms, social justice and international understanding and peace. Its programme needs to respect national, regional traditional, religious, cultural, linguistic and other characteristics of the constitutive peoples and all citizens

382. *Ibid.*, Art. 41; the Statute of RTVFBiH, Art. 9.
383. Statute of the RTVFBiH, Art. 4.
384. This is in contrast with the Law on RTVFBiH, Art. 38, which stipulates equal use of both alphabets.
385. *Ibid.*, Art. 8.
386. *Ibid.*, Specific Programmatic Conditions for FTV.
387. RTRS Law, Art. 7.

of BiH, and will also promote cultural and other needs of national minorities in BiH. Furthermore, the programme of the RTRS should respect the constitutional rights of constituent people and citizens of BiH and will be edited equally in all three official languages and two alphabets.[388]

190. The RTRS must provide factual, timely, impartial information and news, and ensure open and free deliberation on issues of public interest, taking care that all interests and tastes are presented, thus supporting the pluralism of political, religious and other ideas and strengthening democracy, mutual understanding and tolerance. The broadcaster is also required to nurture and develop all forms of creativity in culture, art and entertainment, and contribute to the respect and promotion of fundamental human rights and freedoms, democratic values and institutions, and promote a culture of public dialogue. Additionally, it is required to respect privacy, dignity and honour of individuals, and especially of youth and children. The programmes of RTRS are to be adjusted to the needs of persons with hearing impairment and other special needs.[389]

191. Incitement of national, racial or religious hatred and intolerance, anti-Semitism, xenophobia, or discrimination against individuals or groups based on their origin, race, political beliefs, religion, health, gender, sexual orientation and any other characteristics are strictly prohibited. The RTRS should not broadcast immoral or pornographic content, and will not instigate violence and criminal behaviour or promote the use of alcohol, drugs, narcotics or tobacco products among youth. It will not broadcast any programmes that can have a negative impact on the physical, psychological or moral development of children and youth in the period when children and youth are likely to be exposed to such programmes. The broadcaster shall not violate generally accepted cultural standards of decency.[390]

192. The RTRS must ensure that most of its programmes will be reserved for European production whenever possible, except for the time dedicated to the news, sports events, entertainment, advertising, and teletext and teleshopping services. At least 40% of the time will be reserved for domestic programmes, except news and sports programmes. At least 10% of broadcasting time, except informative broadcasts, sports programmes, and advertising must be commissioned from independent producers and/or commercial broadcasters.[391] Specific programme requirements for the RTRS as the same as those for FTV, including at least: 9 hours of informative programmes, 6 hours of children and youth programmes, 3 hours of sports programmes, 2 hours of educative programmes, 1.5 hours of culture and art programmes, the same amount of music and entertainment programmes, and 1 hour of religious programmes.[392]

388. *Ibid.*, Art. 13 (Programming Principles).
389. *Ibid.*, Art. 14 (Fulfilling the Programming Principles).
390. *Ibid.*, Art. 15 (Programming Limitations).
391. *Ibid.*, Art. 16 (Programme Share).
392. *Ibid.*, Specific Programmatic Conditions for TVRS.

§2. THE ORGANIZATION OF PUBLIC SERVICE BROADCASTING

193. The PSB System of BiH consists of three broadcasters: *RTVFBiH*, *RTRS*, and *BHRT*. The managing body of the PSB System of BiH is the System Board. It consists of twelve members, who come from the Boards of Directors of the three broadcasters, and it coordinates programme schemes among broadcasters, is in charge of the collection of the subscription fee, is envisioned to be a Supervisory Board of the Joint Corporation (once it is eventually established), and adopts codes of conduct for the PSB System.[393]

194. The governing bodies of each of the three broadcasters – BHRT, RTVFBiH, and RTRS – are the Board of Directors (*Upravni odbor*) and Managing Board (*Poslovodni odbor*).[394] The Managing Board, made up of the Director General and sector managers, oversees the daily work of public broadcasters.[395] The Board of Directors represents the public interest in respect to the programme, supervises the business operations, is in charge of the property management, and appoints the Director General.[396]

195. Each Board of Directors of the three public service broadcasters has four members – one member comes from each of the three constituent people (Bosniaks, Croats, and Serbs) and the 'others'. Members of the Board of Directors of entities and state broadcasters are appointed by their respective entities and state parliaments.[397] In the case of RTRS and BHRT, the appointment of the members of their Board of Directors is made based on the list of candidates submitted by the CRA to their respective Parliaments, while in the case of RTVFBiH the appointment is made by appointment commissions of both houses of the Parliament of FBiH. Members of the Board of Directors of each of the three broadcasters cannot be persons from executive, legislative and judicial branches of the government, members of the bodies of political parties, employees of BHRT, RTRS and RTVFBiH, employees and affiliates of other companies involved in the broadcasting sector.[398]

196. It is generally considered that the members of the boards of directors are appointed based on their political loyalty and in some cases lack professional credentials.[399] The procedure to have the CRA submit the list of the candidates for the BHRT and the RTRS was created with the idea to make the process more transparent and to reduce the potential political influence on the appointments. Nevertheless, the principle on occasions failed in practice as the parliamentary bodies have

393. Article 7 and 8 of the Law on Public RTV System of BiH. See also Jusić & Džihana, Bosnia and Herzegovina, 101–102.

394. BHRT Law, Art. 23; RTVFBiH Law, Art. 22; RTRS Law, Art. 43.

395. *Ibid.*

396. BHRT Law, Arts 24, 29 & 31; RTVFBiH Law, Arts 23, 28 & 34; RTRS Law, Arts 44, 48 & 51.

397. BHRT Law, Art. 25; RTVFBiH Law, Art. 25; RTRS Law, Art. 46.

398. *Ibid.* and the Law on BHRT, Article 26.

399. *See* Sanela Hodžić, The Credibility and Competence of PSB Boards are Questioned. *See* Mediaobservatory 2013, https://mediaobservatory.net/radar/flash-report-bosnia-and-herzegovina, accessed 3 Oct. 2020.

a decisive role in the appointments. For instance, in 2011, the CRA submitted the list of candidates for the Board of Directors of the state-level public broadcaster BHRT, but the appointments were blocked in the second chamber of the BiH Parliament – the House of Peoples – which 'failed to appoint the candidates from the submitted lists despite the legal requirement to do so'.[400] As a consequence, terms have been extended for the previous members of the Board.[401] However, the CRA notes that in the recent appointments of the Board of Directors of the BHRT, the procedure was respected, and the Board members were appointed based on the list submitted to the Parliament.[402] When it comes to the public broadcaster of Republika Srpska, the RTRS, the amendments to the Law on RTRS adopted in 2013 ousted the CRA from the appointment procedure, stipulating that the members of the Board are to be appointed directly by the National Assembly of RS. These changes enabled further politicization of the appointment procedures. The latest call for new Board members was published in June 2020. In the case of the public service broadcaster of the Federation of BiH, RTVFBiH, it is stipulated that only one member of the Board of Directors should be appointed per year, which was supposed to prevent one party or coalition from determining the appointment of the majority of members of the Board. However, due to a lack of political agreements, the process of the appointment has been under a blockade since 2012. In 2012, the Parliament of FBiH, contrary to the Law on RTVFBiH, discharged the old and appointed a new Board, but after a strong resistance by the media community and civil society, as well as international actors, this decision was abandoned.[403] The Parliament failed to appoint new members, and since mid-2020, only one of the Board members (the term of which is long expired) is still formally performing this duty.[404]

§3. The Financing of Public Service Broadcasting

197. Regular activities of public service broadcasters are financed from monthly licence fees,[405] advertising revenues, and revenues from additional services such as selling of programmes, authorship rights, etc.[406] Regular activities are preparation, production, transmission and broadcasting of its programmes; production of printed materials related to its programmes and broadcasting issues in general; archiving of audio and video materials; organization of cultural, music and other events; public

400. Commun. Regulatory Agency, *Annual Report 2011*, 18.
401. *Ibid.*, 18; *Also see*: E. Gorinjac, *RAK mora dva puta raditi isti posao: Novi Parlament BiH tako er želi podobne u UO BHRT-a* (Sarajevo-x.com; 29 August 2011); http://www.sarajevo-x.com/bih/novi-parlament-bih-takodjer-zeli-podobne-u-uo-bhrt-a/110829097, accessed 28 Jan. 2012.
402. Written reply by Commun. Regulatory Agency, 23 Oct. 2020. *Also see* Commun. Regulatory Agency Annual Report for 2017, 12.
403. Hodžić, The Credibility and Competence of PB Boards are Questioned.
404. Website of RTV FBiH, at: http://www.rtvfbih.ba/loc/template.wbsp?wbf_id=191&section=info, accessed 3 Oct. 2020.
405. The licence fee is defined as a tax on possession of television and radio sets and it is presumed that one person in each household as well as legal entities is in possession of at least one radio or television receiver.
406. BHRT Law, Art. 20; RTVFBiH Law, Art. 18; RTRS Law, Art. 38.

opinion polls, marketing and advertising services; provision of teletext and other related services. Additional programming services, such as online provision of programmes or Pay-TV, may be offered in accordance with relevant laws and licensing rules and regulations of the CRA. Furthermore, within the PSB of BiH, the three broadcasters can jointly obtain certain programmes and introduce new broadcasting technologies.[407]

198. The mix of sources of funding is meant to provide for greater financial independence of public broadcasters, especially from the state influence. While the commercial revenues are an important source of funds, the duration of advertising cannot exceed four minutes per hour on public service TV channels or six minutes on public service radio programmes.[408]

199. The public RTV system is having severe difficulties with collecting the licence fees. The previous system of collection through landline telephone bills had been increasingly inefficient due to the sharp fall of the number of landline users.[409] However, political disagreements and lack of will for a joint solution halted new collection solutions. In 2017, the BHRT and RTVFBiH started collecting the fees through electricity bills, while the RTRS has been collecting the fees partly on its own and partly through the public postal company Pošte RS. This fragmented system is at odds with the Law on public RTV system that stipulates that the licence fees are collected at a central account and then distributed among the three public broadcasters, so that 50% belongs to the BHRT, while each entity broadcaster, the RTVFBiH and RTRS, receives 25%.[410] Although in the previous system the distribution did not work well in practice, with both entity broadcasters having large debts towards BHRT, the new system of collection of RTV only adds to the problem. From 2017 RTRS completely stopped redistributing the collected licence fees to the other two broadcasters.[411]

200. According to the same law, advertising revenues are to be distributed in line with the same formula as the licence fee (50:25:25) but that aspect of the law has never been put into practice due to the politically and financially driven obstructions in the implementation of the Law. The provisions of the law that relate to the distribution of advertising revenues according to the 50:25:25% formula faced a particular resistance from the side of the RTVFBiH who would lose much of its

407. BHRT Law, Art. 7; RTVFBiH Law, Art. 7; RTRS Law, Art. 17.
408. Code on Commercial Communications, Art. 9 (Duration of Television Advertising and Teleshopping) and Art. 13 (Duration of Advertising and Teleshopping in Radio Programmes), https://rak.ba/en/articles/107, accessed 3 Oct. 2020.
409. BHRT's 2006 Annual Business Report, March 2007, 26; BHRT's 2010 Annual Business Report, 2011, 10; https://bhrt.ba/wp-content/uploads/2020/08/IZVJE%C5%A0TAJ-O-RADU-I-POSLOVANJU-BHRT-a-ZA-2010.-GODINU.pdf, accessed 4 Oct. 2020.
410. Art. 23 of the PSB System Law.
411. Izvještaj o radu i poslovanju RTVFBiH za 2017. godinu, 5 [The activity and business report for 2017] http://www.rtvfbih.ba/loc/template.wbsp?wbf_id=166&section=info, accessed 4 Oct. 2020.

advertising revenues in that case.[412] Moreover, Article 18.3 of the Law on RTVFBiH is inconsistent with the Law on Public RTV system, since it stipulates that the RTVFBiH primarily uses advertising revenues for financing its own operations.

201. There is a lack of data on revenues in the media market. In 2018, as in 2017, the overall advertising revenues were estimated at EUR 38 million, out of which EUR 25.8 acquired in the TV media market.[413] The advertising revenues have been dropping and in 2018 are estimated to around 61% of its value from 2008.[414] The three Public Service Broadcasters – primarily RTVFBiH, together with the largest commercial broadcasters – primarily Nova BH and OBN, have the largest advertising shares.[415] On the other hand, funding by the public sector makes up an important part of overall revenues, amounting to between EUR 15 and EUR 50 million per year.[416] Public Service Broadcasters also can receive direct funding from government budgets, and particularly the RTRS has been receiving such support: around EUR 2.1 million in 2018, mostly from the Government of Republika Srpska[417] The overall revenues of the RTRS amounted to BAM 26.627.793 (EUR 13.6 mil) in 2017 and BAM 32.354.878 (EUR 16.5 mil) in 2018, while revenues of the RTVFBiH in 2017 amounted to BAM 27.058.737 (EUR 13.8 mil). There is a slight trend of increase in the collection of RTV fees, however, the RTVFBiH reports that the advertising revenues are dropping due to increasing competition from commercial media.[418] The BHRT particularly reports on financial difficulties, pointing out that in 2016, the revenues dropped by around 25% as compared to 2010.[419]

---

412. For analysis of the financial aspects of operation of public service broadcasters in BiH see for example: Jusić & Džihana, *Bosnia and Herzegovina*, 97–100; Auth. Commun. Guarantees & Commun. Regulatory Agency, *Overview of the Communications Sector*, 111–113.
413. Sanela Hodžić and Anida Sokol. Sustainability of Professional Journalism in the Media Business Environment of Western Balkans: National Data Overview Bosnia and Herzegovina (TACSO 2020), 10, http://tacso.eu/wp-content/uploads/2020/09/Sustainability-of-Professional-Journalism-in-WB-Study-National-Data-Overview-BiH-final.pdf, accessed 4 Oct. 2020.
414. *Ibid.*, 9.
415. In 2006 the public service broadcasters earned 65% of the market revenue in 2006, while three largest private broadcasters at that time – NTV Hayat, Pink BH, and OBN – earned 20%. The remaining 15% is shared among the smaller local and regional stations. Commun. Guarantees & Commun. Regulatory Agency, *Overview of the Communications Sector*, 119.
416. Hodžić and Sokol. Sustainability of Professional Journalism in the Media Business Environment of Western Balkans: National data Overview Bosnia and Herzegovina. Also see Auth. Commun. Guarantees & Commun. Regulatory Agency, *Overview of the Communications Sector*, 111–113. for older data.
417. Annual report of RTRS for 2018, 23. https://lat.rtrs.tv/comp/doc/Izvjestaj%20o%20radu%20jp%20rtrs%20za%202018.%20godinu%20-%20Cirilica.pdf, accessed 4 Oct. 2020.
418. There is a long-lasting trend of decrease in advertising share of public service broadcasters. *See* Mareco Index Bosnia, 2006, cited in: Aida Hozić, *Democratizing Media, Welcoming Big Brother: Media in Bosnia and Herzegovina, in Finding the Right Place on the Map: Central and Eastern European Media Change in a Global Perspective* 154 (Karol Jakubowicz & Miklos Sukosd eds, Intellect 2008).
419. Izvještaj o radu i poslovanju RTVBiH za 2016. godinu, 12. https://bhrt.ba/wp-content/uploads/2020/08/Izvje%C5%A1taj-o-radu-i-poslovanju-Radiotelevizije-Bosne-i-Hercegovine-za-2016.-godinu-bosanski.pdf, accessed 4 Oct. 2020.

202. The radio market is much smaller than the TV market, with estimated total revenues of EUR 2.66 million in 2018.[420] Like in the TV sector, a dozen of main radio stations acquire a large part of revenues[421] Except for the three radio channels of BHRT, RTRS and RTVFBiH, sixty-four radio stations are majority-owned or financed by municipal or cantonal governments. On the other hand, seventy-seven radio stations are private.[422] Hence, public financing is a significant source of income for a significant part of the radio stations on the market.

420. Hodić and Sokol. Sustainability of Professional Journalism in the Media Business Environment of Western Balkans: National data Overview Bosnia and Herzegovina, 10.

421. In 2006, some 60% of revenue on the radio market was distributed among more than 130 stations, while 40% was shared among 10 main radio stations. Auth. Commun. Guarantees & Commun. Regulatory Agency, *Overview of the Communications Sector.*

422. Commun. Regulatory Agency, *Annual Report for 2019*, 13.

Chapter 2. Private Broadcasting

§1. Different Categories of Private Broadcasters

203. In the BiH, there are radio and TV stations at local, cantonal, regional, entity and state levels in respect to their formal status, but their coverage is conditioned by geography rather than by administrative boundaries, meaning that those broadcasters have local, regional or state-wide coverage. Apart from commercial private broadcasters, there is also a possibility to establish a non-profit community radio station. Officially, categories of private broadcasters are primarily defined in terms of types of licences awarded and /or the means of transmission used and do not necessarily emphasize the territorial dimension/coverage of the broadcasters, though the territorial dimension is defined through the coverage range of allocated frequencies. This means that the private broadcasters can be divided into the following categories according to the relevant CRA rules:[423]

- television broadcasting over a terrestrial broadcasting service;
- television broadcasting over other electronic communication networks, excluding terrestrial broadcasting service;
- on-demand audiovisual media services;
- radio broadcasting over a terrestrial broadcasting service;
- radio broadcasting over other electronic communication networks, excluding terrestrial broadcasting service;
- non-profit radio;
- temporary licence for the coverage of individual events;
- on-demand radio service.

§2. Licensing Requirements

204. The Council of Ministers of BiH is responsible for the development of the policies in the communication sector, while the CRA is responsible for the regulation of broadcasting and telecommunications, including issuing of licenses, planning coordination, purpose, and awarding of the radio frequency spectrum.[424]

205. The criteria for the issuance of licences for the provision of audiovisual and radio services, as well as the rights and obligations of providers of such services are defined in the relevant rules of the CRA.[425] The primary purpose of these rules is to ensure the protection of media pluralism, public interest, and equal and efficient competition on the market of audiovisual and radio services in BiH.

423. Rule 77/2015 on the Provision of Audiovisual Media Services; Rule 76/2015 on the Provision of Radio Media Services.
424. The Communications Law of BiH, Art. 3.
425. Rule 77/2015 on the Provision of Audiovisual Media Services, and Rule 76/2015 on the Provision of Radio Media Services.

I. Licence for Television Broadcasting[426]

206. Acquiring a licence issued by the CRA is the basic precondition for the start of the provision of TV broadcasting services. During the period of validity of the licence, the user of the licence must fulfil requirements and conditions upon which the licence was issued, and the failure to do so can result in the revocation of the license.[427]

207. There are two main types of licence for TV broadcasting: *the Licence for the terrestrial broadcasting of TV programmes*, and *the Licence for television broadcasting over other electronic communication networks, excluding terrestrial broadcasting service*. The licence for the terrestrial broadcasting of TV programmes is issued through the public bid,[428] while licence for television broadcasting over other electronic communication networks, excluding terrestrial broadcasting service, is granted on a non-exclusive basis.[429] All legal entities registered in BiH can participate in the public bid for the licence for the terrestrial broadcasting of TV programmes.[430]

208. Both types of licences for TV broadcasting are issued based on programme, economic and technical criteria.[431] Programme criteria include the following:[432]

a. Compliance of the weekly programme schedule, programme segments and programme structure, with the rules of the Agency (i.e., CRA).
b. Overall level of skill and experience of staff, evaluated on the basis of organizational structure, education, and work experience of staff in charge of the programme.

209. Additional programme criteria that only applies to the licence for the terrestrial broadcasting of TV programmes (and not to licence for television broadcasting over other electronic communication networks, excluding terrestrial broadcasting service) is:

- Specificity of programme content in a particular geographic area, evaluated by the degree to which the planned programme schedule together with programme segments and programming structure is already present in that particular geographic area.[433]

426. Rule 77/2015 on the Provision of Audiovisual Mia Services.
427. *Ibid.*, Art. 4 (General Principles).
428. *Ibid.*, Art. 5.
429. *Ibid.*, Art. 10.
430. *Ibid.*, Art. 5.
431. *Ibid.*, Art. 5.
432. *Ibid.*, Arts 7 and 11.
433. *Ibid.*, Art. 7.

210. The economic criteria for both types of TV broadcasting licence are:[434]

a. Economic viability of an applicant in terms of the amount of share and subscribed capital and other sources of funding.
b. Economic performance of an applicant in terms of the structure of assets and sources of funds including measures of liquidity, solvency, debt, etc.
c. Business efficiency of an applicant in terms of analyzing the profitability on the basis of profit rate, internal rate of return, return on capital employed rate, etc.
d. Assessment of business, i.e., producing the study of the economic viability of investments.

211. For the terrestrial TV broadcasting licence, additional criteria include the manner of financial realization for each frequency resource, whereby it is estimated if the applicant has provided funding for each frequency resource for which it applied.

212. In the case of a public bid for the licence for the terrestrial broadcasting of TV programmes, the comparative analysis is used when several bidders that satisfy programme, economic and technical criteria, apply for a licence in the same geographical area. The comparative analysis is conducted for each applicant's planned programme with regard to the programmes that are already available in a given geographic area, and will be scored in the following way:

a. Up to eight points to the applicant that offers programme content that is in no way or only slightly present in a given geographic area.
b. Up to four points to the applicant that offers programmes with a larger share of his own production, European audiovisual works, and works of independent producers.
c. Up to three points, taking into account the list of priorities for each frequency resource.[435]

II. Licence Terms and Conditions

213. There are a number of programme terms and conditions to be met in order to obtain and maintain a licence. In respect to the responsibility and liability, the licensee, *inter alia*:

1. Shall be fully responsible for all programme content regardless of its origin.
2. The content of the licensee, during the entire validity of the license, shall be in accordance with the programme terms of the license, the rules of the Agency, as well as other regulations related to broadcasting.

---

434. *Ibid.*, Arts 8 and 11.
435. *Ibid.*, Art. 9.

3. Public television stations shall have the additional obligation to ensure that their programmes are in compliance with the provisions specified in this Rule (Part 4).
4. The licensee is free to address any other issues related to the provision of audiovisual media services that are not regulated under the Agency's rules and regulations, nor other regulations related to broadcasting, through self-regulation.[436]

214. Rule 77/2015 on the Provision of Audiovisual Media Services also regulates the percentage of originally produced programmes and the limits on rebroadcasts. Hence, it stipulates that:

> (5) At least 20 percent of total weekly programming shall be the licensee's in-house production, at least 75 minutes of which shall be broadcast daily between 17:00 and 23:00 hours.[437] (…) (7) The licensee may rebroadcast programs provided that they do not exceed 20 percent of the total daily programming.(…) (9) Any change in program segments and programming structure exceeding 20 per cent, excluding the shift between summer and winter program schedules, shall be subject to prior written approval of the Agency. (…) (10) The Agency reserves the right to reject the approval under paragraph (9) of this Article, if it determines that it would lead to a lack of variety of programme segments and structure of the programme for which the license has been granted.[438]

215. Furthermore, 'in the event of war, natural disasters or any other situation that may pose a risk for the health and lives of citizens, security or public peace and order, the Licensee shall broadcast public service announcements and notifications at the request of competent authorities free of charge'.[439]

216. The licensee is required to make its services accessible to people with visual or hearing disabilities.[440]

217. In respect to the quota for European works, the licensee must reserve a majority proportion (51%) of their programme content for European works, whereby the time appointed to news, sports events, games, advertising, teletext services and teleshopping are excluded. The European work includes work originating in EU member states, in European third states parties to the European Convention on Transfrontier Television of the Council of Europe, as well as the works co-produced in audiovisual agreements between European Union and third countries. The European works include BiH works and own productions of the licensee.

436. *Ibid.*, Art. 13 (Programme Terms and Conditions).
437. Paragraph (5) of this Art. 13 does not apply to thematic channels, including the channels exclusively devoted to teleshopping or self-promotion.
438. Rule 77/2015 on the Provision of Audiovisual Media Services, Art. 13 (Programme Terms and Conditions).
439. *Ibid.*, Art. 13.
440. *Ibid.*, Art. 13.

Services of an entirely local nature and thematic channels, including channels exclusively devoted to teleshopping or self-promotion, are excluded from this obligation. Moreover, the licensee has to reserve at least 10% of his programme content for European works created by independent producers, excluding the time appointed to news, sports events, games, advertising, teletext services and teleshopping, out of which at least 50% of work has to be produced within the last five years.[441]

218. Next to European works, the licensee also has to reserve for BiH works at least 20% of its programme content on a weekly level, hereby excluding the time appointed to news, sports events, games, advertising, teletext services, and teleshopping. These obligations do not apply to thematic channels, including the channels exclusively devoted to teleshopping or self-promotion.[442]

219. The right to use short news extracts is also granted by Rule 77/2015. A licensee with exclusive access to an event of high interest to the public must grant, under equal conditions, access to this event to all broadcasters established in BiH or the European Union. Short news reporting is an extract which is no longer than ninety seconds and is solely to be used for news programmes.[443]

220. The licensee is obliged to identify its content by means of its logo. Furthermore, the licensee must make the following information, easily, directly and permanently accessible to the public: (a) the name of the licensee; (b) the geographical address at which the licensee is established or has its head office; (c) the details of the licensee, including his electronic mail address or website; and (d) the information that it has been granted a licence by the Agency.[444]

221. Use of material protected by copyright or other rights is allowed under the condition that the licensee has valid contracts for broadcasting all such materials. Upon request of the Agency, the licensee shall submit the proof of holding the rights to broadcast material protected by copyright or other rights. In order to inform the public on current affairs and only, for this reason, the licensee may use copyrighted material that appears as an integral part of the current affair concerned, provided that a clear attribution to the source is given. In general, such excerpts shall not exceed ninety seconds. In addition, the licensee shall not broadcast cinematographic works outside the time periods agreed with the rights holders.[445]

222. The licensee has to keep separate financial records of incomes and expenditures for the activity regulated under Rule 77/2015.[446]

223. Also, the licensee has to provide information and/or recordings of the programme to the Agency. The CRA can request this information when required for the

441. *Ibid.*, Art. 14 and 15.
442. *Ibid.*, Art. 16.
443. *Ibid.*, Art. 17.
444. *Ibid.*, Art. 18.
445. *Ibid.*, Art. 19.
446. *Ibid.*, Art. 20.

purposes of ensuring compliance with licence terms and conditions or other regulatory work. The licensee must make and retain complete recordings of all broadcast programmes in such a manner that the continuity and integrity of programmes are maintained. Such recordings shall be kept for a minimum of six weeks or longer upon request of the CRA.[447]

224. The conditions for the transfer of licence are strictly regulated. The licensee is not authorized to transfer or assign the licence wholly or partly by sale or any other contract to other entities. However, the CRA can approve, upon the request of a licensee, a transfer of the licence to another natural or legal person, in the case of a business reorganization with the licensee, for instance, a merger, acquisition, division or change in the type of a legal person or a crafts business that holds the license, provided that a written consent of all owners/co-owners of the licence is obtained. Any change in the ownership of a licensee exceeding 5% share will constitute a partial transfer of ownership and will thus require a written approval of the CRA. If the transfer of ownership is approved, the licensee shall notify the CRA about all relevant changes in the court registry or the registry of securities.[448]

225. The licensee has to adopt procedures for handling complaints received by the public as regards all programme content and must ensure that these procedures are duly observed. Amongst other things, these procedures require that complainants are informed of the possibility to refer their complaint to the CRA. The licensee is obliged to keep a written record of the complaints for the period of one year and must communicate this record upon request of the CRA.[449]

226. The CRA has the task to monitor the licensee's performance in order to ensure compliance with the applicable rules and regulations. If the Agency issues an order, the licensee will comply in a timely manner. In the case of an emergency order issued by the Agency, the licensee will immediately implement this order. The licensee will grant access to its premises to authorized personnel of the Agency in order to inspect or examine any facilities, including official records, equipment, etc., for purposes of verifying compliance with the rules concerning the use of radio-frequency spectrum, lawful orders, instructions and/or CRA's rules and regulations.[450]

227. The duration of a licence for Television broadcasting over a terrestrial broadcasting service and over other electronic communication networks is ten years. The licensee will begin the broadcast operations in accordance with granted or altered licence terms and conditions within ninety days from the date of issuance of the licence or the approval of alterations to licence terms and conditions. If the licensee does not begin the scheduled broadcast operations within ninety days, the CRA shall revoke the licence or alter the licence terms and conditions. However, an

447. *Ibid.*, Art. 21.
448. *Ibid.*, Art. 22.
449. *Ibid.*, Art. 24.
450. *Ibid.*, Art. 26.

exception can be made if the beginning of the scheduled broadcast is contingent on appropriate authorizations by other responsible authorities, unfavourable weather conditions or other objective and warranted circumstances, on the condition that the licensee has notified the Agency of this particular situation and requested the Agency to extend the initial issuance date. In this case, the Agency can grant an extension, taking into account the circumstances of each individual case. Such an extension cannot exceed six months after the decision on the extension request is made. If the licensee fails to start the broadcasting operations within the extension period, the Agency will revoke the licence or programme terms and conditions. The licence may be renewed from the date of expiration thereof, in which case the licensee is obliged to apply for renewal of the licence not later than three months before the expiration date of the licence.[451]

228. The licence can be revoked not only as a possible sanction for breach of the rules and regulations of the CRA but also if the CRA finds out that the licensee has provided false information or has withheld information with the intention of misleading the CRA; if there have been frequent or lengthy interruptions in broadcasting; if the licensee fails to fulfil its financial obligations towards the CRA; and at the licensee's request.[452]

229. Any breach of, or failure to comply with Rule 77/2015 on the Provision of Audiovisual Media Services will lead to appropriate sanctions in accordance with the Communications Law and the by-law adopted on the basis thereof.[453]

III. Technical Terms and Conditions of the License

230. Article 40 of Rule 77/2015/2011 on the Provision of Audiovisual Media Services applies to technical operations of the holders of the licence for television broadcasting over a terrestrial broadcasting service until the switchover to digital terrestrial television broadcasting in BiH. Article 40 regulates the issues of compatibility of the equipment with international standards; the compliance with specific rules and regulations; safety issues; provisions for the maximum time available for the start of the broadcasting upon the issuance of the license; conditions for the alteration of technical operations; the criteria for production, transmission and broadcast; and the issues related to the human resources of the licensee.

231. The licensee is required to undertake everything necessary in order to maintain and modify its broadcasting equipment in accordance with technical provisions of the International Telecommunications Union (ITU).[454]

451. *Ibid.*, Art. 27.
452. *Ibid.*, Art. 27.
453. *Ibid.*, Art. 39.
454. *Ibid.*, Art. 40.

232. It is stipulated that the licensee comply with all CRA's rules on technical operations for television broadcasters, and to adhere to all other relevant rules in BiH.[455]

233. The licensee is required to act in accordance with the CRA's rules on restricting the emissions of electromagnetic radiation when operating its broadcast systems and facilities in order to protect people from the harmful effects of electromagnetic fields. Any equipment that might, due to its failure or damage, cause harmful consequences to health or people's lives must immediately be put out of use, while the CRA must be notified of any such event. The CRA has the right to order the licensee to put any potentially harmful equipment out of use until such danger is eliminated.[456]

234. In accordance with the technical terms and conditions, the scheduled broadcasting must start within ninety days from the date of issuance of the licence or the approval of alterations to technical terms and conditions by the CRA. If the licensee does not meet this condition, the licence or altered technical terms and conditions shall be revoked.[457] The extension of the scheduled start of broadcasting can be granted in exceptional cases, described earlier. The extension can be granted for the period not longer than six months, but only when the licensee had approached the CRA with such a request prior to the expiration thereof. In the case when the licensee does not begin the broadcast operations even after the granted extension has expired, the CRA shall revoke the licence or technical terms and conditions without exceptions.[458]

235. The licensee can request the alteration of its licensed technical operations. In such a case, the CRA uses specific technical criteria to assess the technical feasibility for a specific frequency resource. The criteria consist of the production part and the transmission and broadcast part.[459] The criteria for the production part include organizational structure, the qualifications and experience of technical staff responsible for the production of the programme; studio equipment reliability and quality, availability of spare equipment; maintenance strategy for studio equipment (regular, preventive, emergency); and the control of signal in production, including the procedures applied in signal monitoring, as well as the technical characteristics of the equipment used for monitoring and restricting the signal to the baseband layer.[460] The criteria for the transmission and broadcast part include transmission and broadcast equipment in terms of its reliability and quality; maintenance strategy for transmission and broadcast equipment; and the control of signal in a radio-frequency band (RF) in transmission and broadcast part of the chain, taking into account the procedures applied by the personnel in signal monitoring, as well as the technical data and equipment used for monitoring and restricting the signal in RF

455. *Ibid.*, Art. 40.
456. *Ibid.*, Art. 40.
457. *Ibid.*, Art. 40(13).
458. *Ibid.*, Art. 40(14).
459. *Ibid.*, Art. 40(8).
460. *Ibid.*, Art. 403(9).

band.[461] Only the licensees that have adequate human and technical resources to manage their broadcast signal according to the relevant rules and regulations can fulfil the criteria.[462]

IV. Licence for on-demand Audiovisual Media Services

236. The conditions and procedures for the authorization of provision of on-demand audiovisual media services are outlined in section 5 of Rule 77/2015 – Provision of On-demand Audiovisual Media Service. All natural and legal persons are required to obtain authorization from the CRA before they would start with the provision of on-demand audiovisual media services. Any natural or legal person registered for the relevant activities in BiH that has no unfulfilled financial obligations towards the Agency can request such authorization.[463]

237. The full responsibility, in accordance with rules and regulations of the CRA, for all programme content it provides regardless of its origin rests with the on-demand audiovisual media service provider. All relevant CRA's codes and rules in the audiovisual field shall, where appropriate, apply to on-demand audiovisual media services.[464]

238. The on-demand audiovisual media service provider is required to promote the production of and access to BiH and European works, either through the financial contribution made by on-demand audiovisual media services to the production and rights acquisition of such works or through the share of BiH and European works in their programme catalogue.[465]

239. Services of the on-demand audiovisual media service provider need to be made accessible to people with visual and/or hearing disabilities.[466]

240. Finally, the on-demand audiovisual media service provider is required to identify itself in its catalogues of programme content. More specifically, its name, address of its head office, electronic mail address or website, and the information that it has been registered for the provision of on demand audiovisual media services with the CRA must be easily, directly and permanently accessible to the public.[467]

461. *Ibid.*, Art. 40(10).
462. *Ibid.*, Art. 40(11).
463. *Ibid.*, Art. 34.
464. *Ibid.*, Art. 35.
465. *Ibid.*, Art. 35.
466. *Ibid.*, Art. 30(5).
467. *Ibid.*, Art. 36.

V. Radio Broadcasting Licenses

241. Rule 76/2015 on the Provision of Radio Media Services 'defines the criteria for the provision of radio media services in BiH, as well as the rules and obligations of the providers of radio media services in the country'. The purpose of the Rule is to create conditions for the protection of public interest, media pluralism, and fair competition in the market of radio services in BiH. The rule does not apply to public broadcasting services.[468]

242. The licensee is obliged to adhere to the terms and conditions of the license. The CRA reserves the right to monitor and estimate the actual quality of a licensee's compliance with the terms and conditions of the licence at any given moment of the licence period. Non-compliance with the terms and conditions of the licence may result in the revocation of the license.[469]

243. The CRA issues the following types of radio broadcasting licences:

– General licence for radio broadcasting (over terrestrial radio broadcasting and other electronic communication networks).
– Licence for non-profit radio, and
– Temporary licence for coverage of individual events.[470]

A. *General Licence for Radio Broadcasting over a Terrestrial Broadcasting Service*

244. General licence for radio broadcasting over a terrestrial broadcasting service is awarded exclusively, through a public tender procedure. Licence can be granted to any natural and legal persons registered for relevant activities in BiH.[471]

245. Within the public tender procedure, the Agency shall apply: programme criteria; technical criteria; and economic criteria. When two or more applicants that fulfil criteria apply for one frequency resource, the CRA shall conduct a comparative analysis to determine who should be granted the license.[472]

246. Programme criteria consist of the compliance of the weekly programme schedule, segments and programme structure with the relevant codes and rules of

468. Rule 76/2015, Art. 1.
469. *Ibid.*, Art. 3.
470. *Ibid.*, Art. 3.
471. *Ibid.*, Art. 4.
472. *Ibid.*, Art. 4.

the CRA and the overall level of skill and experience of staff in charge of programme matters, as well as to what extent the planned programme schedule, programme structure and programme segments are already represented in the particular geographical area.[473]

247. Technical criteria are those concerning the technical personnel for programme production, e.g., organizational structure, qualifications and experience; quality of studio, transmission and broadcasting equipment; strategy for the maintenance of the equipment; the control of the signal in the production as well as in the radio-frequency range within the transmission and broadcasting segment and the feasibility of technical implementation for each specific frequency resource.[474]

248. Economic criteria are: economic viability of an applicant; economic performance in terms of the structure of assets and sources of assets, i.e., measures of liquidity, solvency, debt, etc.; business efficiency in terms of profitability; the evaluation of business plan in terms of economic justifiability of investment, the manner of financial realization, i.e., whether the applicant has secured funding for each frequency resource for which the application is submitted.[475]

249. According to Article 8, the comparative analysis will be undertaken in the case when two or more applicants fulfil special criteria for the frequency resource that is offered in a public tender procedure. The comparative analysis focuses on the programme of bidders and compares them to the programmes that already exist in the geographic area of the frequency range that is the subject of the bid. Hence, the advantage is given to the applicant which offers programme segments which are not adequately available in the geographic area of the frequency range that is the subject of the bid, and which has a larger segment of its own production of the programme. The advantage is also given to those applicants who better correspond to the list of priorities for each frequency resource.[476]

B. General Licence for Radio Broadcasting over Other Electronic Communication Networks, Excluding Terrestrial Broadcasting Service

250. General licence for radio broadcasting over other electronic communication networks, excluding terrestrial broadcasting service, is granted on a non-exclusive basis. All natural and legal persons registered for the pursuit of relevant activities in BiH can apply for the licence. The integral parts of the licence are programme segments and the structure of the programme.[477]

473. *Ibid.*, Art. 5.
474. *Ibid.*, Art. 7.
475. *Ibid.*, Art. 6.
476. *Ibid.*, Art. 8.
477. *Ibid.*, Art. 9.

251. Article 10 sets out the programme and economic criteria for granting the licence for radio broadcasting over other electronic communication networks, excluding terrestrial broadcasting services. The programme criteria are in compliance with the weekly programme schedule, segments and programme structure with the relevant codes and rules of the CRA and the overall level of skill and experience of staff.[478] The economic criteria are economic viability of an applicant; economic performance in terms of the structure of assets and sources of assets, i.e., measures of liquidity, solvency, debt, etc.; business efficiency of an applicant in terms of analysing the profitability; and the development plan in terms of economic justifiability of investment.[479]

252. The yearly licence fee for the General licence for radio broadcasting over other electronic communication networks, excluding terrestrial broadcasting service, is set at BAM 750.[480]

C. Licence for Non-profit Radio

253. Licence for non-profit radio is granted, on a non-exclusive basis, to the legal persons that are registered as non-profit organizations, and are established with the goal of protection and promotion of rights and interests of specific social groups. The same radio-frequency resource can be allocated by the CRA to several different users of the licence, which would then use the frequency in different time periods.[481]

254. Apart from the formal requirements, the licence is issued under the condition that the planned programme, in its content and language, is fully oriented towards a social group which is represented by the legal person, or which rights and interests the legal person stands for.[482]

255. All rules of the CRA related to the programme standards, which are outlined in the CAVRMS and other relevant rules of the CRA, are applicable to the non-profit radio licence.[483]

256. Importantly, the programme of the non-profit radio cannot contain any commercial communications, except self promotion and advertisements in the public interest if those are broadcast without charges.[484]

257. Critics emphasize that these stipulations point to two major 'misconceptions of what community media must be and can be: a misconception that stations

478. *Ibid.*, Art. 10.
479. *Ibid.*, Art. 10.
480. *Ibid.*, Art. 11.
481. *Ibid.*, Art. 12.
482. *Ibid.*, Art. 12(4).
483. *Ibid.*, Art. 12(5).
484. *Ibid.*, Art. 12(6).

must not be community media if they take advertising; and that community media must speak to a very narrowly defined social group, rather than the local community as a whole'.[485]

258. Consequently, the licence for non-profit radio, by prohibiting commercial funding and at the same time 'failing to provide or encourage any other means of financial support, or other incentives for non-profit groups, reveals a lack of understanding of the mission of community media and what kind of enabling legislation actually fosters an emergent community media sector'.[486] According to the same authors, the practice in most European countries is rather different, allowing community radio stations to broadcast limited commercials and to seek sponsorships. The key characteristic of the non-profit radio concept is that stations reinvest revenue generated through advertising and sponsorship back into the station, and not for personal gains of its management and owners.[487]

259. In respect to the definition of the social group which is targeted by the community radio station, in most European countries, the social mission of community media is fulfilled not by requesting the stations to speak for a single, specific social group, but by programming and participation requirements and criteria that guarantee the stations actively engage community groups.[488]

D. Temporary Licence for the Coverage of Individual Events

260. The *Temporary licence for the coverage of individual events* is issued for the period no longer than twenty-eight days, exclusively for the purpose of coverage of individual events, such as fairs, festivals, sports events, etc. The licence is issued on a non-exclusive basis, in accordance with the available frequency spectrum. All relevant rules and codes of the CRA apply to the use of this type of licence as well.[489]

VI. Terms and Conditions for the Radio Licences

261. The licensee holds full responsibility for all programme content regardless of its origin. The programmes must comply with the relevant rules, regulations, codes, licence terms, and conditions related to programme matters and broadcasting

485. Kate Coyer & Joost van Beek, *Community Radio in Bosnia and Herzegovina: Opportunities and Challenges* in *Communication and Community: Citizens, Media and Local Governance in Bosnia and Herzegovina* 150–151 (Tarik Jusić ed., Mediacentar Sarajevo & Analitika – Center for Social Research 2010).
486. *Ibid.*
487. *Ibid.*
488. *Ibid.*
489. *Ibid.*, Art. 14.

throughout the licence period. Radio stations in public ownership need to ensure that their programmes fulfil additional requirements, defined in Part 4 of Rule 76/2015.[490]

262. In situations that may pose a risk for the health and lives of citizens, security or public peace and order, such as war or natural disasters, the radio station is obliged to broadcast public service announcements and notifications free of charge if requested by competent authorities.[491]

263. Any change in segments and structure of the programme exceeding 20%, excluding the shift between summer and winter programme schedules, is subject to prior written approval by the CRA. The approval can be denied if such a change would cause a deficiency of particular programme segments on which the licence was issued in the first place.[492]

264. Radio station is required to have at least 70% of the total daily programming of its own production. Out of that, at least 50% must be produced in-house. Thematic channels, including the channels exclusively devoted to teleshopping or self-promotion, are excluded from this provision.[493]

265. Up to 20% of the daily programming may consist of rebroadcast programmes. The source of the rebroadcast programme must be clearly identified, and any rebroadcasting must be based on a written contract between the radio station and the media provider whose programme is being rebroadcast.[494] Furthermore, several licence holders may exchange programme segments from their in-house production, based on appropriate contracts.[495]

266. Article 18 of the Technical Terms and Conditions for radio broadcasting outlines provisions regarding compliance with international standards, safety requirements, and the start of operation. Hence, radio stations are required to maintain and modify their broadcasting equipment in accordance with technical provisions of the ITU and to comply with all the rules of the CRA regarding technical operations for television broadcasters, as well as all other applicable rules in BiH.[496] Broadcast systems and facilities will be operated with due regard to the protection of people from harmful effects of electromagnetic fields, in accordance with restrictions of the emissions of electromagnetic radiation as stipulated in the CRA's relevant rules. In the case of failure or damage to equipment that might jeopardize safety, health or people's lives, the radio stations must put such equipment out of

490. *Ibid.*, Art. 15 (Programme Terms and Conditions).
491. *Ibid.*, Art. 15(5).
492. *Ibid.*, Art. 15(10, 11).
493. *Ibid.*, Art. 15(6,7).
494. *Ibid.*, Art. 15(8).
495. *Ibid.*, Art. 15(9).
496. *Ibid.*, Art. 16(1, 2).

use and notify the CRA about the incident. The CRA has the right to issue an order requiring the radio station to put such equipment out of use until the problem is eliminated.[497]

267. The scheduled broadcasting must start within ninety days from the date of issuance of the license[498] or the approval of alterations to technical terms and conditions by the CRA. If this condition is not met, the licence or altered technical terms and conditions will be revoked. In exceptional cases, the CRA can grant the extension of the planned start of broadcasting, such as for example, when additional authorizations might be required from other responsible authorities or due to unfavourable weather conditions, and if the licensee had approached the CRA with the request prior to the expiration of the originally scheduled start of the broadcasting. The extension can be granted for a period not longer than six months. In case the radio station does not start broadcasting within the extended schedule, the licence or technical terms and conditions will be revoked without exceptions.[499] The licence can also be renewed from the day of the expiration if the licensee applied for the renewal three months before the expiration, where possible. For non-profit radio stations, the request is to be made at least one month before the expiration.[500]

268. The radio station has to regularly identify itself by its official name at least once every thirty minutes during the broadcasting of its programmes.[501] Provider of on-demand radio media service shall ensure its identification in the catalogue of programme content.[502]

269. When using material protected by copyright or other rights the licensee needs to have contracts for broadcasting of such material, which they can be requested to present to the Agency. For purposes of provision of information on current affairs only, the radio station is allowed to use copyrighted material as an integral part of the current affair item, under the condition that clear attribution to the source is given, and that such excerpts do not exceed ninety seconds.[503]

270. The licensee is required to provide relevant information and/or recordings of the programmes as might be required by the CRA for the purposes of ensuring compliance with licence terms and conditions.[504] Furthermore, the licensee must 'make and retain complete audio recordings of all broadcast programmes in such a manner that the continuity and integrity of programmes is maintained. Such recordings shall be kept for a minimum of six weeks, or longer if required by the Agency'.

497. *Ibid.*, Art. 16(3, 4).
498. *Ibid.*, Art. 26(5, 6).
499. *Ibid.*, Art. 26(7).
500. *Ibid.*, Art. 26 (8).
501. *Ibid.*, Art. 17.
502. *Ibid.*, Art. 34.
503. *Ibid.*, Art. 18.
504. *Ibid.*, Art. 20(1).

Additionally, the licensee has to maintain daily records of the broadcast programmes and keep them for the period of two years. Records of the broadcast programmes shall contain information on the exact time of broadcast of each programme content, its name, type of programme segment and its duration. [505]

271. Transfer of licence by sale or other contracts to another natural or legal person is strictly prohibited without prior approval by the CRA. The Agency may approve a transfer of the licence in the event of business reorganization, such as merger, acquisition, division or changes in the type of legal persons that hold the license. The transfer can be granted under the condition that a written consent of all owners/co-owners of the licence holder has been obtained. Any change in the ownership of more than a 5% share of interests constitutes a partial transfer of ownership and must be approved by the CRA in writing. All relevant changes in the court registry or the registry of securities related to the transfer of ownership must be reported to the CRA.[506]

272. The radio station is required to adopt procedures for handling complaints received from the public regarding its programmes. The procedures must contain, *inter alia*, a requirement that individuals or organizations who complain about the stations' programme are informed that they also have a right to refer their complaints to the CRA. Such complaints received from the public will be kept for a period of one year and made available upon the request of the CRA.[507]

273. The CRA monitors the licensee's performance and ensures compliance with the rules and regulations. The licensee is required to comply in a timely manner with any decision issued by the Agency and shall grant access to its premises to authorized personnel from the CRA in order for them to inspect any facilities, official records, equipment, etc.[508]

274. The General licence for radio broadcasting over a terrestrial broadcasting service and the General licence for radio broadcasting over other electronic communication networks are each valid for a period of ten years. Licence for the non-profit radio is valid for a period of one year while the temporary licence for the coverage of individual events can be valid for no longer than twenty-eight days. The license may be renewed, in which case the licensee is obliged to apply for renewal of the licence not later than three months (or one month for non-profit radio) before the date on which it would otherwise cease to be valid.[509]

275. The licence can be revoked in the cases of breach of the relevant rules and regulations of the CRA; if the licensee has provided false information or has withheld information with the intention of misleading the CRA; if there are frequent or

505. *Ibid.*, Art. 20(2, 3).
506. *Ibid.*, Art. 21.
507. *Ibid.*, Art. 23.
508. *Ibid.*, Art. 25.
509. *Ibid.*, Art. 26.

lengthy interruptions in broadcasting; if the licensee fails to fulfil its financial obligations towards the CRA; and at the licensee's request.[510]

276. Failure to comply with the relevant rules of the CRA will lead to appropriate sanctions in accordance with the Communications Law of BiH and the related by-law documents.[511]

VII. Licence for On-Demand Radio Service

277. Provision of on-demand radio media services is subject to prior authorization from the CRA. All natural and legal persons registered for the pursuit of relevant activities in BiH may request authorization for the provision of on-demand radio media service. The on-demand radio media service provider has an obligation to inform the CRA about its programme orientation and the available catalogues of programmes.[512]

278. Full responsibility for programme content, disregarding the origin of the programme rests with the provider of on-demand radio media service. Relevant CRA's rules and codes also apply to the on-demand radio media service.[513]

279. Furthermore, the CRA 'shall keep the Register of on-demand radio media service providers that shall contain the following information: name of an on-demand radio media service provider, its official address, contact information and programme orientation'.[514]

280. The authorization for the provision of on-demand radio media service shall be revoked in following cases: if the on-demand radio media service provider has provided false information or has withheld information with the intention of misleading the CRA; if the provider has not provided the service for more than one year; or when requested by the provider.[515]

281. The issuance of the authorization for the provision of on-demand radio media service is free of charge.[516]

510. *Ibid.*, Art. 26.
511. *Ibid.*, Art. 37.
512. *Ibid.*, Art. 33.
513. *Ibid.*, Art. 33.
514. *Ibid.*, Art. 33.
515. *Ibid.*, Art. 33(9).
516. *Ibid.*, Art. 33(10).

Chapter 3. Programme Standards

282. The CAVRMS 'sets basic principles of programme content of audiovisual media services and radio media services in BiH in accordance with the Constitution of BiH, Communications Law, EU Audiovisual Media Services Directive and other applicable domestic and international legal documents'.[517]

283. Article 3 of the CAVRMS sets out the Basic Principles for the audiovisual and radio media services:

1. respect of the dignity of the human being and the fundamental rights of others;
2. respect of ethnic, cultural and religious diversity in BiH;
3. prohibition of content that includes 'any discrimination or prejudice based on gender, race, ethnicity, nationality, religion or belief, disability, special needs, age, sexual orientation, social origin, or any other content which has the purpose or effect to nullify or to impair the recognition, enjoyment or exercise, on an equal footing, of any person's rights and freedoms on equal basis';
4. freedom of media service providers in creating and editing their content while ensuring respect for professional and generally accepted values and ethical standards;
5. respect of the generally accepted standards of decency in audiovisual media content;
6. prohibition of abuse and/or manipulation with superstition, fears or credulity of individuals or the public, as well as the encouragement of potentially harmful behaviour;
7. the treatment of vulnerable persons who appear in audiovisual and radio content shall require due attention; and
8. the audiovisual and radio media services shall not contain 'material which carries a clear and immediate risk of causing negative consequences which include, but are not limited to death, injury, property damage or other type of violence, or obstruction of police activities, medical services or activities of other services related to maintenance of public order and security'.

284. Additionally, 'the media service providers are responsible for all content, regardless of its source, as well as for professional activities of their employees. This includes in-house production, purchased/procured, rebroadcast and exchanged programmes, programme announcements, text messages and other messages of the public, as well as commercial communications'.[518]

285. Further provisions on programming standards are stipulated in the relevant rules and regulations of the CRA, as well as in the laws on public service broadcasters and their Statutes as outlined in the following sections.

---

517. CAVRMS, Official Gazette of BiH 3/16, Art. 1.
518. *Ibid.*, Art. 3(7).

§1. IMPARTIALITY

286. When it comes to impartiality and fairness in audiovisual and radio programmes, the CAVRMS in Article 5 (Fairness and Impartiality) stipulates that accuracy of information must be ensured in all programming, and especially in news and current affairs programmes. The providers of audiovisual and radio media services are required to correct any detected mistakes with respect to the accuracy of its programmes.[519]

287. Fairness, impartiality and balance in all programme segments, in particular in news and current affairs programmes, must be ensured by presenting all differing viewpoints, be it in the same programme or within a sequence of other programmes that represent a whole in dealing with a certain topic.[520] Audiovisual and radio programmes cannot promote the interests of an individual political party, group or individual, nor will they allow the prevalence of one opinion or position when dealing with controversial political, economic and other topics of public interest.[521]

288. Presenters and reporters, authors of programmes, moderators of political, current affairs, as well as the debates and discussion programmes, are allowed to express their own opinions and views, but must not compromise due impartiality and balance by misusing the advantage of regular appearances in such programmes for the promotion of their own personal views and opinions. In case such personal views and opinions are expressed, they must be clearly signalled as such to the audience.[522] When it comes to news programmes, presenters are required to present the information in an unbiased manner, without expressing their own opinions.[523] Comments must be clearly separated from the news.[524]

289. Individuals or organizations present in the audiovisual and radio programmes must be treated fairly.[525] In the case when alleged wrongdoing, incompetence, or any negative connotations is attached to a person or an organization, those concerned must be given an opportunity to adequately respond to such allegations in the same programme. If the person or organization refuses to appear in a programme or make a statement in response to the allegations, this will be noted by the media service provider. In urgent cases, where it was in the public interest to publish such information even without response to the concerned person or organization in the very same programme, they will be offered an opportunity to respond as soon as circumstances allow.[526]

519. CAVRMS, Art. 5(1).
520. *Ibid.*, Art. 5(2).
521. *Ibid.*, Art. 5(3).
522. *Ibid.*, Art. 5(4).
523. *Ibid.*, Art. 5(5).
524. *Ibid.*, Art. 5(6).
525. *Ibid.*, Art. 5(7).
526. *Ibid.*, Art. 5(8).

290. Relevant provisions in line with the CAVRMS are also contained in the RTVFBiH Law and the RTRS Law. Hence, the editorial independence of RTVF-BiH is granted in Article 37 of the RTVFBIH Law, followed by provisions on programming standards which stipulate the obligation of the broadcaster to ensure balanced radio and TV programmes in accordance with the highest ethical and professional principles, and in line with relevant rules and regulations of the CRA.[527] Basically, identical provisions are contained in the RTRS Law.[528] The statutes of three public service broadcasters also point out that the content has to be in accord with professional standards and CRA rules and regulations.[529]

§2. Cultural Diversity

I. Access to Airtime for Cultural Groupings

291. There is no legal provision containing explicit measures that require commercial broadcasters to offer minority and cultural groupings programming and access to airtime.

292. Such possibility exists through the *licence for non-profit radio*[530] that is granted, on a non-exclusive basis, to the legal persons that are registered as non-profit organizations, and are established with the goal of protection and promotion of rights and interests of specific social groups. Apart from the formal requirements, the licence is issued under the condition that the planned programme, in its content and language, is fully oriented towards a social group which is represented by the legal person, or which rights and interests the legal person is promoting and protecting.[531]

293. Unlike commercial media, public service broadcasters are explicitly required to offer programmes that reflect the cultural diversity of the country. Hence, all three laws on public service broadcasters[532] stipulate that BHRT, RTVFBiH and RTRS in their activities and human resources policy must follow relevant Constitutional requirements when it comes to the equality of constituent peoples and other ethnocultural groups living in the country/respective BiH entity. Also, the programmes of the BHRT must correspond to the needs of constituent peoples and citizens of BiH, and broadcast equally in three official languages and two alphabets.

527. RTVFBiH Law, Arts 38 and 39.
528. RTRS Law, Arts 13 and 14.
529. Statute of RTRS, Art. 10; Statute of RTVFBiH, Art. 7, Statute of BHRT also mentions respect of CRA rules and regulations and international standards in Art. 10.
530. Rule 76/2015 on the Provision of Radio Media Services, Art. 12.
531. See, ch. 2 Private Broadcasting, section on non-profit radio, *supra.*
532. The BHRT Law, Art. 8; The RTVFBiH Law, Art. 8; RTRS Law Art. 18(Representation according to the Constitution of BiH).

294. Similarly, the RTRS[533] and RTVFBiH[534] programmes must respect national, regional, traditional, religious, cultural, linguistic and other characteristics of the three constituent peoples and all citizens of BiH, and should promote cultural and other needs of national minorities in BiH. The programmes of the RTRS and RTVFBiH need to be edited equally in three official languages – Bosnian, Croatian and Serbian – and two alphabets, Cyrillic and Latin. In the production of its programmes, the RTRS and RTVFBiH should ensure equal representation of content that reflects the tradition of the three constituent people, and ensure adequate presence of the three constituent people and others.

295. Additional available mechanisms that have the potential to enhance the chance for minorities and cultural groupings to have adequate access to airtime are Programme Councils which must be established by each public service broadcaster. Each public radio and TV station is required to have a programme council that will reflect ethnic, cultural and religious characteristics of the population to which the broadcaster is offering its services.[535] Accordingly, Article 50 of the RTRS Law stipulates that the Programme Council of the RTRS has eleven members coming from different social groups (youth, retired, employers, unions, national minorities, religious communities, university, civil society organizations, etc.). The RTRS Programme Council has an advisory role especially in relation to the adoption of the editorial policy and programme plans of RTRS. Basically, identical provisions on the Programme Council of RTVFBiH are contained in the RTVFBiH Law.[536] BHRT Law also envisages the possibility of establishing advisory bodies.[537] However, the information on Programme Council is available only on the website of RTRS, where few meetings per year are organized,[538] while in BHRT there is a lack of information on the work of this body and in the case of RTVFBiH, the Council (with currently only one member working under a technical mandate) is not functioning at all.

II. Content Obligations (Quota)

296. There are no specific programming quota requirements for commercial broadcasters in relevant rules and legislation.

297. Nevertheless, public broadcasters[539] must have at least 40% of weekly programmes consisting of news and other informative and educational programmes.

533. The RTRS Law, Art. 13 (Programme principles).
534. The RTVFBiH Law, Art. 38 (Programme principles).
535. Rules 76/2015 and 77/2015 of the Commun. Regulatory Agency.
536. The RTVFBiH Law, Arts 30, 31, 32 and 33.
537. Law on RTVFBiH, Art. 30.
538. Information on the Programme Council at: https://www.rtrs.tv/comp/psavjet.php, also see annual reports of RTRS at https://lat.rtrs.tv/comp/dokumenti.php, accessed 3 Oct. 2020.
539. Rule 76/2015 on Provision of Radio Media Services, Art. 28, and Rule 77/2015 on Provision of Audiovisual Media Services, Art. 29 (Programme obligations).

Moreover, out of the total weekly news and other informative and educational programmes, 10% must be dedicated to specific socially relevant topics, such as refugees and displaced persons; national minorities; and vulnerable groups.[540] The three public service broadcasters have specific programme quotas, defined in the System Licence including informative, educational, programmes for children and youth, programmes on art and culture and religious programmes.[541] However, relevant laws and regulations do not specify precisely how to implement these programme quotas in practice in respect to the representation of different ethnic groups, nor do they define what equal and adequate representation actually means. The implementation of these requirements is at the discretion of individual editors.[542] Also, no systematic data are available to demonstrate the level of compliance of public broadcasters with the provisions on content obligation (i.e., quota).[543] Analysis conducted by the CRA from 2019, however, indicates an extremely low presence of the content on minorities, vulnerable groups and persons with disabilities in programmes of both public and private broadcasters, while the educational content is somewhat better represented.[544]

298. The *licence for non-profit radio*[545] also requires that the programme of community radio, in its content and language, is fully oriented towards the social group which is represented by the station, or which rights and interests are promoted and protected by the community radio station.

299. All licensed broadcasters are required to reserve a majority proportion of their programme content for European works,[546] excluding the news, sports events, games, advertising, teletext services and teleshopping. The proportion of European

540. Programming statistics for earlier periods (2004–2006) indicate that none of the Public Service Broadcasters fulfils the CRA rules that require a minimum of 40% of programmes to be of public interest. Source: RTVFBiH and RTRS Business Reports for 2004–2006 and BHRT Business Report for 2006, cited in Jusić & Džihana, *Bosnia and Herzegovina*, 108.
541. For more, *see* the Chapter 1 on Public Service Broadcasting.
542. Jusić & Džihana, *Bosnia and Herzegovina*, 110.
543. *Ibid.*, 110.
544. Commun. Regulatory Agency. Analiza dječijih i obrazovnih programa, programa koji su namijenjeni ili se bave manjinama i ranjivim grupama stanovništva, te programa prilagođenih osobama sa invaliditetom u audiovizuelnim medijskim uslugama i medijskim uslugama radija u Bosni i Hercegovin, [The analysis of children and education programmes, programmes for or about minorities and vulnerable groups, as well as programmes adapted to persons with invalidity in audiovisual media services and radio media services in BiH] Commun. Regulatory Agency, 2019. https://docs.rak.ba//documents/a2949dad-09fe-4c5c-9485-51c6a31d66ab.docx, accessed 5 Oct. 2020.
545. Rule 76/2015 on the Provision of Radio Media Services, Art. 12(4b).
546. According to the Art. 14 (European Works) of Rule 77/2015 on the Provision of Audiovisual Media Services, European works mean the following: '(a) works originating in Member States of the European Union; (b) works originating in European third states party to the European Convention on Transfrontier Television of the Council of Europe, (c) works co-produced within the framework of agreements related to the audiovisual sector concluded between the European Union and third countries and fulfilling the conditions defined in each of those agreements. The European works are works mainly made in accordance with one of the following conditions: (a) they are made by one or more producers established in one or more of those states, or (b) production of an individual work is supervised and actually controlled by one or more producers established in one or more of

works also includes BiH works, as well as the licensee's own production.[547] Furthermore, the licensee is required[548] to reserve at least 10% of their programme content for European works created by independent producers.[549]

300. Finally, the licensee is required to reserve for BiH works[550] at least 20% of its weekly programme content, excluding the news, sports events, games, advertising, teletext services, and teleshopping.[551]

301. Additionally, Article 41 of the RTVFBiH Law and Article 16 of the Law on RTRS also set out similar quota requirements on its programming content.

III. Language Requirements

302. Commercial broadcasters are not required by the law to use any specific languages of different cultural groups or minorities. This is the obligation of the three public service broadcasters – BHRTV, RTVFBiH and RTRS – which are explicitly required to use three official languages and two alphabets in their programmes. Hence, the BHRT Law stipulates that the programmes of the BHRT are

---

those states, or (c) the contribution of co-producers from those states to the total co-production costs is preponderant and the co-production is not controlled by one or more producers established outside those states'.

547. *Ibid.*, Art. 14.

548. *Ibid.*, Art. 15 (European Works Created by Independent Producers).

549. According to the Art. 15 of Rule 77/2015 on the Provision of Audiovisual Media Services: '(1) an independent producer shall mean the natural or legal person that fulfils the following conditions: (a) it is registered in accordance with the Law for the pursuit of relevant activities in line with a valid classification of economic activities in Bosnia and Herzegovina or appropriately registered in one of the Member States of the European Union; (b) it has the seat in Bosnia and Herzegovina or in one of the Member States of the European Union; (c) it is not included within the organizational structure of the Licensee; (d) in which the Licensee has not more than 25% share in capital or managerial/voting rights; (e) its proportion of production done upon Licensee's request does not exceed one half of their entire annual production; (f) its average share in the total cost of production or co-production has exceeded 10% over the last three years. (2) An independent producer can also be the natural or legal person who has the seat in a third country provided that European works have comprised the major part in their entire audiovisual production over the last three years and that they fulfil the conditions set out in paragraph (1), subparagraphs c), d) and f).'

550. According to the Art. 16 (Bosnian and Herzegovinian works) of Rule 77/2015 on the Provision of Audiovisual Media Services, '(1) ... Bosnian and Herzegovinian works ... mean the following: (a) Works originating from Bosnia and Herzegovina; (b) Works originally produced in the languages of constitutive peoples in Bosnia and Herzegovina, or in languages of national minorities, i.e., works aimed at national minorities in their languages, as well as works of Bosnian and Herzegovinian cultural heritage. (2) Works referred to in paragraph 1 of this Article are works mainly made by authors and workers residing in Bosnia and Herzegovina, provided that they comply with one of the following conditions: (a) They are made by one or more producers registered in Bosnia and Herzegovina, or (b) the production of an individual work is supervised and actually controlled by one or more producers registered in Bosnia and Herzegovina, or (c) the contribution of co-producers from Bosnia and Herzegovina to the total co-production costs is preponderant and the co-production is not controlled by one or more producers established outside Bosnia and Herzegovina.'

551. *Ibid.*, Art. 16 (Bosnian and Herzegovinian works).

to be adjusted to the needs of constituent peoples and citizens of BiH, and edited and broadcasted equally in three official languages and two alphabets.[552]

303. Also, the RTRS Law requires from RTRS that the programme of this broadcaster must respect national, regional, traditional, religious, cultural, linguistic and other characteristics of constituent people and all citizens of BiH. The programme of the RTRS must be edited equally in three official languages and two alphabets.[553]

304. Finally, the RTVFBiH is required to respect national, regional, traditional, religious, cultural, linguistic, and other characteristics of constituent people and all citizens of BiH. The programme of the RTVFBiH should be edited equally in three official languages and two alphabets.[554] However, the Statute of RTVFBiH, Article 8, stipulates that the Latin alphabet will be used in TV programmes.

305. Nevertheless, there are no specific obligations to use languages other than those of three constituent people, such as the languages of other minority and cultural groups.[555]

IV. Representation of Minorities on the Screen

306. In the context of representation of minorities on the screen, references can be made to the relevant legislation on three public service broadcasters – BHRTV, RTVFBiH and RTRS – which are required to offer programmes that correspond to the cultural diversity of the country. As noted earlier, the BHRT Law,[556] the RTRS Law,[557] and the RTVFBiH Law[558] all stipulate that both the services and the human resources policies of public broadcasters have to implement relevant Constitutional requirements with respect to the equality of constituent peoples and others in BiH. Their programmes are to be adjusted to the needs of constituent peoples and citizens of BiH and edited and broadcasted equally in three official languages and two alphabets. The programmes of public broadcasters must respect national, regional, traditional, religious, cultural, linguistic, and other characteristics of constituent people and all citizens of BiH and must promote cultural and other needs of national minorities in BiH. Nevertheless, no specific quota requirements are given for the implementation of these provisions.

552. The BHRT Law, Art. 8 (Representation according to the Constitution of BiH).
553. The RTRS Law, Art. 13 (Programme principles).
554. The RTVFBiH Law, Art. 38 (Programme principles).
555. On issues related to language requirements see Jusić & Džihana, *Bosnia and Herzegovina*, 111–112.
556. The BHRT Law, Art. 8 (Representation according to the Constitution of BiH).
557. The RTRS Law, Art. 18 (Representation according to the Constitution of BiH) and 13 (Programme principles).
558. The RTVFBiH Law, Art. 8 (Representation according to the Constitution of BiH) and 38 (Programme principles).

307. Additionally, the *licence for non-profit radio* is issued under the condition that the planned programme, in its content and language, is fully oriented towards a social group whose rights and interests the community radio station is promoting and protecting.[559]

§3. Protection of Minors

308. The CAVRMS offers a rather elaborate set of measures for the protection of minors. Hence, the content aimed primarily at minors cannot feature the use of tobacco products, alcohol and drugs, and forms of violence or dangerous behaviour that can be easily imitated by minors, unless the aim of such a programme is to raise awareness about harmful consequences of such behaviour.[560]

309. Any misuse of children in audiovisual and radio media content is prohibited, and prior parental or guardian consent must be obtained for minors who take part in audiovisual and radio media content. Prizes given out to minors must be appropriate to their age. Due care must be taken over the emotional and physical welfare and dignity of minors taking part in audiovisual and radio media content, and they must not cause any unnecessary distress or anxiety. It is prohibited to use minors for political purposes and to question them about private family matters or matters that might be beyond their judgment ability.[561]

310. In the case of the coverage of criminal acts or proceedings involving minors, the identity of minors must be protected. Hence, the name and other information that may disclose the identity of a minor involved in criminal proceedings cannot be revealed. This also means that legally binding judgments in such cases can be published but without any personal or other information that reveals the identity of the minors involved. Consequently, media service providers must be especially careful not to publish content that could reveal the identity of minors involved as victims, witnesses, or indicted in relation to the criminal offence. Special attention must be paid to protecting the identity of the most vulnerable minors involved in the case either as victims or witnesses or in any way involved in sexual assaults. The information on the identity of minors in such cases may be published only upon the previously obtained approval by relevant authorities.[562]

311. The media service providers are required to ensure that minors are protected from inappropriate and potentially harmful content. Content that might seriously impair the physical, mental or moral development of minors (including but not limited to displays of brutal and extreme violence, pornographic content and similar) cannot be shown unless it is offered through on-demand audiovisual media

559. Rule 76/2015 on the Provision of Radio Media Services, Art. 12(4); Also see *supra*: Part III. Regulation of Audiovisual Media, ch. 2 Private Broadcasting, section on non-profit radio; for more details see ch. 3. Programme Standards, I. Access to Airtime for Cultural Groupings.
560. CAVRM, Art. 19 (Audiovisual and Radio Media Content Intended for Minors).
561. *Ibid.*, Art. 20 (Participation of Minors in Audiovisual and Radio Media Content).
562. *Ibid.*, Art. 21 (Reporting on Criminal Acts/Proceedings Involving Minors).

services with technical protection measures in place.[563] Furthermore, media service providers must protect minors from potentially harmful and inappropriate content, which is likely to impair their physical, mental or moral development. The protection involves technical protection, appropriate scheduling and categorization. Content that is likely to harm minors involves the portrayal of coarse violence, sex, profane language and scenes depicting the abuse of alcohol and drugs. It is prohibited to show pornographic content without technical protection. In addition, in on-demand media services, pornographic content should be distinguished from other content as a separate part of the catalogue.[564] Content which is likely to impair the physical, mental or moral development of minors, broadcast without technical protection, shall be marked with appropriate graphic identification that will be clearly visible on the screen for the entire duration of the content.[565]

312. The content of the media service providers must be classified according to their possible ethical and other social consequences. The key criteria for the categorisation are: whether depicted violence or other harmful behaviour is presented as socially acceptable or a means for solving problems/conflicts; the role of minors i.e., whether they are portrayed as objects/victims; the level of realism in the portrayals of violence; frequency, vividness and detail in scenes of violence, sexual activity, inappropriate language, suggestive behaviour; frequency, intensity and duration of verbal, graphic and/or textual descriptions of brutality and vulgarity, whether the behaviour is offensive towards human dignity, whether the music, masks, makeup and other effects can be disturbing or create fear and what is the context and/or genre in which the content appears.[566] Content categorized as not suitable for minors under the age of 12 can be broadcast between 20:00 to 06:00, content not suitable for minors under the age of 16 can be broadcast between 22:00 and 06:00, and finally content not suitable for minors under the age of 18 — between 24:00 and 06:00.[567]

313. Additionally, *Rule 79/2016 on the Licenses for the Distribution of Audiovisual Media Services and Radio Media Services*, in Article 10, stipulates that:

> Content with detailed portrayal of sexual activities whose primary purpose is not sexual arousal or stimulation, or content whose primary purpose is sexual arousal and stimulation of the audience and which shows nudity in seductive, provocative sexual positions but without explicit portrayal of sexual organs during sexual intercourse, can be shown in the period between 24:00 and 06:00 hours only. In addition, reality and pseudo-reality programmes can be shown

563. *Ibid.*, Art. 23 (Content that might seriously impair physical, mental or moral development of minors).
564. *Ibid.*, Art. 24.
565. *Ibid.*, Art. 25.
566. *Ibid.*, Art. 22.
567. *Ibid.*, Art. 25.

also only between 24:00 and 6:00. These provisions do not apply to the distribution of such content with technical protection. The screening of pornographic content without technical protection is prohibited.[568]

§4. Human Dignity (Prohibition of Hate Speech)

314. Incitement to hatred, violence or discrimination against a person or a group based on sex, race, ethnicity, nationality, religion or belief, disability, age, sexual orientation, social background or any other circumstance which can nullify or impair the recognition, enjoyment or exercise of personal rights and freedoms is strictly prohibited in the audiovisual and radio media programmes. The material with clear and immediate risk of inciting ethnic or religious hatred, violence or discrimination or which could be interpreted as incitement of hatred, violence and disorder or encourage criminal activities shall not be included in the audiovisual and radio media services. Such content is only allowed as a part of a scientific, copyright, documentary work, or journalistic report published with no intention to incite hatred, violence or discrimination, but is intended to criticize such actions.[569] Furthermore, the RTRS Law in Article 15(1), and the RTVFBiH Law in Article 40 (Programme Limitations) stipulate that these broadcasters shall not broadcast material which can incite national, ethnic, religious or racial hatred, intolerance or discrimination against a person or a group. Moreover, the Press and Online Media Code in its Articles 3, states that the press is 'obliged to do its utmost not to incite and/or inflame hatred and/or inequality on the basis of ethnicity, nationality, race, religion, gender, sexual orientation, physical or mental disability'. In Article 4, the Code states that journalists must avoid prejudicial references to persons ethnic group, nationality, race, religion, gender, sexual orientation, physical or mental disability, and that references to such identities can be made only when directly related to the occurrence being reported.

315. Finally, the Criminal codes on the level of the state, entities and Brčko District prohibit incitement to hatred. However, they are not fully harmonized with EU acquis insomuch as entity-level Criminal Codes pertain only to incitement of national, racial and religious hatred, while other bases for hate speech are not included. Furthermore, the stipulations involve terms such as 'incitement', 'hatred', 'hostility', etc., which are not specified further which enables arbitrary implementation. The cases of hate speech are overall processed rarely and inconsistently in the judiciary practice.[570]

---

568. Rule 79/2016 on the Licenses for the Distribution of Audiovisual Media Services and Radio Media Services, Art. 10.
569. CAVRM, Art. 4 (Hate Speech).
570. *See* Sanela Hodžić, 2019. Mediji i društvene mreže: Uloga i (samo) regulacija problematičnih medijskih sadržaja, In: Surfanje po tankom ledu: Mladi, mediji I problematini medijski sadržaji. Mediacentar Sarajevo 2019, *also see* Marija Lučić-Catić and Dina Bajraktarević Pajević, Nedostaci kaznene politike tužiteljstva BiH i SUDA BiH u slučajevima zločina iz mržnje i govora mržnje. Kriminalističke studije, 2019.

§5. Right of Reply

316. The right of reply is guaranteed by Article 6 of the CAVRMS to any natural or legal person whose rights or interests have been damaged by the information published in a television or a radio programme. The reply must be submitted in writing within fourteen days of the publication of information, and shall only refer to the correction of incorrect or incomplete information. The media service provider has the obligation to publish the reply in the next issue of the programme in which the information requiring a reply was published. If this is not possible, the reply must be published in the most similar programme, in terms of scheduling and topic, to the programme to which the request for reply refers. Importantly, the reply cannot be followed by a counter-reply or additional comment; though the media service provider can publish additional information on the subject matter the reply refers to.

317. Nevertheless, the media service provider can refuse to publish the reply if such a reply has unlawful aspects or if it can put the media service provider into a situation of liability under the civil law or if it violates the provisions of CAVRM.[571] If the publication of a reply is refused, the media service provider must notify in writing the person claiming a right of reply, explaining the rejection.[572]

318. Moreover, the right to reply is also defined by the laws on public service broadcasters. Hence, the RTVFBiH Law[573] and the RTRS Law[574] both outline basically the same principles as stipulated in Article 6 of the CAVRMS.

319. Both laws also stipulate that in the case the broadcaster refuses to publish the reply, the person requesting the right to reply can within eight days submit the complaint to the Governing Board of the public broadcaster. If the person submitting the complaint is not satisfied with the decision of the Governing Board, he/she has the right to seek judicial protection through litigation.

320. Moreover, the right to submit a correction is also defined by the laws on public service broadcasters. Hence, the RTVFBiH Law[575] and the RTRS Law[576] both stipulate that for the request for correction of mistakes the same procedure applies as in the case of the right to reply.

§6. Right to Privacy in Electronic Media

321. General principles of protection of privacy as outlined in the CAVRMS require that 'any infringement of privacy must be justified by a demonstrable public

571. *Ibid.*, Art. 6(4) (Right of Reply).
572. *Ibid.*, Art. 6(5).
573. RTVFBiH Law, Art. 49 (Right to Reply).
574. RTRS Law, Art. 34 (Right to Reply).
575. RTVFBiH Law, Art. 50 (Correction).
576. RTRS Law, Art. 35 (Correction).

interest, in particular if it involves minors and persons who are not public figures or otherwise in the public eye'. It is only in the case of unambiguous and legitimate public interest that the publishing of information from the private life of an individual without their knowledge or consent is permitted.[577]

322. Furthermore, audiovisual and radio programmes reporting on consequences of violence, natural disasters, accidents or family tragedies must achieve a balance between the need to inform the public and the desire to show compassion with victims. In such circumstances, the sensationalism that can cause distress or unwarranted invasion of privacy must be avoided while the right to privacy of victims must be ensured. Persons in a state of distress or shock must not be pressured to provide interviews or participate in an audiovisual or radio programme.[578]

323. It is forbidden to reveal in audiovisual and radio programmes personal information and private and family matters of a minor that could cause harm. Prior written consent of parents or other legally responsible persons must be obtained before asking any questions about private matters of minors and vulnerable persons who are not able to take care of themselves. The content which discloses their difficult position, and whose primary goal is to animate the public to provide assistance shall clearly specify the manner in which assistance can be provided. However, their identity and personal data shall not be disclosed in cases where there is a reasonable doubt, as it could jeopardize their wellbeing and dignity.[579]

324. The use of recordings of telephone conversations with individuals in audiovisual and radio programmes is allowed only when the person in question has given prior consent and was adequately informed about the purpose of the call. Exceptions are possible in the cases of public interest. Broadcasting of footage featuring anonymous persons that were filmed by chance does not require prior consent from such persons. If passers-by are filmed and interviewed in a public place, for the purpose of street surveys, hidden cameras and alike, broadcasting of such content is possible only with the consent of those persons.[580]

325. Also, audiovisual and radio programmes are required to comply with the right to privacy of all persons involved in the criminal proceeding. Minors, other vulnerable persons, as well as victims, witnesses and families of the victims, suspects, the accused, and the convicted persons, must be granted special protection for their privacy. Media service providers must pay particular intention not to publish any information that might reveal or lead to the identification of witnesses in cases in which statutory prohibitions or restrictions on disclosing the identity of witnesses are applicable. Furthermore, the identity of the sexual assault victims must not be revealed unless the victim gives prior consent, or legal authorization is obtained.[581]

---

577. CAVRMS, Art. 17 (Privacy Policy).
578. *Ibid.*, Art. 17.
579. *Ibid.*, Art. 17(6) and 17(7).
580. *Ibid.*, Art. 17 (8, 9 &10).
581. *Ibid.*, Art. 15 (The Coverage of Court Proceedings).

326. Public service broadcasters, such as the RTVFBIH and RTRS are required to respect the privacy, dignity, reputation and honour of individual persons as well as those of minors.[582]

---

582. The RTVFBiH Law, Art. 39; The RTRS Law, Art. 14.

Chapter 4. Political Broadcasting

§1. Rules on Political Independence of Broadcasters

327. The key underlying regulatory principle of broadcasting in BiH is the separation of broadcasters from political control and manipulation, in order to strengthen democratic principles and market economy.[583] This is to be achieved in several ways: First, the persons authorized to represent a public broadcaster and editor-in-chief of a public radio and television station cannot be an elected public official or members of bodies of a political party (coalition, or independent candidate or list of candidates). Second, elected public officials cannot be members of the Editorial Council of public broadcasters. And third, editor-in-chief, persons with power of representation, and members of the Editorial Council of a public broadcaster are required to submit to the CRA a statement that confirms that they are not affiliated to political institutions/elected officials.[584]

328. The RTVFBiH Law stipulates that the RTVFBiH needs to be functionally and editorially independent and have institutional autonomy especially with respect to its programming, news presentation and editing, assets management, employment policy, and budget execution, etc.[585] The same is granted in Article 8 of the RTRS Law.

§2. Fair Representation in Election Periods

329. Election Law of BiH requires the media to fairly, professionally and competently cover electoral activities, in accordance with the journalistic code. During the elections, the media must respect generally accepted democratic principles and rules, especially the principles of freedom of expression. The broadcast media are required to respect the principles of balance, honesty and impartiality while covering elections.[586] Principles of balance, honesty and impartiality must be particularly respected in informative programmes, such as current news broadcasts, interviews, and debates on current political issues.[587] Broadcasters have to enable paid political advertising to each political subject, under equal terms, while public broadcasters additionally must reserve a part of their programme for direct address by candidates, political parties and their programmes, under equal conditions and free of charge. Private broadcasters are free to reserve such time for direct speaking, but it

583. Communications Law of BiH, Art. 4(1c).
584. Rule 77/2015 on Provision of Audiovisual Media Services, Arts 30 and 32; Rule 76/2015 on Provision of Radio Media Services, Arts 29 and 31.
585. The RTVFBiH Law, Art. 37 (Independence).
586. Election Law of BiH (*Izborni zakon BiH,* Official Gazette of BiH 23/01, 7/02, 9/02, 20/02, 25/02, 4/04, 20/04,25/05, 52/05, 65/05, 77/05, 11/06, 24/06, 32/07, 233/08, 37/08, 32/10, 18/13, 7/14 and 31/16), Ch. 16 – Media in Electoral Campaign, Arts 16.1 and 16.2.
587. *Ibid.*, Art. 16.4.

must be done under equal conditions for all candidates.[588] Public service broadcasters, RTVFBiH and RTRS, are obliged to enable political parties and candidates to present their electoral programmes under equal conditions during the electoral campaign period. It is also stated that these public radio and television broadcasters must make available a part of their programme time for the presentation of candidates and political parties, free of charge.[589]

330. All political actors must have equal treatment by broadcast media, without any preferences. Candidates for the elections who are at the same time officials at any level of government cannot have preferential treatment by broadcasters in comparison to other candidates. Broadcasters can provide information on the regular activities of the government officials when such activities are part of the defined scope of activities of the government bodies in which they work, but no reference to their candidacy for elections or their party affiliation can be made.[590]

331. The results of opinion pools must be published with due care. The media must always name the institution that conducted the survey, the source funding for the survey, the period when the survey was conducted, and the sample. Additionally, in the case of phone surveys and street surveys, the media outlet must point out the limitations of such survey methods in respect to their reliability.[591]

332. Journalists and editors in broadcast media are not allowed to express their party affiliation and preference in regular or special programmes.[592]

333. The order of time slots for candidates and party representatives in special broadcasts is determined by the draw, in the presence of representatives of political actors.[593] These time slots cannot be changed once they are determined.[594]

334. The electoral blackout period starts forty-eight hours prior to the opening and lasts until the closing of electoral booths. During the period, no results of the public opinion survey about voting and elections will be published. Additionally, twenty-four hours prior to the opening of the election booths, there will be no reporting on any activity related to the political or electoral campaign.[595]

335. The CRA is in charge in relation to all breaches of the provisions on the role of the media in electoral campaigns, while the complaints on conduct of print media are to be addressed to the Press Council, as defined by the Election Law of

588. *Ibid.*, Arts 16.12, 16.14 and 16.15.
589. The RTRS Law, Art. 30 (Advertisement during an Electoral Campaign), RTVFBiH Law, Art. 46 (Advertisement during an Electoral Campaign)
590. The Election Law of BiH, Art. 16.3.
591. *Ibid.*, Art. 16.5.
592. *Ibid.*, Art. 16.6.
593. *Ibid.*, Art. 16.7.
594. *Ibid.*, Art. 16.8.
595. *Ibid.*, Arts 16.10 and 16.11.

BiH.[596] More specific regulation of the media's conduct during the electoral campaign is offered in the *Rulebook on the media representation of political actors during the election period.*[597]

§3. News and Current Affairs Programmes

336. The most important provisions relevant for the news and current affairs programmes are contained in Article 5 (Fairness and impartiality) of the CAVRMS, which stipulate that audiovisual and radio programmes must ensure due accuracy, fairness, impartiality and balance of presented information in all programming, in particular news and current affairs programmes. This can be ensured by 'publication of all conflicting views, either in the same programme or in a sequence of other programmes that represent a whole in dealing with a certain topic'.[598] Audiovisual and radio programmes are not allowed to promote the interests of any political party, group or individual while the opinions and views of journalists and moderators on controversial political or industrial matters must be clearly signalled as such, while comments must be clearly distinguished from news items. If any negative connotations to a person or an organization are expressed in a programme, those concerned must be given an opportunity to respond to such allegations.

337. In respect to public service broadcasters, when it comes to informing the public on political, economic, educational, scientific, religious, cultural, sports and other events in the country and the world, RTVFBIH and RTRS are required to do it truthfully, comprehensively, impartially and timely. They must also ensure open and free debate on issues of public interest, taking into consideration a variety of existing interests and tastes, and promoting the pluralism of political, religious and other ideas. All political, economic, educational, scientific, religious, cultural, sports and other issues must be treated impartially. Broadcasters must contribute to 'the respect and promotion of basic human rights and freedoms, democratic values and institutions, and promotion of the culture of public dialogue'.[599]

338. News must be impartial, factual and independent. Before broadcasting, one must verify the content, origin and truthfulness of the information material for the news, while commentaries must be clearly marked and separated from the news.[600] Additionally, the sponsorship of news and information programmes is prohibited.[601]

---

596. *Ibid.*, Arts 16.16 and 16.17.
597. The Rulebook on the Media Representation of Political Subjects during the Electoral Campaign (*Pravilnik o medijskom predstavljanju političkih subjekata u razdoblju od dana raspisivanja izbora do dana održavanja izbora)*, from February 2018, adopted by the Central Electoral Commission of BiH in compliance with the Art. 16.18 of the Election Law of BiH, published in the Official Gazette of BiH 29/18.
598. CAVRMS, Art. 5 (Fairness and Impartiality).
599. The RTVFBiH Law, Art. 39; also see the RTRS Law, Arts 14 and 7.
600. *Ibid.*
601. The RTVFBiH Law, Art. 45 and Law on RTRS, Art. 32 (Sponsorship).

§4. Political Advertising

339. Paid political advertising is allowed during the electoral campaign. Hence, broadcast media are required to offer equal conditions for paid political advertising to all political subjects during the period of thirty days before the elections. Paid political advertising must be clearly separated from the remaining editorial programme. Such advertising has to fit within the allowed time limits for advertising, in accordance with the rules and regulations of the CRA. The price for political advertising cannot be higher than the existing price list for marketing services at the particular broadcast media.[602] It is not allowed to broadcast promotional messages of political parties and candidates outside of the official electoral campaign period.[603]

340. During the period from the official announcement of the elections to the day of the official start of the electoral campaign, paid electoral advertising is prohibited, both in broadcast and print media or through any type of paid public advertising. It is only allowed to promote internal party meetings. Campaigns cannot involve content that is stereotypical and offensive towards any gender group.[604]

341. During the period of thirty days before the elections, public broadcasters must provide the possibility of paid political advertising of political subjects. Such advertising cannot be longer than thirty minutes per week, under the same conditions for all electoral candidates and parties. Public broadcasters must enable slots to political subjects, under the same conditions. [605]

342. The similar requirements apply to private broadcast media as well, which are required to enable, under the same conditions during the period of thirty days before the elections, paid political advertising of political subjects in the maximum duration of sixty minutes per week. During the same period, private broadcast media can also provide free time slots to political subjects, but only under the same conditions for all.[606]

343. The *Rulebook on the media representation of political actors during the election period* elaborates further some of the provisions from the Election Law of BiH.[607]

602. Election Law of BiH, Art. 16.12.
603. The RTRS Law, Art. 30 (Advertisement during an Electoral Campaign) as well as the RTVFBiH Law, Art. 46 (Advertisement during an Electoral Campaign).
604. Election Law of BiH, Art. 16.14.
605. *Ibid.*, Art. 16.14.
606. *Ibid.*, Art. 16.15.
607. The Rulebook on the Media Representation of Political Subjects during the Electoral Campaign.

Chapter 5. Advertising Rules

344. Pursuant to Article 39, paragraph 1, of the Communications Law of BiH, the Council of the CRA adopted the Code on Commercial Communications.[608] The Code sets basic principles of commercial communications in the programme content of all audiovisual media service providers and radio media services in BiH. This Code does not apply to political advertising which is regulated under the relevant provisions of the Election Law of BiH as well as the rules and regulations adopted by the Central Election Commission of BiH.[609]

§1. Different Forms of Commercial Communications

345. The Code on Commercial Communications defines the audiovisual commercial communication and commercial communication in radio media services:

> Audiovisual commercial communication means images with or without sound which are designed to promote, directly or indirectly, the goods, services or image of a natural or legal person engaged in economic activity. (…)The commercial communication in radio media services means sound and voice content which is designed to promote, directly or indirectly, the goods, services or image of a natural or legal person engaged in economic activity.[610] The commercial communications are included in a programme in return for payment, similar types of compensation, or for self-promotional purposes.[611] Forms of audiovisual commercial communication and commercial communication in radio media services include, *inter alia*, advertising, sponsorship, teleshopping, and product placement.[612]

346. Advertising is 'any form of announcement related to a trade, business activity, craft or profession, which is broadcast in order to promote the supply of goods or services, including immovable property, rights and obligations of a public or private legal or natural person, in return for payment or for similar consideration, or for the purpose of self-promotion'.[613] When an existing advertising message is replaced in a programme or inserted on billboards shown in the programme, appearing as an integral part of the original broadcast where it actually did not exist, it is considered as an instance of virtual advertising, which is normally prohibited.[614] Split-screen advertising is the simultaneous transmission of editorial and advertising content, while tele-promotion or radio promotion is advertising based on the

---

608. Code on Commercial Communications, Part One – Scope and Definitions; Art. 1 (Scope).
609. For more detail refer to the ch. 4 – Political Broadcasting; sec. 2. Fair Representation in Election Periods, *infra*.
610. Code on Commercial Communications, Art. 2 (Definitions).
611. *Ibid.*
612. *Ibid.*
613. *Ibid.*
614. *Ibid.*

interruption of the editorial content in such a way that the programme presenter acts as a promoter of the goods or services presented.[615]

347. Sponsorship is an instance when any part of production or broadcasting costs of programmes are covered by a sponsor in order to promote specific names, trademarks, images, activities or products.[616]

348. Teleshopping is a form of commercial communication where direct offers of supply of goods or services in return for payment are broadcast to the public.[617]

349. Finally, product placement is when a reference to a product, a service or a trademark is featured within a programme of audiovisual or radio media services in return for payment or for similar compensation.[618]

§2. Restrictions on Content

350. There is a comprehensive set of restrictions related to commercial communication in BiH. Audiovisual and radio media service providers are required to make any commercial communications clearly recognizable as such. It is prohibited to broadcast covert or misleading commercial communications or to use subliminal techniques.[619]

351. The Code on Commercial Communications stipulates that such communications shall not:

a. prejudice respect for human dignity;
b. demean or intimidate anyone or incite to violence or discrimination against a person or a group based on gender, race, ethnicity, nationality, religion or belief, disability, special needs, age, sexual orientation, social background or any other circumstance which has the purpose or effect to nullify or to impair the recognition, enjoyment or exercise, on an equal footing, of any person's rights and freedoms;
c. be offensive or contrary to general standards of public decency;
d. encourage behaviour that is prejudicial to health or safety;
e. encourage behaviour that is harmful to the environment.[620]

352. It is prohibited to broadcast commercial communications that display gratuitous use of force or threat of use of force.[621] Also, persons regularly presenting audiovisual news and current affairs programmes cannot be featured in television or

615. *Ibid.*
616. *Ibid.*
617. *Ibid.*
618. *Ibid.*
619. *Ibid.*, Art. 3 (General Principles of Commercial Communications).
620. *Ibid.*
621. *Ibid.*

radio advertising and teleshopping programmes.[622] It is also prohibited to exploit or manipulate superstitions, fears or credulity, encourage potentially harmful behaviour or promote quackery.[623]

353. In order to encourage healthy competition and inform the public, comparative commercial communications are permitted. Nevertheless, such communications must respect the principles of fair competition, must compare goods or services that meet the same needs and cannot be misleading. It is not allowed to discredit the competitor, its product, service, or trademark. Comparative prices used in such broadcasts must reflect the actual state at the time of broadcast.[624]

354. Commercial communications for cigarettes and other tobacco products, weapons and ammunition, pyrotechnic devices and drugs, in all of their forms, is prohibited.[625] In respect to alcoholic beverages, commercial communication needs to comply with the following criteria:

a. they shall not be aimed specifically at minors and persons appearing in the commercial communications associated with the consumption of alcoholic beverage cannot be or look like a minor;
b. they shall not link the consumption of alcohol to enhanced physical performance or to operating a motor vehicle;
c. they shall not claim that alcohol has medicinal properties or that it is a stimulant, a sedative or a means of resolving personal conflicts;
d. they shall not encourage immoderate consumption of alcohol or present abstinence or moderation in a negative light;
e. they shall not place emphasis on high alcoholic content as being a positive quality of the alcoholic beverage;
f. they shall not create the impression that the consumption of alcohol contributes to social or sexual success.[626]

355. It is not allowed to have commercial communications for medicines, medical devices and medical treatments which are available only on prescription or a referral. Nevertheless, commercial communications for all other medicines, medical devices, medical treatments and dietary supplements that do not require a prescription, must be recognizable as such, honest, truthful, verifiable and must protect the individual from harm. Commercial communications for medical institutions and private practices can contain only the name and address of a medical institution or private practice, the activities listed in the relevant proof of registration for performing medical practice, operating hours and contact details. Teleshopping for medicines, medical devices and medical treatments is prohibited.[627]

622. *Ibid.*
623. *Ibid.*
624. *Ibid.*, Art. 4 (Comparisons and Claims about Prices).
625. *Ibid.*, Art. 5 (Commercial Communications of Certain Products and Services).
626. *Ibid.*
627. *Ibid.*

356. Special attention is given to the protection of minors[628] with respect to commercial communication. It is prohibited to encourage behaviour that can endanger health, mental and/or moral development of minors.[629] Such communication must not contain any false information or value judgments with respect to the information on the product or service, in terms of its actual size, value, nature, durability, speed, colour and other characteristics. It is prohibited to recommend products or services that are not suitable or are dangerous for minors, such as medicines, medical treatments, means of regulating body weight and flammable substances or to convey religious messages or erotic content. Minors cannot be shown in dangerous situations unless such commercial communications have educational purposes indicating a hazard to a minor's health and security. Furthermore, commercial communication that aims at minors cannot contain scenes of violence or suggest that promoted products or services will enhance minors' physical and intellectual characteristics or social skills. It is prohibited to encourage minors to purchase products or services by exploiting their inexperience or credulity, or to urge them to persuade their parents or others to purchase the promoted products. Finally, commercial communication must not exploit the minors' trust in parents and teachers, or uphold social discrimination based on physical appearance, other aesthetic categories or success based on weight loss.[630]

357. Additionally, in the cases:

> when a commercial communication shows the result of drawing, drafting, assembling and modelling, the ability to achieve such result shall match the average ability of target minors. Such commercial communication shall indicate the age of a minor it targets.[631]

358. Apart from the Code on Commercial Communications, the restrictions on commercial communications also exist in relevant laws on public broadcasters which largely correspond to the provisions of the Code.[632]

§3. Time and Frequency Restrictions

359. Commercial communications that directly or indirectly refers to erotic content or pornography (hot-lines, advertising and teleshopping for pornographic magazines and films) or the content that promotes paranormal phenomena or

628. Please *see*: Part III. Regulation of Audiovisual Media, ch. 3. Programme Standards, sec. 3. Protection of Minors, *supra.*
629. Code on Commercial Communications, Art. 6 (Commercial Communications and Minors).
630. *Ibid.*, Art. 6; *also see* the RTVFBiH Law, Art. 42 (Marketing and Advertising Principles).
631. Code on Commercial Communications, Art. 6.
632. The RTVFBiH Law, Arts 42, 43, 44, 45 and 46; the RTRS Law, Arts 29, 30, 31 and 32.

parapsychology, may be broadcast only between 24:00 and 6:00 hours. This does not apply to content broadcast with technical protection or for on-demand audiovisual and radio media services.[633]

360. Television and radio advertising and teleshopping must be clearly distinguishable from editorial content by optical, spatial and/or acoustic means. Such commercial content must be broadcast in blocks and can be inserted between or during programmes, but without undermining the integrity of the programmes. Isolated advertising and teleshopping spots must be avoided, except during the broadcasting of sports and other live events.[634] Films made for television, cinematographic works, as well as news and children's programmes if their duration is longer than thirty minutes (except series, serials, and documentary programmes), may be interrupted by television advertising or teleshopping once for each period of thirty minutes. In television broadcasting, news and children's programmes of up to thirty minutes may not be interrupted by advertising or teleshopping. In radio programmes, advertising and teleshopping cannot be broadcast in news programmes.[635]

361. Television advertising or teleshopping is not allowed during religious services.[636] Also, television and radio advertising and teleshopping for alcoholic drinks, medicines, medical treatments, aids and devices, including dietary supplements, medical institutions, means of regulating body weight, ignition devices, inflammable and other hazardous substances, as well as religious messages and games of chance must not be broadcast fifteen minutes before, during or fifteen minutes after children's programmes.[637]

362. Duration of television advertising and teleshopping (including split-screen advertising and tele-promotion and excluding teleshopping windows) for commercial television broadcasters is limited to twelve minutes per hour, while for public television broadcasters, it is limited to four minutes per hour. This does not apply to the promotion of own programmes and services (or promotion of media services of affiliated companies or companies in their ownership), as well as ancillary products and services directly derived from these programmes and services, sponsorship announcements, product placements, as well as public service announcements and charity appeals, broadcast free of charge.[638]

---

633. Code on Commercial Communications, Art. 3 (General Principles of Commercial Communications).
634. *Ibid.*, Part III – Television Advertising and Teleshopping, Art. 8 (Scheduling of Television Advertising and Teleshopping); Art. 12 (Scheduling of Advertising and Teleshopping in Radio Programmes).
635. *Ibid.*
636. *Ibid.*, Art. 8.
637. *Ibid.*, Art. 8; Art. 12 (Scheduling of Television Advertising and Teleshopping and Scheduling of Advertising and Teleshopping in Radio Programmes).
638. *Ibid.*, Art. 9 (Duration of Television Advertising and Teleshopping).

363. Duration of advertising and teleshopping (including radio promotion and excluding teleshopping windows) for commercial radio broadcasters is limited to twelve minutes per hour while for public radio broadcasters, it shall not exceed six minutes per hour.[639] Commercial radio broadcasters may reallocate freely the time allowed for advertising, but this time cannot exceed 20% of the daily transmission time. These limitations do not apply to the promotion of own programmes (or programmes of affiliated companies), sponsorship announcements, product placements, public service announcements and charity appeals broadcast free of charge.[640]

364. Furthermore, teleshopping windows, in both radio and television programmes, need to have a minimum uninterrupted duration of fifteen minutes and must be clearly identified by optical or acoustic means at the beginning and the end of the window. The maximum number of teleshopping windows per day is eight while their total duration cannot exceed three hours per day.[641]

365. Split-screen advertising[642] on television is permitted, but it should not be excessive in a way that would compromise the unobstructed viewing of the editorial content. Split-screen advertising and tele-promotion are prohibited in children's, religious, and news and current affairs programmes. All relevant provisions of the Code on Commercial Communications in respect to scheduling and duration also apply to split-screen advertising and tele-promotion.[643]

366. Virtual advertising[644] is permitted only during the transmission of sports events. The event organizer has to give its prior consent and the viewers are to be informed about the presence of virtual advertising if such advertising is to take place. Furthermore:

> The virtual advertisement shall appear only in places that are usually used for advertising, but shall not be more noticeable than the advertisements that are present in those places, nor shall it appear on people's faces, clothing or equipment. Furthermore, it shall not compromise the integrity of the programme and the rights of the rights holders.[645]

---

639. *Ibid.*, Art. 13 (Duration of Advertising and Teleshopping in Radio Programmes).
640. *Ibid.*
641. *Ibid.*, Art. 9 (Duration of Television Advertising and Teleshopping); Art. 13 (Duration of Advertising and Teleshopping in Radio Programmes).
642. Split-screen advertising means simultaneous or parallel transmission of editorial and advertising content.
643. Code on Commercial Communications, Art. 10 (Split-Screen Advertising, Tele-promotion and Virtual Advertising).
644. Virtual advertising means the advertising technique whereby an existing advertising message in the broadcast programme (placed on advertising boards etc.) is changed or a new advertisement is inserted in places where it does not exist in the actual programme, in such a manner that the virtual advertising appears as part of the original transmission of the programme in question.
645. Code on Commercial Communications. Art. 10.

367. Radio promotion[646] is subjected to the same rules on scheduling and duration of radio advertising and teleshopping as set forth by the Code on Commercial Communications.[647]

368. The Code on Commercial Communications also applies to television and radio channels exclusively devoted to advertising, teleshopping, and self-promotion. Nevertheless, the rules on scheduling and duration of television and radio advertising and teleshopping do not apply to these channels.[648]

369. According to the relevant laws on public service broadcasters, 'the duration of advertisements and other paid messages, as well as their redistribution in the prime-time, cannot be longer than the duration defined by the CRA'.[649] The Code on Commercial Communications, Article 20, stipulates that the duration of advertising and teleshopping in television and radio programmes of public service broadcasters (RTRS, RTVFBiH and BHRT) shall not exceed six minutes.

370. Additionally, advertisement is prohibited in non-profit community radio programmes.[650]

§4. Sponsorship

371. Sponsorship of audiovisual or radio media services or programmes must not influence the content or schedule of sponsored services or programmes in a way that would affect editorial responsibility and independence. The media service provider must retain full editorial control over the sponsored programme. The media service provider is obliged to inform its viewers or listeners of the existence of a sponsorship agreement. This also means that the sponsored programmes shall be clearly identified as such by the name, logo or any other reference to the sponsor, in the beginning, during or the end of the programmes. However, the identification of the sponsor must be brief and neutral, without additional information or promotional references to its products and services. It is not allowed to directly encourage the purchase or rental of goods or services of the sponsor in sponsored programmes.[651]

372. Audiovisual or radio media services or programmes cannot be sponsored by public or private, legal or natural persons whose main activity is the production

646. Radio promotion means a form of advertising during the transmission of a programme based on the interruption of the editorial content, whereby the programme presenter temporarily assumes the role of a promoter of the goods or services presented.
647. Code on Commercial Communications, Art. 14 (Radio promotion).
648. *Ibid.*, Art. 11 (Teleshopping and Self-Promotional Television Channels), and Art. 15 (Radio Channels for Teleshopping and Self-Promotion).
649. The RTVFBiH Law, Art. 43 (Duration of advertising); the RTRS Law.
650. Rule 76/2015 on the Provision of Radio Media Services.
651. Code on Commercial Communications, Part IV – Sponsorship, Art. 16 (General Principles of Sponsorship).

or sale of cigarettes and other tobacco products, weapons, ammunition, pyrotechnic devices, and narcotics. Programmes can be sponsored by private or legal persons engaged in the manufacture or sale of medicinal products and services, but without promoting specific products or medical treatments which are available only on prescription or referral. Sponsorship is not allowed in news and current affairs programmes.[652]

373. The laws on public service broadcasters correspond with the provisions of the Code on Commercial Communications.[653]

§5. Product Placement

374. Product placement is prohibited except in cinematographic works, films and series made for audiovisual media services or radio media services, sports programmes and light entertainment programmes. This exception does not apply to children's and religious programmes. Also, product placement is allowed in other programmes but under the condition that the audiovisual media service or the radio media service provider is not receiving the payment but only the provision of certain goods or services free of charge from the sponsor.[654]

375. Product placement must not influence content or scheduling or the programme in a way that affects editorial independence and responsibility of the audiovisual media service or the radio media service provider. Additionally, it is forbidden to directly encourage the purchase or rental of goods or services, in particular by making special promotional references to those goods or services that are the subject of the product placement, as well as to give undue prominence to the products and services in question.[655]

376. The media service provider is obliged to inform viewers and listeners about the existence of product placement in specific audiovisual or radio programmes. A visual sign 'PP' must appear on screen for at least thirty seconds at the start and the end of the audiovisual programme, as well as after each advertising break in the programme. The beginning of the programme should also include a textual announcement. In radio programmes, an acoustic notification shall be broadcast at the beginning and end of the programme, and after each advertising break. It is only if a specific programme has neither been produced nor commissioned by the media service provider itself or its affiliated company, that the media service provider has no obligation to inform viewers about the existence of product placement.[656]

---

652. *Ibid.*, Art. 17 (Prohibited Sponsorship).
653. The RTVFBiH Law, Art. 45 (Sponsorship); the RTRS Law, Art. 32 (Sponsorship).
654. Code on Commercial Communications, Part 5 – Product Placement, Art. 18 (General Principles of Product Placement).
655. *Ibid.*
656. *Ibid.*, Art. 17 (Identification of Product Placement).

Chapter 6. Right to Information

§1. Access to Major Events

377. Access to major cultural, sport, entertainment and other events in BiH and abroad can be obtained only by broadcasters whose programmes are available to the whole population of the country. Broadcasters whose programmes do not reach the whole population cannot have exclusive rights for most prominent events, such as Olympic games; world and European cups in football, basketball, and other sports; official international competitions in which the representation of BiH participates; and international competitions taking place in BiH.[657]

378. Public broadcasters, RTVFBiH and RTRS, have the right to access public, cultural, sport and other events for the purpose of informing the widest possible population. In the cases of reports on events broadcasted without acquiring rights, they cannot last longer than it was necessary to inform the public through the news format.[658]

379. Public broadcasters also have the right to cover the sessions of the parliaments at entity and state levels and are obliged to inform the public on parliamentary activities. For these purposes, they are granted free access to the parliamentary sessions.[659]

380. Under specific conditions, broadcasters can report on court proceedings. Namely, audiovisual and radio programmes are required to report on court proceedings in an objective and correct manner, and to respect the presumption of innocence until a legally valid decision enters into force. Privacy of all persons in any way involved in the proceeding must be respected within the audiovisual and radio programmes. In that respect, special protection must be granted to minors and other vulnerable persons, victims, witnesses, families of the victims, the suspect, accused and the convicted persons. Media service providers are required to comply with relevant legal provisions regarding the protection of witnesses. In particular, it is prohibited to publish any information that might reveal or lead to the identification of witnesses in cases in which statutory prohibitions or restrictions on disclosing the identity of witnesses are applicable. The identity of the victims of sexual assaults can only be revealed in cases where the victim gives previous consent or based on prior legal authorization. Finally, direct reporting from, and recording in the courtroom requires authorization issued by the relevant authorities.[660]

---

657. The BHRT Law, Art. 10 (International exchange and exclusive rights).
658. The RTVFBiH Law, Art. 53 (Access to and Broadcasting of Events) as well as the RTRS Law, Art. 37 (Access to and Broadcasting of Events).
659. The RTVFBiH Law, Art. 38; the RTRS Law, Art. 13.
660. CAVRMS, Art. 15 (The Coverage of Court Proceedings); also see, Part II. Regulation of Print Media, ch. 5. Access to public information, sec. 2. Court Hearings and Documents, *supra.*

§2. SHORT NEWS REPORTING

381. A licensee that has exclusive rights to the transmission from the event of high interest to the public shall, under equal conditions, grant access to the event, for the purpose of short news reports (extract not longer than ninety seconds used for news programmes), to all broadcasters that are established in BiH or the European Union. Compensation can only be required for actual costs incurred in the fulfilment of this obligation. The licensee that broadcasts such a short extract from the event is required to identify its source.[661]

382. Copyrighted material can only be used by a licensee for the purposes of informing the public on current affairs if the clear attribution to the source is provided and if such excerpts do not exceed ninety seconds.[662]

383. Public broadcasters, RTVFBiH and RTRS, must be granted access to public, cultural and sports and other events in order to be able to inform the widest possible population in the country. If the reports are broadcast without paying for the broadcasting rights, such broadcasts cannot be longer than necessary to inform the public in the news format.[663] Moreover, RTVFBIH and RTRS have the right to broadcast excerpts of the programmes of other broadcasters within their regular information programme, under the condition that such excerpts are not longer than ninety seconds, and that the source is clearly stated.[664] The same applies to all other radio and TV broadcasters in respect to the programmes of RTVFBiH and RTRS.

661. Rule 77/2015 on the Provision of Audiovisual Media Services, Art. 17 (Right to Use Short News Extracts).
662. *Ibid.*, Art. 19 (Use of Material Protected by Copyright or Other Rights).
663. The RTVFBiH Law, Art. 53 (Access to Events); the RTRS Law, Art. 37 (Access to Events).
664. *Ibid.*

Chapter 7. Access to Networks and Platforms

§1. Introduction

384. It is generally agreed that 'detailed and effective regulation of access and interconnection to existing networks is a crucial issue, especially at the earlier steps of liberalization, in order to allow competition to be fully operational'.[665] There is an important difference between, on the one hand, the access of end-users and content providers to distribution channels of audiovisual media services and radio media services, and, on the other hand, the access to telecommunications infrastructure for different telecommunications operators. The access of users and content providers to distribution channels of audiovisual and radio media services is regulated by Rule 79/2016 on Licenses for the Distribution of Audiovisual Media Services and Radio Media Services. The access to the telecommunications infrastructure is regulated by the CRA's Rule 51/2010 on Interconnection, and Rule 35/2008 on Unbundled Access to the Local Loop.

385. The process and the criteria for awarding licences for the distribution of audiovisual and radio media services are specified in Rule 79/2016 on Licenses for the Distribution of Audiovisual Media Services and Radio Media Services.[666] According to Article 1, the purpose of this Rule is to 'ensure access to communication services for all users on transparent, objective and non-discriminatory basis; to protect interests of all users and to ensure the quality in provision of services in accordance with the generally accepted standards in the European Union'.

386. Additionally, the reception and retransmission of audiovisual media services from the EU Member States and other European countries that are signatory to the European Convention on Transfrontier Television are free on the territory of BiH.[667] The licence is issued under the same conditions to all interested parties[668] on a non-exclusive basis, and is valid for a period of ten years,[669] with the possibility of renewal. The licensee is required to apply for the renewal no later than three months prior to the expiration of the license. [670]

---

665. Auth. Commun. Guarantees & Commun. Regulatory Agency, *Overview of the Communications Sector*, 199.
666. Rule 79/2016 on the Licenses for the Distribution of Audiovisual Media Services and Radio Media Services replaces the previous Rule 56/2011, with identical title (Official Gazette of BiH 98/11 and 52/15).
667. Rule 79/2016 on the Licenses for the Distribution of Audiovisual Media Services and Radio Media Services, Art. 3 (General Principles).
668. *Ibid.*, Arts 3 and 4.
669. *Ibid.*, Art. 6 (License Validity and Renewal).
670. *Ibid.*

387. Rule 51/2010 on Interconnection[671] regulates issues related to the interconnection[672] of public telecommunication networks and the provision of interconnection services by operators and service providers. The interconnection of networks and the provision of interconnection services is achieved according to the Interconnection Contracts while 'contractual interconnection services that are established by this Rule will be applicable to the licensed public operators of telecommunications and service providers'.[673]

388. Rule 35/2008 on Unbundled Access to the Local Loop sets obligations and conditions for access to local loop[674] unbundled[675] and related facilities, as well as obligation content of the Reference Offer.[676]

§2. Must-Carry Rules

389. There is a must-carry obligation for the distribution of programmes of Public Service Broadcasters of BiH, which are BHRT, RTVFBiH, and RTRS. The licensed distributor of audiovisual media services and of radio media services is required to distribute programmes of the Public Service Broadcasters without any compensation, in accordance with its technical capacities. The licence holder will not distribute the programmes for which the Public broadcasters do not possess distribution rights.[677]

390. The licensee is also obligated to distribute all programmes of the holders of the Agency's Licence for television broadcasting via terrestrial broadcasting service, whose zone of broadcasting is situated within the zone of the licensed telecommunications network. These programmes are to be distributed free of charge

671. Rule 51/2010 on Interconnection, Art. 1 (Purpose).
672. According to Rule 51/2010 on Interconnection, Art. 2(3): '"Interconnection" is physical and logical connection of telecommunication networks used by one or more operators, for the purpose of enabling users from one operator to communicate with users from the same or the other operator, or for the purpose of access to the services offered by the other operator. The services can be provided by involved parties, or by other parties that have access to the network.' (*Translation by the author*).
673. *Ibid.*, Art. 1 (Purpose).
674. According to Rule 35/2008 on Unbundled Access to the Local Loop, Art. 2(9), '*Local Loop* means metal wire (twisted-pair copper wire) connecting network end point at the location of end user of service (subscriber) with connection at the main distribution frame of local switchboard or distant subscription level or some equivalent part of fixed public network (ITU-T Recommendation G.101 and P.10); Terms "subscription loop" and "subscription line" refer to local loop.'
675. According to Rule 35/2008 on Unbundled Access to the Local Loop, Art. 2 (Definitions), '(6) *Unbundling* means making network elements and related facilities, equipment, functions or services at disposal of another operator and/or service provider for the purpose of providing electronic communications services. This option is enabled for an operator and/or service provider that orders network elements by its choice, paying only for required capacities or functions. This does not mean transfer of ownership over capacities and equipment used to enable access.'
676. Rule 35/2008 on Unbundled Access to the Local Loop, Art. 1 (Scope of the Rule).
677. The 79/2016 on Licenses for the Distribution of Audiovisual Media Services and Radio Media Services, Art. 8.

and without any preconditions unless the broadcaster states in writing that it does not allow distribution of its programmes or conditions such distribution with any fees.[678]

§3. Obligations for Conditional Access Providers

391. On 5 May 2010 BiH signed and accepted the European Convention on the Legal Protection of Services based on, or consisting of, Conditional Access (CETS No. 178). According to the Summary of the Treaty:

> The Convention seeks to protect operators and providers of paid radio, TV and online services against unlawful reception of such services. It supplements a similar European Union directive by extending protection throughout Europe. The States Parties to the Convention undertake to make it a criminal offence to manufacture, import, distribute, sell, offer for hire, possess or install decoders or smart cards enabling access to be obtained unlawfully to the above-mentioned services. They will also prohibit promotion, marketing or advertising of illicit devices. The penalties provided for by the Convention include seizure and confiscation of the devices or material and of any profits or financial gain resulting from the unlawful activity. The Council of Europe's aim in adopting this Convention is to help European providers of audiovisual and online services to reduce financial losses sustained as a result of electronic and computer piracy, in the interests of both service operators and the public.[679]

392. Accordingly, the distribution of audiovisual and radio media services is allowed only upon acquiring prior written approval from the owners of the programme content or from their authorized representatives. The licence holder is required to submit to CRA the updated programme list with the statement of acquired rights for distribution of media content prior to the distribution of such programmes. The licence holder cannot perform unauthorized distribution of encrypted or unencrypted satellite or terrestrial audiovisual media services and radio media services including, but not limited to the services received through signal spill-over from neighbouring countries, as well as unlicensed audiovisual media services.[680]

393. The services offered through the use of the system of conditional access can also be subject to control by the CRA. The licensee must, upon request by CRA, enable full access to the distribution services, including those provided through a conditional access system.[681]

---

678. *Ibid.*
679. Summary of the treaty, available at http://conventions.coe.int/Treaty/en/Summaries/Html/178.htm, accessed 12 Oct. 2020.
680. Rule 79/2016 on Licenses for the Distribution of Audiovisual Media Services and Radio Media Services, Art. 7 (Right to Distribution).
681. *Ibid.*, Art. 18 (Control).

§4. Other Access Obligations for Network Operators

394. Granting equal access on non-discriminatory basis to all subscribers is ensured by Rule 79/2016 on the Licenses for the Distribution of Audiovisual Media Services and Radio Media Services.[682] It is prohibited to 'limit the access to subscribers based on national, religious, property or any other basis, nor will it select the distributed programmes in a way that implies interests of only one ethnic or religious community in Bosnia and Herzegovina'. The service must be offered on a non-discriminatory basis so that any citizen has the right to establish a subscription contract. The access will not be conditioned by requiring the user to stop using such services offered by competing providers.[683]

395. Granting equal access for all providers of audiovisual and radio media services to the distribution systems is also granted.[684] Hence, with respect to the distribution, each provider of audiovisual and radio media service must be treated under the same conditions. The licence holder is required to distribute, free of charge, the programme of all public service broadcasters and all other broadcasters whose zone of transmission is in the zone of the distribution. The licensee is however free to distribute services of other broadcasters. The distribution price list must be published if the licence holder charges for the distribution of these audiovisual and radio media services.[685]

396. The telecommunications operator which provides a public telecommunications network is obliged to make an interconnection offer to other operators when requested. If telecommunications operators providing public telecommunications networks cannot reach an agreement on interconnection, the involved parties can apply to the CRA for mediation and resolution of the problem. The CRA can request 'from telecommunications operators with significant market power to establish a list of standard interconnection offers for their public telecommunications networks'.[686]

397. A telecommunications operator with significant market power is required to enable other users to access its public telecommunications network or unbundled parts of such network. Agreements on network access and interconnection must be provided on a non-discriminatory basis.[687]

398. The interconnection comprises of the following basic services:

682. *Ibid.*, Art. 3 (General Principles).
683. *Ibid.*, Art. 3.
684. *Ibid.*, Art. 9.
685. *Ibid.*, Art. 9.
686. Law on Communications of BiH, Art. 16 (Obligation to Negotiate).
687. *Ibid.*, Art. 18 (Access to and Interconnection of Public Telecommunications Networks).

a. Access by an alternative telecommunications operator to the network of the telecommunications operator with significant market power through programmed network selection or dialling of selection codes according to the numbering plan.
b. Provision of the necessary traffic data of the relevant connection to the interconnecting telecommunications operator.
c. Switching of calls to users of other interconnecting telecommunications operators.
d. Provision of accounting data in a suitable form for the interconnecting telecommunications operator.[688]

399. The CRA is required to provide detailed rules on provisions relating to interconnection while taking into consideration the protection of competition, service quality, and compliance with relevant international regulations, as well as to determine a minimum number of unbundled network elements that need to be offered. The CRA is also required to resolve disputes by deciding if the costs are appropriate and if network access and interconnection are technically feasible.[689]

400. The telecommunications operators[690] have the right to establish contractual interconnection relationships with any other telecommunications operator. Whenever requested, such telecommunication operators are obliged to enter into a contractual interconnection relationship with any other operator.[691]

401. Furthermore, the CRA has the right to impose special obligations on individual licensed operators based on their market share. Such obligations must entail non-discriminatory compensation for the interconnection and transparent availability of interconnection points. Other operators will be granted the same capacity of interconnection under equal conditions, with the same quality as that which the operator provides for its own services'.[692]

402. An operator of public fixed telephony with significant power on the market of fixed public telephony services is obliged to offer a service of unbundled access to the local loop and related facilities. The unbundled access to the local loop can be requested by operators who offer telecommunications services and meet the criteria to unbundled access to the local loop and related facilities.[693] The unbundled

688. *Ibid.*, Art. 19 (Scope of Interconnection).
689. *Ibid.*, Art. 19.
690. Fixed public telephone network; public voice telephone service; mobile network public telephony; mobile public telephony service; leased lines; etc.
691. Rule 51/2010 on Interconnection, Art. 3 (Translation by the Author).
692. *Ibid.*, Art. 5 (Special provisions).
693. Rule 35/2008 on Unbundled Access to the Local Loop, Art. 3 (Obligation of enabling access).

access to the local loop and related facilities will be offered objectively, transparently, and on a non-discriminatory basis, and such offers will be published.[694] Finally, unbundled access to the local loop and related facilities must be offered under the same conditions and quality that is offered to its own subscribers.[695]

694. *Ibid.*, Art. 4(1) (General terms of access).
695. *Ibid.*, Art. 6(Principle of non-discrimination).

Chapter 8. Standards and Interoperability

403. Decision on the Electronic Sector Policy of BiH for the period 2017 – 2021[696] adopted by the Council of Ministers of BiH in May 2017 sets out the basic policy framework for the improvement of infrastructure and services in the sector. According to the Decision, the developments in the sector should be accorded with the main goals of the International Telecommunication Union, aimed at socially, economically, and environmentally sustainable development enabled and boosted by telecommunications/information technologies. The decision also envisages harmonization of regulation with EU standards and initiatives aimed at strengthening the digital market based on high-speed internet and interoperable applications, as well as those aimed at convergence of sectors of telecommunication, media and information technologies.[697]

404. According to the Communication Law, radio and telecommunications equipment must protect health and safety and meet the requirements regarding electromagnetic compatibility. The equipment that meets the relevant European Union standards is considered to comply with these requirements. If the equipment complies with the requirements of the Communication Law of BiH, operators cannot refuse to connect it to appropriate interfaces unless the equipment 'causes serious damage to the network, harmful radio interference or damage to the operation of the network, the telecommunications operator of a public telecommunications network may be authorized to refuse connection, to disconnect such apparatus or to withdraw it from service'.[698]

405. When it comes to the interoperability of interconnected networks, the Rule on Interconnection in Article 3(5) stipulates that the interconnection will be established upon the following principles:

a. connection of networks 'any with any', so that it will be possible to establish communication of one network with another network, and the services of one telecommunications operator will be accessible to users of another operator;
b. interoperability, so that communication can be transferred from one to another network;
c. timely offering of interconnection; and
d. uninterrupted access to adequate equipment and its equipment with a goal to minimize duplication of the resources of the whole network.[699]

---

696. Official Gazette of BiH 46/17.
697. Decision on the Electronic Communications Sector Policy of Bosnia and Herzegovina for the period 2017–2021 (Council of Ministers of BiH, Official Gazette of BiH 46/17), https://docs.rak.ba//articles/aa3ed3af-d56e-4b8b-a62e-6816c2440397.pdf, accessed 12 Oct. 2020 (*translation by the authors*).
698. Communication Law of BiH, Art. 34 (Essential Requirements) and 35 (Putting in Function and the Right to Connection) (*translation by the authors*).
699. *Translation by the author.*

406. The CRA can require the telecommunication operators to publish a Reference Interconnection Offer (RIO) which would outline the key condition for the provision of services, such as 'location of interconnection points, technical conditions of interconnection, interoperability tests, registration and the control of the traffic, capacity of interconnection lines, etc.'.[700]

407. Also, the CRA can ask operators to meet a set of requirements in respect to network security and functionality in extreme events; network integrity; interoperability of services; quality of services; technical standards; and the conditions for the protection of private data, informational confidentiality and the protection of privacy.[701]

408. Finally, the Rule on Interconnection sets out technical requirements for standardization for interconnection services.[702] Hence, operators are required to adhere to the relevant CRA rules[703] whose purpose is to regulate the usage of radio and telecommunications equipment in BiH. The basic requirements are the protection of health and safety, electromagnetic compatibility, and efficient usage of the radio spectrum.[704] Also, the CRA can require that specific types of equipment must be able to function in networks with other devices and that it can be connected to certain interfaces; that it does not damage the network functionality and service quality; that it contains protective measures to ensure the protection of private data and of the privacy of users; that it supports specific functions for the prevention of fraud; that it supports specific functions that ensure the access to emergency services, and that it supports specific functions to enable persons with limited capabilities to use the equipment.[705]

409. Hence, any device 'must be labeled in accordance with basic requirements as defined in relevant EU directives, such as the existence of proper CE-markings or undergoing the procedure for the evaluation of conformity by the relevant national body'.[706]

410. In the case that Rule 12/2001 on Technical Requirements for Radio and Telecommunications Equipment in Public Telecommunications Networks does not provide all necessary standards, Article 10 of the Rule on Interconnection[707] requires that the operators will provide technical interfaces for interconnection in accordance with the following standards:

700. Rule 51/2010 on Interconnection, Art. 4 (Reference Interconnection Offer).
701. *Ibid.*, Art. 8.
702. *Ibid.*, Art. 10.
703. Rule 12/2001 on Technical Requirements for Radio and Telecommunications Equipment in Public Telecommunications Networks, Art. 1.
704. *Ibid.*, Art. 3.
705. *Ibid.*
706. *Ibid.*, Art. 4.
707. Rule 51/2010 on Interconnection.

a. standards adopted by European standardization bodies, such as The European Telecommunications Standards Institute (ETSI) or the European Committee for Electrotechnical Standardization (CENELEC);
b. international standards or recommendations adopted by the ITU, International Organization for Standardization, or the International Electrotechnical Commission;
c. standards approved by the CRA.

411. Additionally, the operators are required to accept the standards published in the Official Journal of the European Union.[708]

708. *Ibid.*, Art. 10(2).

Part IV. Cross-Ownership Regulation

§1. Introduction

412. Initially, the legal framework regarding media concentration in BiH was defined by Rule 21/2003 on Media Concentration and Cross-ownership that entered into force on 1 April 2004. Nevertheless, Article 6 of Rule 21/2003 on Media Concentration and Cross-ownership stipulated that the Rule 'shall be in force for the period of eighteen months after entry into force, after which time it may be reviewed and amended according to experience and changing circumstances'. Since in the meantime the Competition Act[709] was adopted, Rule 21/2003 on Media Concentration and Cross-ownership was not re-enacted after the eighteen months period expired. However, the Competition Act is implemented only on a case-by-case basis, upon complaints concerning competition, and there are no strategic actions to prevent media concentration. So far, the relevant institutions showed a lack of interest in developing such policies concerning all media sectors, as even with the previous Rule CRA did not have means of enforcement beyond the broadcasting sector. In 2019, the Ministry of Communication has established a working group for the purpose of developing a law on electronic communication that should address the issues of media ownership concentration and transparency, but again this law would be applicable to the broadcasting sector only. In sum, for almost fifteen years, the progress towards better regulation of ownership concentration in the media sector has been negligible.[710]

413. The body for implementation of protection of market competition in terms of the Competition Act is the Council of Competition[711] which is an independent body tasked to ensure the implementation of the Competition Act, with exclusive competence in making decisions regarding the presence of prohibited competition practices in the market.[712] The Competition Act 'regulates the rules, measures and

709. The Competition Act (*Zakon o konkurenciji BiH*, Official Gazette of BiH 48/05, 76/07 and 80/09).
710. Hodžić, Media Integrity Matters, 123; Also see U potrazi za boljom regulacijom transparentnosti vlasništva i finansiranja iz javnog budžeta, [In search of the better regulation of transparency of ownership and funding from public budgets]. Consortium Media and Public Reputation, 2017, and Nedim Porobić, Transparentnost vlasništva nad medijima u Bosni i Hezcegovini [Transparency of ownership of media in Bosnia and Herzegovina] BH novinari 2019.
711. The Competition Act.
712. *Ibid.*, Art. 21(1) (Status of the Council of Competition).

methods of protection of market competition, the jurisdiction and the way of operation of the Council of Competition on protection and promotion of market competition in Bosnia and Herzegovina'.[713] It applies to all natural and legal persons who can prevent, restrict or distort competition in the entire territory of the country or a significant part of the market, such as private and public enterprises, state administration institutions and local self-governments. It also applies to any other natural and legal persons who participate in the market, regardless of their legal status, ownership, or residence (associations, sports organizations, holders of intellectual property, etc.).[714]

414. The Competition Act 'also applies to the economic entities that have control over other economic entity, and the economic entities under their control'[715] in terms of more than 50% direct or indirect control of shares, voting rights, or appointments of the members of management and supervisory board. The Act also applies to economic entities with headquarters and residence outside of BiH, if they exercise significant influence on the market in the country.[716]

415. The Competition Act is in principle based on two prohibitions: the prohibition of agreements that can damage the market competition,[717] and the prohibition of abuse of dominant market position.[718] Additionally, the prohibition of concentration is related directly to the prohibition of abuse of dominant market position. These main prohibitions are based on the definition of the 'relevant market'.[719]

§2. Definition of 'Relevant Market'

416. According to the Competition Act, the relevant market is a market of certain products or services of economic entities in a particular geographic area. Relevant geographic market comprises a significant part of the territory of BiH with equal conditions for operations of economic entities. Nevertheless, the relevant geographic market may be determined at the international level as well.[720] The Regulation on the Definition of a Relevant Market 'determines the method, criteria and the procedures for defining the relevant market … as the basis for the calculation of market shares of undertakings concerned (…)'.[721]

417. The methodology for the analysis and assessment of the relevant electronic communications markets including the procedure for declaring which operators have significant market power is defined in the CRA Rule 54/2011 on Electronic

713. *Ibid.*, Art. 1 (Subject matter).
714. *Ibid.*, Art. 2 (Application), para. (1).
715. *Ibid.*, Art. 2(2).
716. *Ibid.*, Art. 2(2).
717. *Ibid.*, Art. 4.
718. *Ibid.*, Arts 9 and 10.
719. *Ibid.*, Art. 13.
720. *Ibid.*, Art. 3 (Relevant market).
721. *Ibid.*, Art. 1 (Subject Matter).

Communications Market Analysis. The same Rule 54/2011 also defines the procedure for imposing obligations on operators with significant market power on the relevant market.[722] Accordingly:

> An operator shall be deemed to have significant market power if, either individually or jointly with others, it enjoys a position equivalent to dominance, that is to say a position of economic strength affording it the power to behave to an appreciable extent independently of competitors, customers and ultimately consumers.[723]

418. The CRA must rely on EU practice and cooperate with the Council of Competition of BiH when assessing the market share of economic entities and when evaluating the significant market power.[724] The criteria for assessing significant market power of an operator on the market are the following: market share; barriers for entering the market; level of countervailing buying power; elasticity of demand; phase in the development of the relevant market; technological advantage; sales and distribution network; economies of scale; economies of scope; vertical integration; a variety of products or services; access to capital markets or financial assets; and control over infrastructure.[725]

§3. Restrictions of Cooperation Agreements

419. The Competition Act prohibits agreements and contracts that prevent, restrict or distort the market competition. This restriction relates to any of the following:

a. direct or indirect fixing of selling and purchase prices or any other trade conditions;
b. limit or control on production, markets, technical development or investment;
c. share of markets or sources of supply;
d. application of dissimilar conditions to equivalent transactions with other economic entities, thereby placing them at a competitive disadvantage; and
e. conclusion of contracts subject to acceptance by the other parties of additional obligations which, by their nature or according to commercial usage, have no connection with the subject of such contracts.[726]

420. The Council of Competition can issue a decision on individual or group exemptions to the above restriction. The group exemption can be granted in the case

722. Rule 54/2011 on Electronic Communications Market Analysis. Art. 1 (Scope), (Official Gazette of BiH 85/2011).
723. *Ibid.*, Art. 6.
724. *Ibid.*, Art. 8(2).
725. *Ibid.*, Arts 7 and 8.
726. The Competition Act, sec. II – Prohibited Competitive Activities, Art. 4 (Agreements).

of horizontal agreements (e.g., on research and development) and vertical agreements (e.g., the agreements on exclusive distribution or purchase). Also, group exemption can be granted in the cases of agreements on transfer of technology, licence, and *know-how* agreements.[727]

§4. Restrictions of Dominant Market Position

421. It is considered that an economic entity has a dominant position in the relevant market when it has such a market power that it can behave relatively independently from its competitors, buyers, consumers or suppliers. With respect to the market share, a single economic entity has a dominant position in the market when it has more than 40% market share. Several economic entities have a dominant position in the market, when two or three economic entities together have more than 60% market share, or when four or five economic entities jointly have more than 80% market share.[728]

422. The Competition Act, Article 10, prohibits any abuse of dominant position, which in particular relates to the following:

a. directly or indirectly imposing unfair purchase and selling prices or other trading conditions which restrict competition;
b. limiting production, markets or technical development to the prejudice of consumers;
c. applying dissimilar conditions to equivalent or similar transactions with other parties, thereby placing them at unequal and unfavourable competitive position; and
d. conclusion of the contracts subject to acceptance by the other party of additional obligations which, by their nature or according to commercial practice, have no connection with a subject of such contract.[729]

423. If there is an absence of effective competition on the market, the CRA can declare, in the form of an administrative act, the operators with significant market power on the market. The operators with significant market power can be subject to the CRA's imposition of the regulatory obligations of transparency, non-discrimination, accounting separation, access to a network, price control, cost accounting, provision of a minimum set of leased lines, etc.[730] Also, the CRA 'is competent (…) to impose on the operator with significant market power the obligation to ensure equal treatment in the provision of interconnection and/or access services'.[731]

727. *Ibid.*, Art. 5 (Individual Exemptions) and Art. 7 (Group Exemptions).
728. *Ibid.*, Art. 9 (Dominant Position).
729. *Ibid.*, Art. 10 (Abuse of Dominant Position).
730. Rule 54/2011 on Electronic Communications Market Analysis (Official Gazette of BiH 85/2011), Art. 12 (Regulatory Obligations).
731. *Ibid.*, Art. 14 (Obligation of Ensuring Equal treatment – Non-Discrimination).

424. A telecommunications operator with significant market power is required to provide competitors with services under comparable circumstances and equal conditions as provided for its own needs. The telecommunications operator with significant market power is not allowed to restrict access to the network except for specific reasons, such as security or integrity of the network, interoperability, and data protection. In the cases of abuse of significant market power, the CRA can impose various measures and sanctions, such as the prohibition of specific actions or termination of problematic contracts.

§5. CONCENTRATION RESTRICTIONS

425. The Competition Act, Article 12, defines concentration as:

a. joining or merger of independent economic entities or parts of economic entities;
b. the acquisition of control or prevailing influence of one or more economic entities over other economic entity, or over more other economic entities or a part of other economic entity, or the parts of other economic entities, as it is: (1) acquisition by purchasing the majority of shares or share capital, or (2) acquisition of majority of voting rights, or (3) otherwise, in accordance with the provisions of the laws governing the establishment of economic entities and their management; and
c. joint venture on a long-lasting basis, of two or more independent economic entities, acting as an independent economic entity.[732]

426. The concentrations that result in a significant distortion of market competition, or those that create new or strengthen an existing dominant position, are prohibited.[733]

427. The intended concentration must be notified to the Council of Competition in the case when the total annual income of all parties to the concentration on the international market is BAM 50 million in the previous year, and the total annual income of at least two partners to the concentration is at least BAM 4 million on the BiH market, or their joint share in the market exceeds 40%.[734]

428. In the cases of intended concentration, the Council of Competition assesses the significant distortion of market competition or potential strengthening of a dominant position. It also considers the market structure, the effects of concentration on competitors, the market share and economic and financial power of competitors, choice of suppliers, barriers to market entry, supply and demand, technical trends, economic development, and consumers' interests.[735]

732. The Competition Act, Art. 12 (Concentration).
733. *Ibid.*, Art. 13 (Prohibited Concentrations).
734. *Ibid.*, Art. 14 (Total Income for the control of concentration).
735. *Ibid.*, Art. 17 (Assessment of intended concentration).

429. It is considered that the TV market in BiH is not overtly concentrated. Namely, as a consequence of the 'specific legacy of the post-war situation, it seems extremely fragmented and features a remarkable number of small and medium size operators both in the terrestrial TV and radio market as well as in the cable distribution market'.[736] No single company dominates the TV market; new TV stations have entered the market in recent decades, while the public service broadcasters – BHRT, RTRS and RTVFBiH – steadily suffer erosion of their market position.[737] Only the government directly owns more than one TV network.[738] There are some examples of joint ownership, such as those over daily Oslobođenje, television O Kanal and related websites and magazines, or joint ownership over dailies Glas Srpske and Nezavisne novine, which however do not constitute an overt ownership concentration. On the other side, some concerns are raised with the growing presence of a regional player, United Group, which owns TV channels (including regional N1, sports channels Sport Klub, children's and light entertainment televisions, Nova TV channels in BiH, Serbia and Montenegro), as well as telecommunications networks, TV distribution businesses, and advertising agencies. So far, the Competition Council did not assess if this constitutes an illegitimate concentration, but it has in few cases over the past years issued a decision confirming that companies belonging to the United Group have violated the Competition Law by imposing different conditions in the distribution of their programmes.[739]

§6. Transparency Obligations

430. In respect to the transparency of ownership in the communications sector, the CRA establishes, manages, and regulates the delivery of information for, the Register of CRA's Licence Users in both the broadcasting and telecommunication sectors.[740] TV and radio broadcasters, providers of on-demand services, distributors of audiovisual and radio media services, providers of telecommunication services, including services of public telecommunication networks, landline and mobile telecommunication and internet access, are all required to deliver ownership information to the CRA. While Rule 71/2013 envisages the establishment of Registry with such data, with the licensees having an obligation to enter and correct the data, [741] for the time being, due to technical reasons this Registry is not in function.[742] The Rule does not specify the type of information that the licensees need to deliver,

736. Auth. Commun. Guarantees & Commun. Regulatory Agency, *Overview of the Communications Sector*, 92.
737. *Ibid.*, 121.
738. *Ibid.*, 124.
739. *See* Sanela Hodžić and Brankica Petković, Sustainability of professional journalism in the Media Business Environment of the Western Balkans. Executive Report. TACSO: 2020, 14-15, as well as Hodžić and Sokol, Country data overview: Bosnia and Herzegovina, TACSO: 2020, 16-18, both reports at: http://tacso.eu/sustainability-of-professional-journalism-in-the-media-business-environment-of-the-western-balkans-executive-report-published/, accessed 12 Oct. 2020.
740. Rule 71/2013 on the Registry of Communications Regulatory Agency Licence Holders (*Pravilo o Registru korisnika dozvola Regulatorne agencije za komunikacije*, Official Gazette of BiH 103/13).
741. *Ibid.*, Art. 2 (Terms and definitions), Art. 3 (Registration).
742. Written reply by Commun. Regulatory Agency from 22 Oct. 2020.

while in its earlier version (Rule 34/2008) it required broadcasters to, *inter alia*, provide information on all levels of ownership structure, up to the physical persons.

431. The CRA publishes basic information about the licensees, including their full names, names of directors and editors-in-chief, address, and contact information.[743]

432. In respect to the issues related to concentration, the 'economic entities, participants to the concentration are required to submit a notification of concentration … within fifteen days of signing the agreement, the publication of public offering or acquisition of control, depending on what happens first'.[744] The Council of Competition must publish the data from the notification of concentration in daily newspapers, including the names of economic entities involved, a form of concentration, and the economic sector in which the concentration occurs.[745] The Council of Competition can require all parties involved in a case of a potentially unlawful concentration to provide all relevant information and enable access to the required information and documents, as well as to provide access to all business premises.[746]

§7. Monitoring of Ownership and Pluralism

433. The key tool for the CRA to monitor the development of the market is the Register of the communications licensees, but until today (i.e., October 2020) it has not been put in function. The Register is supposed to gather regularly updated information on licensees, and the CRA notes that it is working on its establishment.[747] In the meantime, the CRA gathers information on licensees in other forms, including information on media ownership structures. The CRA also gathers, and in its yearly reports provides information on the telecommunication market, number of subscribers, etc.[748]

434. Any change or transfer of ownership over broadcasters of more than 5% of shares requires prior written approval by the CRA. Regarding such ownership transfer, the CRA will consider all relevant regulations and the same conditions applicable to the issuing of the licence.[749] The licence cannot be transferred or wholly or partly to other entities without prior approval by the CRA. Such transfer can be approved by the CRA in the cases of merger, acquisition, division, etc., under the condition that all (co)owners have provided a written consent for such a transfer.[750]

---

743. Register is available at: https://rak.ba/bs-Latn-BA/brdcst-license-holders.
744. The Competition Act, Art. 16 (Notification of Concentration).
745. *Ibid.*
746. *Ibid.*, Art. 35 (Data collection).
747. Commun. Regulatory Agency, written reply from 23 Oct. 2020.
748. *See*, for example, the Commun. Regulatory Agency, annual report for 2019.
749. Rule 76/2015, Art. 21 (Licence Transfer) and 77/2015, Art. 22 (Licence Transfer).
750. *Ibid.*

Moreover, any changes in ownership of more than a 5% share of interests are considered to be a partial transfer of ownership. When the approved transfer of ownership takes place, the licensee must inform the CRA about resulting changes in the court registry or the registry of securities. The CRA will impose sanctions in the case of change in the original ownership of more than a 5% share of interests if such change takes place without prior the CRA's approval.[751] However, the regulation of ownership and transparency of ownership in the broadcasting sector is rather limited. The CRA has only data on nominal owners of their licence users but has no insight into the related and beneficiary ownership that would enable more substantial regulation of ownership and pluralism. Also, the information collected by the CRA is mostly intended for their regulatory operations and the Agency does not publish information on direct ownership, but they are in part available through online registries of business entities and per request.[752]

435. In the print and online media sector, the media ownership transparency is partly assured through data available in registries of business entities, registries of securities and non-profit organizations, but accessing information on related ownership is a complicated task and there is no state institution that systematically monitors the state in the media sector with regard to ownership, concentration and pluralism. There are additional challenges concerning the transparency of online media, many of which are not even registered as business entities and are primarily pursuing particular political and business interests.[753]

751. *Ibid.*
752. *See* Hodžić Bosnia and Herzegovina, in Media Integrity Matters and Porobić, Transparentnost vlasništva nad medijima u Bosni i Hezcegovini.
753. *Ibid.*

Part V. Supervision: Media Regulator

436. The broadcast regulator in BiH is the CRA. To fully understand the role and the current specific position the CRA has, one has to be acquainted with its brief but turbulent history and has to know the specific political and media context in which the CRA was established and in which it operates today.

§1. International Intervention and the CRA

437. The specific character of the CRA position stems from the fact that the CRA is a direct product of the international peace-building intervention in BiH. Namely, after the Dayton Agreement in late 1995 up until mid-1998, the broadcasting sector in the country was virtually unregulated – the actual control over broadcasting was fragmented and divided among three dominant ethnic elites and their respective territories, whereas there were no common regulatory institutions or frameworks at the state level. This has had significant negative consequences for the broadcasting as well as for the political life in the country in general, preventing public debate, not enabling all political parties equal access to the media, and significantly limiting the capacity of opposition parties to challenge ruling ethnonationalist elites.[754]

438. As a consequence, in 1998 the OHR established the IMC[755] tasked to regulate the broadcasting sectors in the country by managing frequency spectrum, issuing licensing, introducing and enforcing codes of conduct, and handling complaints.

754. Media Experts Commission, *Završni izvještaj: Mediji u izborima*; Kurspahić, *Zločin u 19:30 – Balkanski mediji u ratu i miru*; Thompson and De Luce, *Escalating to Success?*

755. Office of the High Representative, *Decision on the Establishment of the Independent Media Commission in Bosnia and Herzegovina*, 11 Jun. 1998, Source: http://www.ohr.int/decision-on-the-establishement-of-the-independent-media-commission/, accessed 12 Oct. 2020.

In 2001, an OHR decision[756] merged the IMC and the Telecommunications Regulatory Agency into the CRA charged to regulate both the broadcasting and telecommunications sectors.[757] Although the Agency emerged under the supervision and protection of the OHR, after several years, it was transformed into a locally-run, independent state agency.[758]

§2. Independent Regulatory Agency

439. The CRA is established as an independent regulatory agency responsible for the regulation of broadcasting and telecommunications sectors, allocation of frequencies to broadcasters including public service broadcasting, and the management of frequency spectrum.[759] The Agency is in charge of overseeing: 38 TV stations; 141 Radio FM stations; 3 radio channels and 3 TV channels of Public Broadcasters (BHRT, RTVFBiH, and RTRS); 2 MW stations; 3 non-profit radio stations; 61 televisions and one radio broadcasted through other-than-terrestrial electronic communication networks; 11 providers of on-demand services; 35 active radio and television programme distributors (28 distributors provide their services via cable, and 7 via IPTV platform (one of these also providers services via satellite, DTH);[760] 3 key landline operators and providers of GSM/UMTS/LTE services; 12 providers of landline telephone services and 8 providers of mobile telephone services, 73 operators of public electronic communications networks and 63 Internet service providers.[761]

440. The CRA is modelled in accord with the best practices and international standards as set out by the Council of Europe.[762] Hence, the CRA is formally well equipped to safeguard its independence and is established as 'a functionally independent and a non-profit making institution with the status of a legal person under the laws of Bosnia and Herzegovina'.[763] The amendments of the *Law on Ministries and Other Bodies of Administration in BiH* from 2003,[764] in its Article 17, listed the

756. Office of the High Representative, *Decision Combining the Competencies of the Independent Media Commission and the Telecommunications Regulatory Agency*, 2 Mar. 2001 (Official Gazette of BiH 8/01; Official Gazette of FBiH 11/01; and Official Gazette of RS 12/01), http://www.ohr.int/decision-combining-the-competencies-of-the-independent-media-commission-and-the-telecommunications-regulatory-agency-3/, accessed 12 Oct. 2020.
757. Hans Bredow Institute for Media Research et al., *INDIREG*, 176, Thompson & De Luce, *Escalating to Success?*
758. Auth. Commun. Guarantees & Commun. Regulatory Agency, *Overview of the Communications Sector*, 30 (Twinning Light Report 2008).
759. Communications Law of BiH.
760. Commun. Regulatory Agency, *Annual Report for the Year 2019*, 13–14.
761. *Ibid.*, 16, 17, 21 and 24. Also see Part I. General Introduction, s. 2. The Media Landscape, *supra.*
762. Council of Europe Recommendation Rec(2000)23 of the Committee of Ministers to Member States on the independence and functions of regulatory authorities for the broadcasting sector.
763. Communications Law of BiH, Art. 36 (The Agency).
764. *Zakon o ministarstvima i drugim organima uprave BiH*, Official Gazette of BiH 42/03, 26/04, 42/04, 45/06, 88/07, 35/09, 59/09, 103/09.

CRA under autonomous administrative bodies whose rights and duties are regulated by the relevant laws that apply to the institutions of public administration,[765] which jeopardized the CRA's independence[766] were retracted in the amendments from 2017. However, the CRA still does not enjoy full financial independence, while political influence over the appointments of its management structures[767] continues to incite strong concerns over the independence and public image of the Agency.

§3. Financial Independence

441. In order for the CRA to be able to properly perform its tasks, it needs adequate financial means and a certain level of financial independence. The yearly budget is first adopted by the CRA Council and then submitted by the Director General to the Council of Ministers of BiH for approval. The CRA operates in accordance with the budget adopted by the CRA Council until the final budget is approved by the Council of Ministers of BiH. CRA funding comes from licence fees and grants or donations. If the grants are received for specific projects they are not part of the formally approved budget but are accounted for separately. Fines collected from the CRA's enforcement measures are included in the budget of the institutions of BiH.[768]

442. Even though the CRA is a self-financed body, its budget is a part of the state budget of BiH.[769] This means that the CRA has no direct control over its funds. Consequently, in the cases when the state budget is not adopted on time (which often happens), the funding for the CRA directly depends on the decisions on temporary financing of state institutions. Due to this situation the provisions of Article 44 of the Communications Law of BiH which provides for a certain level of financial independence of the CRA as described above, are rendered irrelevant. The budget of the CRA has however been relatively stable over the past years and compared to EUR 3.45 million in 2015 it grew to EUR 3.83 million in 2018 and 3.89 million in 2019, to again fall to 3.6 million in 2020.[770]

---

765. Law on Civil Service in the Institutions of Bosnia and Herzegovina (*Zakon o državnoj službi u institucijama Bosne Hercegovine*, Official Gazette of BiH 19/02, 35/03, 4/04, 17/04, 26/04, 37/04, 48/05, 2/06, 32/07, 43/09 and 8/10).
766. European Commission, *Bosnia and Herzegovina Progress Report* (European Commission 2011), http://ec.europa.eu/enlargement/pdf/key_documents/2011/package/ba_rapport_2011_en.pdf 16, accessed 13 Oct. 2020.
767. See Analytical Report of European Commission from 2019, at: https://ec.europa.eu/neighbourhood-enlargement/sites/near/files/20190529-bosnia-and-herzegovina-analytical-report.pdf, accessed 13 Oct. 2020.
768. The Communications Law of BiH, Art. 44.
769. The Law on Financing of Institutions of BiH (*Zakon o finansiranju institucija BiH*, Official Gazette of BiH 61/04), Art. 9(4).
770. Zakon o proračunu institucija Bosne i Hercegovine i međunarodnih obveza Bosne i Hercegovine za 2015 godinu, 2018, 2019 i 2020. [Law on Budget of Institutions of Bosnia and Herzegovina and on international obligations of Bosnia and Herzegovina for 2015; same Law for 2018, 2019 and

§4. ACCOUNTABILITY AND TRANSPARENCY

443. The Supreme Audit Institution (SAI) of BiH undertakes an annual audit review of the CRA, while the Agency publishes and submits to the Council of Ministers of BiH regular annual reports about its activities and finances.[771]

444. The CRA is required by the Law on Communication to publish draft rules and give at least fourteen days for public consultations before any rule is adopted.[772] The Agency regularly practices public consultation by publishing draft rules and organizing consultation meetings with licensees, other relevant institutions, and industry representatives and associations.[773]

445. Although it is not required by the law to do so, the CRA publishes all of its decisions and explanations thereof. Furthermore, all relevant documents and information are easily available on the website of the Agency, while additional information can be requested in accordance with the Freedom of Access to Information Act.

2020], https://www.mft.gov.ba/hrv/index.php?option=com_content&view=article&id=144&Itemid=111, accessed 13 Oct. 2020.

771. The Communications Law of BiH, Art. 44.

772. *Ibid.*, Art. 38.

773. *See*, for example, Commun. Regulatory Agency, *Annual Report for Year 2018 and for Year 2019*.

Chapter 1. Organization

446. The key decision-making bodies of the CRA are the Council of the Agency and the Director General.[774]

§1. Council of the CRA

447. The Council of the CRA provides guidelines for the Agency in strategic issues, adopts codes of practice and rules for broadcasting and telecommunications, and serves as an appellate body for decisions of the Director General.[775] The Council of the CRA has seven members.[776] While previously the CRA Council was mandated to submits the list of candidates for the following term, from 2012 onwards the procedure goes as follows: based on the proposal of the Council of Ministers, the Parliamentary Assembly of BiH establishes an ad hoc Commission, comprised of an equal number of representatives of government and non-governmental sector; the Commission publishes a vacancy call and submits a list of fourteen selected candidates to the Council of Ministers; within thirty days of receiving the list, the Council of Ministers proposes to the Parliamentary Assembly seven candidates from the list.[777] The Parliament can reject one or more nominations, in which case the Council of Ministers is required to nominate other candidate(s) from the list. If the Council of Ministers fails to do so, or the Parliament again rejects the candidates, the Parliament must start a new vacancy procedure. Candidates for the Council Members need to have experience in the telecommunications or broadcasting sectors. The Council members have a four-year term and can be re-appointed once. It is important to note that 'officials in legislative or executive functions at any level of Government, or members of political party organs cannot be candidates for the members of the Council of the Agency'.[778]

448. In principle, decisions of the Council of the Agency are made by consensus. When consensus cannot be reached, the decision is reached by a simple majority vote, under the condition that at least four members are present. Finally, in the case of equal voting, the decisive vote is the vote of the president of the meeting.[779] The members of the CRA must report any conflict of interest with regard to a telecommunication operator or broadcaster and in the case of conflict of interest, they must abstain from decision making.[780] The decisions of the CRA Council are final and binding, but they can be challenged before the state-level Court of BiH.[781]

---

774. The Communications Law of BiH, Art. 36 (2).
775. *Ibid.*, Art. 39(1).
776. *Ibid.*, Art. 39 (2).
777. *Ibid.*, Art. 39 (5 and 6).
778. *Ibid.*, Art. 39(3).
779. *Ibid.*, Art. 41.
780. *Ibid.*, Art. 39(4).
781. *Ibid.*, Art. 47.

449. The members of the Council can be dismissed before the end of their mandate by the Parliament Assembly of BiH in the case of illness that prevents the fulfilment of the duties, conviction of a crime punishable by imprisonment, a conflict of interest (including any members of their household having relevant connections with CRA licence user), violation of the agency's Code of Ethics, resignation or failure to perform their duties.[782]

450. There are many problems when it comes to the appointment of the members of the CRA's Council. Confusing roles of state bodies, non-transparent procedures, non-specified criteria and lack of specifications on the timeframe of the appointment, make the procedure inefficient and exposes the CRA to undue pressures. For instance, it is not specified what qualification should the members of the ad hoc body that selects the candidates should be, how many times the vacancy procedure can be repeated, or how quickly after the term of the Council expires the new vacancy procedure must start. This is how the lack of agreement between the ruling parties lead to the situation in which the six current members of the CRA Council (the seventh resigned and was relieved of his duties in July 2017) continue to perform this duty despite the fact that their terms expired in December 2017. The previous appointments were also halted due to a lack of political agreement.[783] Furthermore, in 2013 when the current members were appointed, the Council of Ministers and Parliamentary Assembly de facto violated the stipulation of the Law on Communications (Article 36) which requires a gender balance in the CRA Council composition.[784]

§2. Director General

451. The CRA is managed by a Director General, nominated by the Council of the Agency and approved by the Council of Ministers.[785] The Director General, who has a term of four years which is renewable only once, reports to the Council of the Agency and is responsible for decision making and management of the CRA.[786] Decisions of the Director General can be challenged before the Council of the agency.[787]

452. The Law on Communication forbids the nominations of government officials or members of political party organs for the position of the Director General

782. *Ibid.*, Art. 42.
783. *See* Hans Bredow Institute for Media Research et al., *INDIREG*, 177–178; European Commission, Bosnia and Herzegovina Progress Report 2011, 16.
784. See more on the appointment of the members of CRA Council in Selma Aščerić, Rak između izvršne i zakonodavne vlasti [CRA between executive and legislative power], Istinomjer, 2 Jul. 2020, https://istinomjer.ba/rak-izmedju-izvrsne-i-zakonodavne-vlasti/, accessed 15 Oct. 2020.
785. The Communications Law of BiH, Art. 40.
786. Commun. Regulatory Agency, https://rak.ba/en/organisational-structure, accessed 14 Oct. 2020.
787. The Communications Law of BiH, Art. 47.

of the CRA.[788] Furthermore, the Director General is not allowed to have any financial relations with broadcasters or telecommunications operators.[789] The Director General can be nominated only from the candidates that have experience in telecommunications or broadcasting sectors.

453. The Director General can be dismissed by the Council of Ministers of BiH only under exceptional circumstances, such as illness, the conviction of a crime punishable by imprisonment, conflict of interest, resignation, failure to perform duties as described in the law, and violation of the Agency's Code of Ethics.[790]

454. As in the case of the appointment of the members of the CRA Council, the appointment of the General Director has been heavily politicized. After the term of the Director General ended in 2007, the Council of Ministers did not give its formal approval to the nominee that was selected according to the legal procedure and proposed to the Council of Ministers by the CRA Council.[791] Although the law does not provide for the possibility of the rejection of the nominee except if the legal procedure is not respected, and although it is not allowed to 'interfere in the decision-making of the Agency in individual cases',[792] the Council of Ministers requested from the CRA to repeat the procedure for the selection of candidates for the position of the Director General. The CRA refused to comply, and the incumbent Director General stayed in a technical mandate for seven years.[793] The political obstructions continued in recent years as well. The term of Predrag Kovač, appointed as an acting director in 2015, and as a director in full capacity in 2016, expired by the end of April 2020. In April, CRA Council proposed Draško Milinović for Director General and the Council of Ministers confirmed his appointment in July 2020. These developments are controversial and are likely to be a large step backwards in terms of the independence of CRA. Namely, not only does Milinović have close political ties with the SNSD party (being a former head of the office of the Prime Minister, as well as of the President of RS),[794] in addition to a member of his family being a chief of the public relations office of a major telecommunication company, but also until December 2020, he was for five years the Director General of public service broadcaster RTRS, thus responsible for a dozen of rulings

788. *Ibid.*, Art. 40.
789. *Ibid.*, Art. 40.
790. *Ibid.*, Art. 42.
791. Halilović, Mehmed, *Disciplining Independent Regulators: Political Pressures on the Communications Regulatory Agency of Bosnia and Herzegovina* (*Puls demokratije / Puls of Democracy*, 10.07.2008), http://www.pulsdemokratije.ba/index.php?l=en&id=1060, accessed 29 May 2012.
792. The Communications Law of BiH, Art. 36.
793. Halilović, *Disciplining Independent Regulators*; Hans Bredow Institute for Media Research et al., *INDIREG*; European Commission, Bosnia and Herzegovina Progress Report (European Commission 2009) (available at http://ec.europa.eu/enlargement/pdf/key_documents/2009/ba_rapport_2009_en.pdf, accessed 15 Oct. 2020).
794. The previous director, Predrag Kovač, was also considered closely politically aligned with another political party, which in the meantime ceased to be a part of ruling majority, which is why his term was not extended in 2020. *See* article on Klix.ba, 27.10.2019, https://www.klix.ba/vijesti/bih/dodikov-propagandista-drasko-milinovic-hoce-u-fotelju-direktora-rak-a/191227014, accessed 15 Oct. 2020.

that CRA issued against RTRS for breach of professional norms, including the lack of balanced reporting and favouritism towards SNSD.[795]

§3. Organizational Structure

455. According to the CRA website, the organizational units of the CRA are the Cabinet of General Director, five specialized sections and several other departments. The five sections, with their specific sub-divisions, are:

- The Section of Telecommunications (consisting of Division of Licensing in Telecommunications; Division of Interconnection and Market Regulation in Telecommunications).
- The Section of Broadcasting (consisting of Division of Licenses, Digitalization, and Coordination in Broadcasting; Division of Programming, Complaints, and Legal Regulation in Broadcasting; Division of Audiovisual Services and International Cooperation in Broadcasting).
- The Section of Legal, Financial, and General Affairs (consisting of Legal Division; Financial – Accounting Division).
- The Section of Frequency Spectrum Management (consisting of Broadcasting Division; Fixed and Mobile Service Division; International Coordination and Regulation Division), and

456. The Section of Radio Monitoring, IT Support, and Control of Compliance with License Terms and Conditions (consisting of Radio Monitoring Division; IT Support Division; Division of Control of Compliance with License Terms and Conditions). Other departments of the CRA are the Public Affairs Department, Regional Office Banja Luka, and Regional Office Mostar.[796]

795. *See*, for instance, Nejra Dzaferagic, New Head of Bosnian Regulator Criticised for War Crime Coverage, BalkanInsight, 13 Aug. 2020, https://balkaninsight.com/2020/08/13/new-head-of-bosnian-tv-regulator-criticised-for-war-crime-coverage/; as well as Slađan Tomić, Rak i političke metastaze. Radnički univerzietet, 21 Jun. 2020. http://radnickiuniverzitet.org/view-more/rak-i-politicke-metastaze/154, accessed 15 Oct. 2020.

796. Commun. Regulatory Agency https://rak.ba/en/organisational-structure, accessed 15 Oct. 2020.

Chapter 2. Tasks

457. According to the Communications Law BiH, the CRA is responsible for:

a. regulating broadcasting and public telecommunications networks and services, including licensing, tariffing, interconnection, and defining the basic conditions for the provision of common and international communications facilities; and
b. planning, co-coordinating, allocating and assigning the use of the radio-frequency spectrum.[797]

458. Within its competencies as defined by the law, the CRA undertakes necessary activities and measures in order to achieve the following objectives pertaining to the broadcasting and telecommunications sector in BiH:

a. Promotion of fair competition in order that users derive maximum benefit in terms of choice, price and quality.
b. Guaranteeing that there is no distortion or restriction of competition in the communications sector according to the Council of Ministers' sector policies.
c. Encouraging efficient investment in infrastructure and innovation.
d. Protection of copyright and other intellectual property as well as personal data and privacy.
e. Ensuring the efficient use and effective management of radio frequencies and numbering resources in accordance with the radio regulations and other recommendations of the ITU, and with other international agreements entered into by BiH.
f. Respect for and promotion of gender equality and elimination of all forms of stereotypical and offensive representation of men and women.[798]

459. Pursuant to the provisions of the Communications Law BiH, Article 37, the duties of the CRA are the following:

a. to promulgate rules on broadcasting and telecommunications, and ensure adherence thereto;
b. to license broadcasters and telecommunications operators pursuant to the provisions of this Law, and monitor their compliance with licence conditions;
c. to plan, manage, allocate and assign frequency spectrum and monitor the use of it as well as to maintain and publish a frequency usage plan for the whole territory of BiH;
d. to require the disclosure of such information as is necessary for the due performance of its regulatory obligations;
e. to apply technical and quality standards, for example, to ensure interconnection and functionality of public telecommunications networks and telecommunications services;

797. The Communications Law BiH, Art. 3(3).
798. *Ibid.*, Art. 3(4).

f. to establish and maintain a technical licence fee system for both broadcasting and telecommunications; and
g. such other duties as are assigned to it under this Law or by the Council of Ministers.[799]

460. CRA has been exercising its powers in a transparent manner, including a regular publishing of its decisions, information on its activities, yearly reports on financial and other indicators and results. There is no evidence of partial decision-making or treatment of media organisations. However, the agency regularly faces criticism from the media outlets subject to its fines, and in particular from public broadcasters. Although in principle such criticism of the Agency has not been valid, it may nevertheless be damaging for the public perception of the CRA.[800] Nevertheless, political pressures have in different periods led to delays in the adoption of decisions in broadcasting and telecommunications and have hampered administrative capacities of CRA, [801] while the recent controversial appointment of its director will likely bring further challenges to the CRA's independence.

461. As noted earlier, the CRA now has a role in the appointment of the Board of Directors of BHRT, while the parliamentary bodies in the Federation of BiH and Republika Srpska have complete control over the appointments of the Board in RTVFBiH and RTRS, respectively. While CRA notes that in recent years the candidates for the Board in BHRT were indeed selected from the list submitted by the CRA, there were previous examples when such stipulations were ignored and the appointments were blocked in the parliamentary bodies. [802] Overall, the role of the parliamentary bodies in these appointments is excessive and there are few measures to prevent politicization and to make sure the best candidates are appointed. Most notably, the appointments of the Board in RTVFBiH have been blocked for eight years.[803]

799. *Ibid.*, Art. 37.
800. Tarik Jusić, Bosnia and Herzegovina, in The Independence of Media Regulatory Authorities in Europe, European Audiovisual Observatory and IRIS 2017, 37.
801. European Commission, *Bosnia and Herzegovina Progress Report 2009*, 52.
802. Commun. Regulatory Agency, Annual Report 2011; *Also see*: E. Gorinjac, Novi Parliament BiH također želi podobne u UO BHRT (klix.ba, 29 August 2020) https://www.klix.ba/vijesti/bih/novi-parlament-bih-takodjer-zeli-podobne-u-uo-bhrt-a/110829097, accessed 26 Oct. 2020.
803. See more in Nejra Džanko. Politički pritisci na javni RTV servis u BiH [Political pressures on public service broadcasting in BiH], Master thesis at the Faculty of the Political Science of the University of Sarajevo: 2019.

Chapter 3. Sanctioning Powers

462. In order to be able to ensure compliance with its codes and rules, the CRA has been awarded enforcement authority in accordance with European regulatory practices. Hence, a set of enforcement measures, which are to be applied proportional to the violations, are available to the CRA:

a. Oral and written warnings.
b. Inspection of licensed facilities.
c. Concrete demands for action or cessation, to be complied with within a specified time limit.
d. Assessment of a financial penalty not to exceed 150,000 km[804] in case of deliberate or negligent violation of individual provisions of the Law or of conditions specified in the licence or in the codes of practice and rules of the Agency. The level of the financial imposition shall be commensurate with the gravity of the infringement and, where applicable, with the gross financial benefits derived from the infringement. In case of repeated violations, the financial imposition may not exceed 300,000 km. The Agency shall devise a schedule of infractions and resulting penalties, which shall be adopted by the Council of Ministers.
e. Orders to interrupt broadcasting or the provision of telecommunications services for a period not exceeding three months.
f. Revocation of a licence.[805]

463. The CRA also has powers to undertake all necessary steps to stop the operation of a telecommunications or broadcasting network or service if it is operated without a licence[806] and has monitoring and information collection powers necessary for the assessment of compliance with licensing conditions, rules and regulations.[807] All law enforcement agencies in BiH must assist the CRA in the enforcement of its decisions if requested by the Agency.[808] In 2019, the Agency issued thirty-nine decisions concerning services in the broadcasting sector, including 18 fines, 13 warnings, 5 suspensions and 3 revocations of licenses.[809] In the period between 2012 and 2019, the CRA issued 530 sanctions, out of which 26 were revocations of (broadcasting and distribution) licences.[810] Between 1998 and 2011, a total of 640 sanctions were issued,[811] including 10 revocations of licenses.

---

804. EUR 1 = BAM 1.95; hence BAM 150.000 = EUR 75,000.
805. The Communications Law BiH, Art. 46.
806. *Ibid.*, Art. 46.
807. Hans Bredow Institute for Media Research et al., *INDIREG*, 299.
808. The Communications Law BiH, Art. 46.
809. CRA, *Izvještaj o slučajevima kršenja pravila u 2019. Godini, (CRA 2020), 5.*
810. *Yearly reports on violations of rules at* https://www.rak.ba/bs-Latn-BA/reports, accessed 15 Oct. 2020.
811. CRA, *Izvještaj o slučajevima kršenja pravila u 2011. godini* (CRA – Communications Regulatory Agency of Bosnia and Herzegovina, 2012), 18; https://www.rak.ba/bs-Latn-BA/reports, accessed 30 May 2012.

Table 1 Overview of Executive Measures Imposed by the CRA Between 1998 and 2019

Sanction Type	Number of Sanctions for the Time Period 1998–2011	Number of Sanctions for the Period 2012–2019
Fines	246	131
Warnings	271	324
Suspensions	60	49
Orders	14	N/A
Revocation of License	10	26
Total	**640**	640

Source: CRA[812]

812. Commun. Regulatory Agency Annual reports at https://rak.ba/bs-Latn-BA/reports, accessed 26 Oct. 2020.

Selected Bibliography

Authority for Communications Guarantees & Communications Regulatory Agency. *Overview of the Communications Sector in Bosnia and Herzegovina*. Sarajevo: Authority for Communications Guarantees & Communications Regulatory Agency, 2008.

Aida Hozić. 'Democratizing Media, Welcoming Big Brother: Media in Bosnia and Herzegovina'. In *Finding the Right Place on the Map: Central and Eastern European Media Change in a Global Perspective*, edited by Karol Jakubowicz & Miklos Sukosd. Bristol, UK/Chicago, USA: Intellect, 2008.

Amer Džihana & Mladen Srdić. 'Zaštita privatnosti'. In *Medijsko pravo u Bosni i Hercegovini.* Edited by Mehmed Halilović & Amer Džihana. Sarajevo: Internews, 2012.

Barbara Krajnc & Selma Kadić Maglajlić. Regulacija tržišta oglašavanja. Mediacentar Sarajevo 2018.

Communications Regulatory Agency. *Annual Reports of the Communications Regulatory Agency for the Years 2011-2019*. Sarajevo: CRA – Communications Regulatory Agency of BiH.

Communications Regulatory Agency. Analiza dječijih i obrazovnih programa, programa koji su namijenjeni ili se bave manjinama i ranjivim grupama stanovništva, te programa prilagođenih osobama sa invaliditetom u audiovizuelnim medijskim uslugama i medijskim uslugama radija u Bosni i Hercegovini, CRA Sarajevo: 2019.

Emina Cerimović, Edin Hodžić & Amra Mehmedić. Anonimizacija sudskih i tužilačkih akata u BiH. Analitika Sarajevo: 2014.

Hans Bredow Institute for Media Research, Interdisciplinary Centre for Law & ICT (ICRI), Katholieke Universiteit Leuven, Center for Media and Communication Studies (CMCS), Central European University, Cullen International, Perspective Associates (eds.). *INDIREG – Indicators for Independence and Efficient Functioning of Audiovisual Media Services Regulatory Bodies for the Purpose of Enforcing the Rules in the AVMS Directive.* Study conducted on behalf of the European Commission, 2011.

Kate Coyer & Joost van Beek. 'Community Radio in Bosnia and Herzegovina: Opportunities and Challenges'. In *Communication and Community: Citizens, Media and Local Governance in Bosnia and Herzegovina*, edited by Tarik Jusić. Sarajevo: Mediacentar Sarajevo & Analitika – Center for Social Research, 2010.

Kemal Kurspahić. *Zločin u 19:30 – Balkanski mediji u ratu i miru.* Mediacentar Sarajevo and South East Europe Media Organization SEEMO, 2003.

Selected Bibliography

Ljubinko Mitrović, Jasminka Džumhur ans Nives Jukić. Specijalni izvještaj o iskustvima u primjeni zakona o slobodi pristupa informacijama u BiH (Ombudsman BiH, 2019).

Maja Čolaković & Lana Bubalo. Građanskopravna odgovornost za klevetu u sudskoj praksi Bosne i Hercegovine [Civil Law Liability for Defamation in the Court Practice of BiH], 2018. URL: https://www.researchgate.net/publication/327824313_Gradanskopravna_odgovornost_za_klevetu_u_sudskoj_praksi_Bosne_i_HercegovineCivil_Liability_for_Defamation_in_Jurispridence_of_Bosnia_and_Herzegovina.

Marija Lučić-Catić and Dina Bajraktarević Pajević, Nedostaci kaznene politike tužiteljstva BiH i SUDA BiH u slučajevima zločina iz mržnje i govora mržnje. Kriminalističke studije, 2019.

Mark Thompson & Dan De Luce. 'Escalating to Success? The Media Intervention in Bosnia and Herzegovina'. In *Forging Peace: Intervention, Human Rights and the Management of Media Space*, edited by Monroe E. Price & Mark Thompson. Edinburgh University Press, 2002.

Media Experts Commission. *Završni izvještaj: Mediji u izborima* (*Media Experts Commission*, OSCE Mission in Bosnia and Herzegovina, 1998).

Mehmed Halilović. 'Zakoni o slobodi pristupa informacijama'. In *Medijsko pravo u Bosni i Hercegovini.* Edited by Mehmed Halilović & Amer Džihana. Sarajevo: Internews, 2012.

Mehmed Halilović & Amer Džihana (ed.). *Medijsko pravo u Bosni i Hercegovini.* Sarajevo: Internews, 2012.

Mehmed Halilović & Mirjana Nadaždin-Defterdarević. 'Ustavno i zakonsko jamstvo slobode izražavanja'. In *Medijsko pravo u Bosni i Hercegovini.* Edited by Mehmed Halilović & Amer Džihana. Sarajevo: Internews, 2012.

Mehmed Halilović & Mladen Srdić. 'Osnovni zaključci o tretmanu klevete pred bh. sudovima'. In *Medijsko pravo u Bosni i Hercegovini.* Edited by Mehmed Halilović & Amer Džihana. Sarajevo: Internews, 2012.

Mehmed Halilović & Mladen Srdić. 'Zakoni o zaštiti od klevete'. In *Medijsko pravo u Bosni i Hercegovini.* Edited by Mehmed Halilović & Amer Džihana. Sarajevo: Internews, 2012.

Merima Tanović. Constitutional Questions about Sovereignty in Context of the Legislative Process in Bosnia and Herzegovina, Pregled - Journal for Social Issues, 2016, Issue 1, 213 221.

Mirjana Nadaždin-Defterdarević. 'Normativni okvir prava na informisanje u Bosni i Hercegovini'. In *Medijsko pravo u Bosni i Hercegovini.* Edited by Mehmed Halilović & Amer Džihana. Sarajevo: Internews, 2012. Mladen Srdić. 'Izražavanje o pitanjima od javnog interesa'. In *Medijsko pravo u Bosni i Hercegovini.* Edited by Mehmed Halilović & Amer Džihana. Sarajevo: Internews, 2012.

Mladen Srdić. 'Kleveta u sudskoj praksi'. In *Medijsko pravo u Bosni i Hercegovini.* Edited by Mehmed Halilović & Amer Džihana. Sarajevo: Internews, 2012.

Mladen Srdić. 'Osnovni standardi postupanja Evropskog suda'. In *Medijsko pravo u Bosni i Hercegovini.* Edited by Mehmed Halilović & Amer Džihana. Sarajevo: Internews, 2012.

Noel Malcolm. *Bosnia: A Short History.* London: Macmillan London Limited, 1994.

Sanela Hodžić, 'Bosnia and Herzegovina', in Brankica Petković (ed.) Media Integrity Matters: Reclaiming Public Service Values in Media and Journalism. Ljubljana: Peace Institute, Institute for Contemporary Social and Political Studies, 2014.

Sanela Hodžić and Brankica Petković Sustainability of Professional Journalism in the Media Business Environment of the Western Balkans. Executive Report. TACSO: 2020.

Sanela Hodžić and Anida Sokol. Sustainability of Professional Journalism in the Media Business Environment of the Western Balkans. National Data Overview: Bosnia and Herzegovina. TACSO: 2020.

Sanela Hodžić and Anida Sokol. Oglašavanje i drugi komercijalni odnosi između javnog sektora i medija. Mediacentar Sarajevo: 2018.

Sanela Hodžić and Anida Sokol: Transparent and legitimate media financing from public budgets. Mediacentar Sarajevo: 2018.

Sevima Sali-Terzić. 'Odavanje tajne u krivičnim zakonima u BiH'. In *Medijsko pravo u Bosni i Hercegovini,* edited by Mehmed Halilović & Amer Džihana. Sarajevo: Internews, 2012.

Srđan Dizdarević, et al. *Democracy Assessment in Bosnia and Herzegovina.* Sarajevo: Open Society Fund Bosnia and Herzegovina, 2006.

Tarik Jusić, 'Bosnia and Herzegovina', in The Independence of Media Regulatory Authorities in Europe, European Audiovisual Observatory and IRIS 2017.

Tarik Jusić & Amer Džihana. 'Bosnia and Herzegovina'. In *Divided they Fall: Public Service Broadcasting in Multiethnic States*, edited by Sandra Bašić-Hrvatin, Mark Thompson & Tarik Jusić. Sarajevo: Mediacentar Sarajevo, 2008.

Tarik Jusić & Sanela Hodžić. 'Local Media and Local Communities: Towards Public Policies for the Promotion of Local Media Content in Bosnia and Herzegovina'. In *Communication and Community: Citizens, Media and Local Governance in Bosnia and Herzegovina*, edited by Tarik Jusić. Sarajevo: Mediacentar Sarajevo & Analitika – Center for Social Research, 2010.

Transparency International. *National Integrity System Study – Bosnia and Herzegovina 2007.* Berlin: Transparency International, 2006.

Selected Bibliography

Index

The numbers here refer to the paragraph numbers.

Index

www.ingramcontent.com/pod-product-compliance
Ingram Content Group UK Ltd.
Pitfield, Milton Keynes, MK11 3LW, UK
UKHW021239300926
15471UKWH00013B/702

9 789403 538549